Sex Differences in Cognitive Abilities

SEX DIFFERENCES IN COGNITIVE ♂♀ ABILITIES

DIANE F. HALPERN
*California State University,
San Bernardino*

LEA LAWRENCE ERLBAUM ASSOCIATES, PUBLISHERS
1986 Hillsdale, New Jersey   London

Lawrence Erlbaum Associates, Inc., Publishers
365 Broadway
Hillsdale, New Jersey 07642

Library of Congress Cataloging in Publication Data

Halpern, Diane F.
   Sex differences in cognitive abilities.

   Bibliography: p.
   Includes indexes.
   1. Cognition.   2. Sex differences (Psychology)
3. Sex role.   I. Title.   [DNLM: 1. Cognition.   Sex
Factors.   BF 311 H195s]
BF311.H295 1986   155.3'3   86-11506
ISBN 0-89859-579-7
ISBN 0-89859-838-9 (pbk.)

Printed in the United States of America
10 9 8 7 6 5 4 3 2 1

Contents

Preface   **vii**

1. Introduction and Overview   **1**
A Hot Issue in Contemporary Psychology   *1*
Nature/Nurture Controversy   *2*
The Notion of Cognitive Abilities   *5*
Values and Science   *7*
Political and Social Ramifications   *10*
Terminology   *11*
Selective Nature of all Reviews   *13*
Plan for This Book   *14*

2. Searching for Sex Differences in Cognitive Abilities   **15**
The Need for Research   *15*
Types of Experimental Investigations   *17*
Understanding Research Results   *23*
Developmental Issues   *39*
Self-Fulfilling Prophecies   *41*
Evaluating Research Claims   *42*

3. Empirical Evidence for Cognitive Sex Differences   **45**
Intelligence   *45*
Verbal Abilities   *47*
Visual-Spatial Abilities   *48*
Quantitative Abilities   *57*
Relationship Between Visual-Spatial Abilities and Quantitative
    Abilities   *59*

v

Magnitude of the Differences   60
Sex Differences in Factor Structures   64
Chapter Summary   66

4. **Biological Hypotheses**   67
The Notion of Biological Determination   68
Genetic Theories   69
Sex-Related Brain Differences   75
Sex Hormones   91
Critique of Biological Hypotheses   102
Chapter Summary   106

5. **Psychosocial Hypotheses**   107
The Importance of Psychosocial Variables   107
Sex Roles and Sex Role Stereotypes   110
Sex-Linked Socialization Practices   121
Ability Differences   132
Extrapolating from Empirical Trends   141
Chapter Summary   142

6. **Understanding Cognitive Sex Differences**   145
The Need for Cross-Cultural Research   145
The Winning Hypothesis Is. . .   149
New Approaches to Old Problems   158
Into the Future   160

References   163
Author Index   175
Subject Index   180

Preface

It seemed like a simple task when I started writing this book. All I had to do was provide a comprehensive synthesis of the theories and research concerning the causes, correlates, and consequences of cognitive sex differences and make some meaningful conclusions that were supported in the literature. My interest in the area grew naturally out of several years of teaching both cognitive psychology and psychology of women to college classes. The idea that women and men might actually think differently, that is have different preferred modes of thinking or different thinking abilities came up in both classes. At the time, it seemed clear to me that any between-sex differences in thinking abilities were due to socialization practices, artifacts and mistakes in the research, and bias and prejudice. After reviewing a pile of journal articles that stood several feet high and numerous books and book chapters that dwarfed the stack of journal articles, I changed my mind. The task I had undertaken certainly wasn't simple and the conclusions that I had expected to make had to be revised.

The literature on sex differences in cognitive abilities is filled with inconsistent findings, contradictory theories, and emotional claims that are unsupported by the research. Yet, despite all of the noise in the data, clear and consistent messages could be heard. There are real, and in some cases sizable, sex differences with respect to some cognitive abilities. Socialization practices are undoubtedly important, but there is also good evidence that biological sex differences play a role in establishing and maintaining cognitive sex differences, a conclusion that I wasn't prepared to make when I began reviewing the relevant literature.

The conclusions that I reached about cognitive sex differences are at odds with those of other authors (e.g., Caplan, MacPherson, & Tobin, 1985; Fairweather, 1976). There are probably several reasons why the conclusions in this review are different from the earlier ones. I believe that the data collected within the last few years provide a convincing case for the importance of biological variables, and that earlier reviews were, of course, unable to consider these findings. Other reviewers were sometimes quick to dismiss inconsistent theories and experimental results as symptomatic of a chaotic field of investigation. If they had reviewed the inconsistencies, they would have found that many of them are resolvable and that some of the theories and research could be eliminated because they had become outdated or had not received experimental support, thereby reducing the dissonance in the literature. Although there is still much that we don't know in this area, plausible conclusions based on the information that is currently available can be made.

This book was written with a broad audience in mind—bright undergraduates and graduates and their professors and general readers who are intrigued with the questions and answers about cognitive sex differences. It could serve as a supplemental book in many courses in psychology and other fields. The issues raised in this book are appropriately addressed in introductory psychology, sociology, education, philosophy, human development, and biology courses. It is also appropriate for advanced courses in sex roles, sex differences, human genetics, child and adult development, education theory and research, social psychology and physiological psychology because of the broad perspective needed in understanding cognitive sex differences.

The topics addressed vary in their complexity, with brain-behavior relationships more difficult to explain than psychosocial influences on the development of cognition. My goal was to make even the advanced topics in biology and statistics comprehensive without oversimplyfying multifacted relationships or losing sight of the fact that the problems are complex. The topics addressed in this book go far beyond the usual "pop" coverage found in the popular press. I hope that despite my efforts to emphasize serious research and conceptual issues, I have been able to convey to readers some of my fascination with one of the most controversial and politically charged topics in modern psychology, the psycholgy of cognitive sex differences.

Acknowledgments

I am very fortunate to have so many wonderful friends and colleagues who were willing to help me with this book. Dr. George Mandler at University of California, San Diego and Dr. Deborah Burke at Pomona College reviewed the entire book. They made numerous helpful comments and suggestions that shaped my thinking in many ways. I am grateful to both of them for sharing their expertise with me and for encouraging me with this project. Dr. Frederick Newton at California State University, San Bernardino and Dr. Richard Lewis at Pomona College and University of California, Los Angeles served as reviewers for Chapter IV (Biological Hypotheses). They provided a neuropsychological perspective to this chapter and helped to clarify my thinking about this topic. Numerous other friends and colleagues provided insights on selected chapters. Dr. Gloria Cowan at California State University, San Bernardino offered helpful comments on Chapters II and III. My good friends Deborah Silverstein and Dr. Stanley Silverstein patiently read through early drafts of several chapters, as did Dr. Harris Halpern, who is a close friend and a relative. They were helpful in pointing out strengths and weaknesses in my own thinking and writing processes. Dr. Katharine Newman, now retired from West Chester University, read most of the book and prodded me to make it the best that I could. I also thank Jack Burton, Vice President at Lawrence Erlbaum Associates, Inc. for his support and confidence in me, and Robert Perine, a friend and artist, for designing the book cover. This book is much better because of the unselfish help and encouragement you have all provided.

Special thanks go to my wonderful family. My husband Sheldon read and commented on the entire book, suffered through the low points in my writing, and encouraged me to succeed at anything that I believe is important. He also drove the extra carpools and assumed the extra household jobs needed to keep a home and family functioning so that I could spend more time on my writing. I also thank my children Evan and Joan for being such wonderful people and for reminding me about the enormity of human potential.

This book is dedicated to
the girls and boys of the next generation —
my own children, Joan and Evan,
my nephews and nieces and God children,
and all children everywhere
In the hope that they will each be able to develop their
unique abilities and interests
without limitations imposed by sex or race or any
stereotypical beliefs that inhibit intellectual growth.

1 Introduction and Overview

CONTENTS
A Hot Issue in Contemporary Psychology
Nature/Nurture Controversy
   Sociobiology
The Notion of Cognitive Abilities
Values and Science
   The Myth of Objectivity
   Feminist Scholarship
Political and Social Ramifications
   The Bugaboo of Biological Explanations
   Censorship in Science
Terminology
   Sex and Gender
   Sex and Sex-Related
   Abilities, Skills, and Performance
   Pronouns
Selective Nature of All Reviews
Plan for This Book

A HOT ISSUE IN CONTEMPORARY PSYCHOLOGY

The furor may be inevitable.

—Gelman et al. (1981)

"She thinks like a man." Many people would interpret this comment as praise for a woman who has demonstrated logical and orderly thought processes. But, what does it mean to "think like a man?" In fact, is there any evidence to suggest that men and women think differently?

Questions of sex differences have been a consuming interest of psychologists in recent years. Virtually every journal in every area of specialization, including the popular press, contains reports of research on differences between women and men. One observer noted that, "women have become the latest academic fad" (Westkott, 1979). But the topic of sex differences isn't just "hot" in the sense of fashionable, it is, in fact, inflammatory. The answers we provide to questions like, "Which is the smarter sex?" or "Do girls have less mathematical

1

ability than boys?'' have implications for present and future societies. The questions are important, and no one is taking the answers lightly.

The political climate with regard to the questions of sex differences and the appropriate roles for men and women has been combative in the approximately 20 years since the Women's Movement began shaking up American society. During the last 2 decades, women have been entering traditional male occupations at an increasing rate and, to a lesser extent, men have assumed a greater role in child care and homemaking. On the other hand, the Equal Rights Amendment failed to obtain ratification, a fact which demonstrates that many Americans are either opposed to social changes in the roles played by men and women in contemporary society or that they believe that a separate amendment ensuring equal protection for women under the law is unnecessary. Political commentators, late-night talk show hosts, teachers, and the rest of us have wrestled with questions concerning the draft exempt status of women (Are women too weak for the rigors of war?), whether women could be good vice presidents or presidents of the United States (Are they too emotional to make reasoned decisions?), whether men should be given equal consideration in child custody suits (Are men able to assume the primary role in parenting?), why are there so few women in the sciences (Are women less able to comprehend advanced scientific concepts?) and whether men are naturally too aggressive to be trusted with world peace (Would there be fewer wars if women ran the military?). In the midst of all of this brouhaha, psychologists and other social scientists have amassed mountains of data about sex differences in the belief that the answers can be determined in a scientific manner. The purpose of this book is to review the data that pertain to sex differences in cognitive abilities and the theories that have guided the way the data were collected and interpreted. The goal is to provide an up-to-date synthesis and summary of this highly complex and controversial area of research.

NATURE/NURTURE CONTROVERSY

Even in an area as complex and replete with contradictory results as the questions of cognitive sex differences, there are a few facts that virtually everyone will agree upon. These facts concern the sex-related differences in the daily activities of a majority of women and men in contemporary Western cultures. The majority of mathematics, science, and engineering majors in coed colleges are male, while the majority of elementary school teachers, nurses, and secretaries are female. When one parent assumes the job of primary homemaker, it is almost always the mother. The number of professions and avocations comprised of a clear majority of one sex is almost limitless. In fact, very few sex-neutral occupations come to mind. Even a casual observation of people going about their daily activities reveals that women and men tend to perform different tasks. The important question for experimental psychology is whether these activities reflect sex-related differences in cognitive or thinking abilities, and if there are cognitive differences, are they due to factors that are inherent in the biology of maleness and femaleness, or are they due to differential sex-related experiences and expectations?

The question being posed here is a familiar one to psychologists: "Does nature or nurture play the greater part in sex-related cognitive differences?" This is a highly controversial and politically charged question. Like all loaded questions, the answers sometimes backfire. The implications of the way psychologists answer this question are similar to those about racial differences in intelligence. Results could be and have been used to justify discrimination and/or affirmative action based on sex.

The nature/nurture dichotomy has guided much of the research in the area of sex differences. Proponents on each side of the issue stack up their data hoping to overwhelm the opposition with the sheer weight of the evidence that supports a favored point of view. Arguments on the nature side of the question point to the folly of denying that the biological manifestations of manhood and womanhood influence how we think and act. The nurture side is quick to point out that individuals develop in a societal context that shapes and interprets thoughts and actions in stereotypical ways. Of course, few modern psychologists maintain a strict "either/or" position. The naturally gifted poet and author, for example, will never develop or publicize this gift if denied an education, or if not allowed to write, or if publishers refuse to publish the creative work. Nature and nurture operate jointly in the development of cognitive abilities.

Although most researchers agree that the better question is *how much* do nature and nurture contribute to the development of cognitive abilities, it is virtually impossible to devise measures that allow for a direct and independent

Copyright Leo Callum, 1985.

comparison. Nature and nurture are like Siamese twins who share a common heart and nervous system. The technology has not yet been developed that will allow them to be separated. Thus, while researchers pay lip service to interactionist positions, the research is, in fact, focused on either biological (nature) variables or environmental (nurture) variables. The nature/nurture controversy has been debated for over 2,000 years without resolution because it is essentially unanswerable. Yet, it has served as a framework for much of the sex differences research.

Sociobiology

The nature/nurture controversy erupted into a full-scale war when E. O. Wilson "sought to establish sociobiology 'as the systematic study of the biological bases of all social behavior' " (Bleier, 1984, p. 15). Sociobiology is a subdiscipline within biology that attempts to use evolutionary principles to explain the behavior of humans and other animals. According to this theory, a species is fit if it reproduces well. A major tenet of sociobiology is that there are genetically programmed universal traits that improve the probabilities of producing many viable offspring. Given the basic assumptions of sociobiology, women, for example, should have a genetically determined predisposition that makes them better child caretakers because they are the ones that gestate and nurse the young. Like the female members of other species, women purportedly possess a "maternal instinct" because such an instinct would be beneficial to the survival of the species. Men, on the other hand, inherit a genetic predisposition that makes them prone to infidelity because multiple sexual encounters is a good reproductive strategy for males.

There are several flaws in this line of reasoning. First, hormones and other between-sex biological differences become decreasingly important as determinants of behavior as we ascend the phylogenetic scale. Second, explaining male infidelity by analogy to the animal kingdom ignores the many species that form monogamous mateships; it is not the natural state of all males across species to have multiple sexual partners. Third, it ignores societal influences on complex behaviors such as child care and mating choices.

Sex differences with respect to cognitive abilities are also explained by the adherents of basic principles of sociobiology. Consider, for example, a sociobiological argument to explain differences in spatial ability. Proponents of sociobiology maintain that because men were the hunters in primitive hunter-gatherer societies, they needed better spatial skills than the women who performed the gathering tasks; therefore, men are genetically superior in spatial ability.

Numerous thoughtful critiques of sociobiology have been offered (Bleier, 1984; Janson-Smith, 1980). The possibility that there are genes that determine specific social behaviors (e.g., child care arrangements, infidelity) and cognitive abilities is extremely remote. In addition, adherents of sociobiology ignore data that are not consistent with the theory. Spatial skills, for example, were also needed for gatherers who often had to travel long distances to gather food. In addition, there were many hunter-gatherer societies in which women hunted (e.g., the Pygmies of the Zaire rain forest and the Tiwi of the Bathurst Islands) (O'Kelly, 1980). Women in these earlier societies had to weave the baskets needed for efficient gathering (a complex spatial skill). Sociobiologists rely heavily on dubious analogies from other animal species to make their point. As Weisstein (1972) noted, this is the same as concluding: "that it is quite useless to teach human infants to speak since it has been tried with chimpanzees and does not work" (p. 218). Sociobiology provides neither an explanation of nor a justification for sex differences.

THE NOTION OF COGNITIVE ABILITIES

Cognitive psychology is the branch of psychology concerned with how people think, learn, and remember. The ability to think, learn, and remember is, in turn, related to the concept of intelligence. Although intelligence has been defined in many ways (see Halpern, 1984a), it is used in this context as the raw material or "stuff" of thought. Intelligence is not a unitary concept. It is comprised of several intellectual abilities that are related to each other, but yet somewhat different. The number and nature of these component abilities are usually identified with a mathematical procedure known as factor analysis. Factor analysis is a useful descriptive technique that allows researchers to discover clusters of correlated variables. These clusters of variables, known as factors, can be thought of as the "underlying dimensions" of intelligence.

Intelligence was one of the first interests of early psychologists, and there is probably more written about intelligence than any other topic in psychology. In a classical factor analytic study of intelligence, Thurstone and Thurstone (1941) administered 60 different ability tests (e.g., arithmetic, spelling) to eighth grade students. They found that scores on these tests formed three sets of clusters or factors which they called verbal, number (quantitative), and perception (visual-spatial) factors. Modern psychologists concerned with cognitive sex differences still refer to these same three factors. In the years since 1941, several other models of intelligence have been proposed (e.g., Cattell, 1963; Guilford, 1967). The question of whether intelligence is comprised of one, two, or sixteen different factors is not relevant to the issues addressed in this book. The fact that only three categories of intellectual abilities are reviewed here is not meant to imply that intelligence is comprised of only these three factors or that a three-factor view of intelligence is being advocated. Verbal, quantitative, and spatial are the three ability factors in which sex differences are most frequently reported.

Underlying abilities are abstract constructs. They are what we believe we are measuring when we give certain tests. But not all tests measure abilities. In fact, it is very difficult to devise a test of ability that isn't also measuring achievement.

An achievement test measures what an individual knows at the time of the test. For example, if I wanted to know how much mathematics you know, I would give you a mathematics achievement test. If you had very few mathematics courses in high school, then I would expect that you wouldn't know much about the type of mathematics taught in the high school courses you didn't take. You wouldn't be able to solve trigonometry or calculus problems, for example. This doesn't mean that you couldn't solve these problems with appropriate instruction, nor does it necessarily mean that you would have difficulty learning these mathematical concepts. A low score on this test would mean only that you can't solve the mathematical problems at the time of the test.

Ability tests attempt to assess the likelihood of your being able to succeed at certain tasks *in the future* if you received proper instruction and if you were motivated to learn and demonstrate the skills needed to perform the task. A low score on a mathematical ability test, for example, is meant to imply that you are less able to learn certain advanced concepts such as calculus or other higher mathematics than someone obtaining a higher score. It can be loosely thought of as the ability to benefit from instruction in a certain area.

There are, however, several important "ifs" in ability testing. Suppose, for example, a young man who believes that language fluency is a "sissy trait" is tested in the area of verbal ability. He certainly would not be motivated to perform well on this test, leading the researcher to conclude that he had little verbal ability. Consider some of the other assumptions implicit in ability testing. We test mathematical ability by presenting individuals with mathematical problems to solve. Wouldn't someone who had taken more or better mathematical courses be expected to answer more questions correctly than someone with a poorer mathematical education background? In other words, aren't we also measuring achievement? To some extent, we are always measuring achievement whenever we try to measure ability. This is a troublesome problem for psychologists who want to understand possible sex differences in ability. In American and other Western societies, girls typically take fewer advanced mathematics courses and receive less encouragement to excel in mathematics than boys. How can we ever be certain that what we are labeling sex differences in ability aren't really sex differences in achievement? We can't.

A pure measure of cognitive ability would separate what each of the sexes do do (achievement) from what each of the sexes can do (ability). This is not yet possible. Instead, we must rely on the only available data that we have. But, we also need to be careful about the kinds of extrapolations we make from it. Just because tests given in the 1980s show sex differences, doesn't mean that tests in the 1990s will. The term "cognitive abilities" is used throughout this book because it is the term that is commonly used in the literature, yet readers are asked to think of these abilities as impure measures that may really be closer to the concept of achievement.

Tests of cognitive abilities, like all tests, contain a "margin of error." That is, they are not perfectly accurate in the kinds of predictions that they make. A good test of mathematical ability, for example, should predict fairly well an individual's ability to acquire mathematical concepts. Ideally, it should be validated by actually comparing scores on the test with achievement in future mathematics courses. Unfortunately, this is rarely done. More often, these tests are validated by comparing scores on one mathematical ability test with scores on another mathematical ability test. If, in general, the scores are in accord, we can probably conclude that they are measuring the same construct, but we still cannot say much about the predictive value of either test or the meaningfulness of the construct we've just measured. The construction of valid and reliable tests is a complex statistical endeavor. Some of the tests cited in the cognitive sex differences literature have poor or unknown psychometric properties (reliabilities and validities). These tests should be considered only as ancillary evidence for or against a particular position and not as primary evidence because of the questionable nature of their construction.

In all psychological measurement, there is always a gap between the test result and what it signifies. Test results are interpretable only to the extent that a plausible theory can link them to meaningful constructs. Although mountains of data exist that address the questions of cognitive sex differences, there are few good theories that can synthesize and interpret the empirical results. Thus, while we can talk about sex differences on various tests, we can't always interpret what these differences mean.

Cognitive abilities are theoretical constructs that represent the underlying components of intelligence. The quality of a construct in the sex differences literature can be assessed by how well it passes three tests: (1) If sex differences are found consistently on several different tests that tend to cluster or load onto a single factor, then we have reason to believe that, in general, the sexes perform differently on whatever these tests are measuring. This first step provides converging evidence from several tests that sex differences exist with respect to the construct being measured; (2) If, in addition, we can use these tests to predict performance on a task that requires the skills we believe that the tests are measuring, then the construct is useful; and (3) If an empirically supported theory or theories has been devised to explain why sex differences exist in the ability being measured, then the construct and the theory that incorporates it have explanatory power. The ability to explain phenomena is a major goal of research. The third requirement is needed to make the construct theoretically meaningful, and is the most controversial and difficult of the tests to satisfy.

VALUES AND SCIENCE

The Myth of Objectivity

When most of us first learned about the scientific method, somewhere back in junior high school, we were told about the disinterested researcher who objectively and methodically went about the business of collecting data with the goal of revealing truth. For those of us involved in research, the imagery that this description brings to mind is somewhat humorous. While it is true that researchers collect data, very little of what most of us do could be considered "disinterested." Whatever the topic, few researchers who invest their energies in an experiment are neutral with respect to the type of outcome they expect or want. This is especially true in an area like cognitive sex differences where there is so much at stake and where the potential for misinterpretation and misuse of experimental outcomes is so great.

There are numerous ways in which personal beliefs and values can influence the experimental procedure. Researchers make many decisions in the course of conducting an experiment and the way the decisions are made can deliberately or unwittingly bias the results. Although this topic is covered more extensively in Chapter 2, let's think about a few of these decisions now: the way subjects are selected; the type of measurement employed (e.g., continuous or discrete); the kinds of items used on tests; how to analyze the data (e.g., multivariate or univariate, parametric or nonparametric tests); the number of subjects to include in the study; and whether to focus the discussion on significance levels or effect sizes. If I were interested, for example, in showing that there are no sex differences in mathematical ability, then I would want a sample in which women with high mathematical ability were included because I would want an overall high score for the women. I could opt for discrete measurement; the test items that I would select would have to include examples drawn from typical female experiences; I could use nonparametric tests which are typically less powerful (less likely to reveal group differences); and I would want to use a small number of subjects. Decisions concerning what to focus on in the discussion could be made post hoc depending on whether they would support or detract from my favored view. None of this is dishonest (although the use of a less powerful or inappropriate statistical test is very close to dishonest), nor are all of the decisions devious, especially if all of the relevant information is provided in the write up of the experiment. In fact, the decision to include test items from typical experiences of girls would make it a fairer test than including examples exclusively from typical boy activities. This discussion is not intended to show that research or researchers are "bad." An experiment is the most objective method for providing answers to questions. It is important to keep in mind, however, that even our most objective method can be slanted in ways that support the researcher's favored outcome.

In a recent discussion about the relationship between values and science, Wittig (1985) stated: "Knowledge about behavior is constructed, not merely deduced. Such constructions are affected by the historical, personal, social, and cultural context. Judgments of the meaning, validity, and usefulness of a particular analysis of human behavior are themselves socially influenced" (p. 803). It is important to remember that research is conducted in a social environment. The kinds of questions that we ask and the kinds of evidence we are willing to accept depends on its compatibility with the prevailing social view and each researcher's personal views on the topic.

Modern researchers can laugh at the evidence Broca provided in 1861 to support his contention that blacks and women are intellectually inferior. According to Gould (1978), Broca won an epochal debate on this topic by citing the following evidence: "In general, the brain is larger in mature adults than in the elderly, in men than in women, in eminent men than in men of mediocre talent, in superior races than in inferior races" (p. 44). Broca failed to consider the relationship between body size and brain size, and had no data at all on his "inferior race–superior race" distinction. Yet, many nineteenth century academics and physicians willingly accepted his "data" as support for the view that they favored on this issue. We can only imagine twenty-first century researchers laughing at our own naivete in the way we sought to understand cognitive sex differences.

In Shields' (1980) cogent discussion of the subservience of science to social values, she explained that the nineteenth century belief that women were intellectually inferior to men because of their smaller frontal lobes in their brain was replaced later in the century with the belief that the parietal lobes were the true seat of intellectual prowess. Not surprisingly, the following report was published soon after the discovery of the importance of the parietal lobes:

> the frontal region is not, as has been supposed, smaller in women. . . . But the parietal lobe is somewhat smaller, a preponderance of the frontal region does not imply intellectual superiority . . . the parietal region is really the more important. (Patrick, 1895, cited in Shields, 1980)

Feminist Scholarship

In recognition of the fact "that science played handmaiden to social values" (Shields, 1975), several psychologists have suggested that sex differences researchers adopt a "feminist scholarship" approach. One of the goals of feminist scholarship is the recognition and elimination of the "androcentric bias in both content and method" in traditional research (Lott, 1985). Men and women who ascribe to the philosophy of feminist research are careful to consider the importance of context or situational variables as potent influences on the results they obtain from research. Sex is not only a subject variable, it is also a stimulus variable, when viewed from this perspective. Women and men may respond differently in certain situations because the other people in that situation are responding to them in a sex-differentiated manner. In other words, women may perform differently from men on a certain type of task because the other people in the setting are giving them more or less encouragement to perform that task than they are giving to the men. In this case, any sex differences in the task performance should be attributed to sex as a stimulus variable rather than to sex as a subject variable.

Advocates of feminist scholarship utilize nontraditional methods in addition to traditional mainstream methods to examine qualitative differences in the psychology of maleness and femaleness. They will sometimes prefer lengthy individual interviews in attempting to understand a phenomenon. Feminist scholars of both sexes are concerned with similarities as well as sex differences. They are also consciously aware of the way sexist assumptions and other stereotypic beliefs guide the kinds of research questions that are investigated and the varieties of evidence researchers are willing to accept. Like all good researchers, they examine the quality of the data that is collected and the logic that links the data to a conclusion. Of course, they are no freer from their own personal biases than other researchers, but hopefully they are more aware of them—an important fact in itself.

POLITICAL AND SOCIAL RAMIFICATIONS

> *As an area of research, sex and gender is fraught with dilemmas and decision points.*
>
> —Deaux (1985)

There are many commonly held stereotypes about differences between women and men. Women, for example, are usually perceived as being less intelligent than men (Broverman, Vogel, Broverman, Clarkson, & Rosenkrantz, 1972). Many people also believe that women *should be* less intelligent than men. In a survey of school teachers, Ernest (1976) found that both men and women teachers believe that boys are superior to girls in mathematical ability. We know that teachers act in ways that convey these beliefs to the children in their classrooms (Sadker & Sadker, 1985). Suppose that after a careful review of the literature, these stereotypes were found to be true! Teachers would knowingly or unknowingly increase the way they encourage and discourage different areas of intellectual development in their students depending upon the student's sex. Advocates of sexual prejudice and discrimination could justify their beliefs and actions by an appeal to scientific findings. The social and political ramifications of such conclusions cannot be ignored.

The Bugaboo of Biological Explanations

It is frightening, and perhaps even unAmerican, to consider the possibility that even a small portion of the sex differences in cognitive abilities may be attributable to biological factors. This is probably because many people confuse biological contributions with the idea of an immutable or unavoidable destiny. Suppose, for example, that after reviewing the literature I conclude that males really are superior in mathematics and that sex differentiated hormones or brain organizations are implicated in these differences. This does not necessarily reduce the importance of psychosocial variables, nor does it imply that the differences are large or that the differences could not be reduced or eliminated with appropriate instruction. What such a conclusion does do, however, is create the potential for misquotation, misuse, and misinterpretation, in an attempt to justify discrimination based on sex. Perhaps the very publication of such research results create a considerable risk.

Censorship in Science

The question that is being raised is whether there should be censorship in science, even self-imposed censorship, when results are likely to be misused. However, the danger inherent in censorship is far greater than the danger in publishing results that could be used for undesirable purposes. The answers provided in this book to the questions of sex differences are complex and contain many qualifiers. Readers who read only the chapter on biological hypotheses or only the chapter on psychosocial hypotheses without reading the final chapter that integrates both approaches will come away with different erroneous conclusions about the area. Quotations taken out of context can be used to support virtually any position because all sides of the issues have been considered.

Keep in mind that results obtained from groups of males and females do not justify discrimination against individuals. Nor can we afford to confuse what has been with what could be. Sex differences that exist in twentieth-century American society do not necessarily exist in other societies or in the American society of the future.

TERMINOLOGY

The terms we use to convey ideas reflect our own biases about the topic being discussed. I have argued elsewhere that different images and meanings are evoked depending on the choice of words that are selected to convey our thoughts (Halpern, 1984a). Consider, for example, differences among the terms "senior citizen," "old man," and "golden ager." While, in some sense, these three terms can be considered synonyms, each conveys a somewhat different meaning. There is a reciprocal relationship between thought and language. The words that are used in the sex differences literature also influence how we think about the issues and the research results; therefore, I have decided to explain why I selected certain controversial terms.

Sex and Gender

Some psychologists prefer to use the term "sex" only when they are referring to biological distinctions between males and females, while reserving the term "gender" to refer to the psychological features or attributes associated with the biological categories (e.g., Deaux, 1985; Unger, 1979). Other psychologists have maintained that sex and gender are independent concepts as in the case of a biological male who may be perceived of as unmanly in his social context (e.g., Money, 1975). I have decided to use the term ''sex'' to refer to both biological and psychosocial aspects of the differences between males and females because these two aspects of human existence are so closely coupled in our society. It is frequently difficult to decide if the differences that are found between females and males are due to biological (*sex*) differences or the psychosocial concomitants (*gender*) of biological sex.

The use of the term *sex* is not meant to imply that biological variables are more important than psychosocial ones or that the results being discussed are caused by differences in genes, hormones, sex glands, or genitals. The point that biological manifestations of sex are confounded with psychosocial variables is made repeatedly throughout this book. The use of different terms to label these two types of contributions to human existence seemed inappropriate in light of the interactionist position that I have taken in several places throughout this book. Because I believe that it is not possible to study sex differences and gender differences independently, I have decided to use the term *sex* to refer to both types of differences and their interaction.

Language purists will agree with my choice of the word *sex* instead of *gender*. Gender was originally a grammatical term used in languages that make a distinction between feminine and masculine nouns. It is not related to maleness or femaleness even in these languages. Gender is also sometimes used as a euphemism for the word *sex* because of the possible physical overtones implied by sex. Thus, for several reasons, gender seems to be an inappropriate label for the differences between females and males.

Sex and Sex-Related

Other psychologists have urged that the term ''sex-related'' differences be used instead of *sex* differences in order to emphasize the fact that many of the differences that are reported are correlates of the biological distinctions between females and males and not necessarily due to biological differences (Sherman, 1978). Once again, the objective of this distinction is to separate biological and psychosocial determinants of between-sex differences. While I am aware of the consciousness raising aspect of this distinction, I have decided to use the shorter term ''sex differences'' in recognition of the close relationship between biological and psychosocial variables, using the term *sex-related* only occasionally for emphasis. The preference for the term *sex differences* is not meant to imply a preference for biological explanations.

Abilities, Skills, and Performance

Because there is considerable disagreement about how well various theories can explain sex differences and whether sex differences could be eliminated with appropriate instruction, other researchers have suggested that the term ''abilities'' should be replaced with other more neutral terms like ''skills'' or ''performance'' (Sherman, 1977). Once again, this distinction is based on the notion that the word ''abilities'' is suggestive of biological or immutable differences while the terms ''skills'' or ''performance'' are not. These three terms are used interchangeably throughout this book. The use of the term ''abilities'' is not meant to imply that the trait under discussion is either biologically determined or genetically linked.

Pronouns

Traditional English usage has required that the masculine pronoun *he* be used whenever the sex of the referent is unknown. The male bias in our language and particularly the use of the male pronoun to refer to either females or males is discussed more fully in Chapter 5. Psycholinguistic research has shown that listeners tend to think of males when the male pronoun is used (MacKay, 1983). For this reason and because of a personal dislike for this convention, I have rejected the exclusive use of the masculine pronoun and have alternated the use of female and male pronouns throughout this book whenever the sex of the referent is unknown. Sex neutral plural constructions (they) have also been used when they didn't interfere with the topic being discussed.

SELECTIVE NATURE OF ALL REVIEWS

The purpose of this book is to provide a comprehensive review and synthesis of the research and theories that pertain to the questions of cognitive sex differences. Thousands, maybe even tens of thousands, of journal articles and books have been written that address this topic. Different experimental methods have sometimes been used to answer the same questions, and the answers don't always agree. Different results have frequently been obtained with the same tests, and similar results have been interpreted in different ways by different experimenters. Decisions had to be made continually as to which research is important and good. In an area as large as this one, only a subset of all of the available information can be presented. In addition, new knowledge is accumulating at an unprecedented rate. Thus, this review, like all reviews of the sex differences literature, is necessarily selective.

I'd like to take this opportunity to apologize to the many researchers who have published in this field, but whose research has not been cited. In deciding which research to include in this review, I followed a few basic guidelines. I decided to include research that is representative of many experiments when several similar investigations were reported on the same topic (e.g., many researchers have found that spatial skills can be learned), to include pivotal or *important* research that helped to clarify a theoretical position or to choose between two or more alternative interpretations of research, and to devote more space to the controversies than to the areas in which a consensus has been reached. I have also attempted to maintain a balanced view in this highly controversial area of psychology. I also believe that the answers we accept as true today will probably seem outdated and will sometimes be proven wrong in several years. There are no final answers, only the questions will endure.

PLAN FOR THIS BOOK

This introductory chapter is designed to set the stage for an examination of sex differences in cognitive abilities. Research methods and philosophies that determine how we answer the questions of cognitive sex differences are discussed in Chapter 2. It is unusual to include a research methods chapter in a book on cognitive sex differences. It is included here in the belief that readers need to understand how the research questions were answered in order to understand the answers. Readers with a good background in experimental methods and statistics can skip or skim this chapter before going on in the book. Chapter 3 examines the question of whether or not sex differences in cognitive abilities exist, and, if so, where? Chapter 4 considers biological hypotheses devised to explain cognitive sex differences, and Chapter 5 considers the psychosocial hypotheses. Competing and complimentary research and theories are integrated in Chapter 6, along with suggestions for further research.

2 Searching for Sex Differences in Cognitive Abilities

CONTENTS
The Need for Research
Types of Experimental Investigations
   Anecdotal Evidence and Surveys
   Correlational Approaches with Nonrandom Assignment of Subjects
   Observational Techniques
   True Experiments
   Factor Analytic Approaches
Understanding Research Results
   The Logic of Hypothesis Testing
   Sampling Issues
   Measurement
   Multivariate Indicators
   Variability and Shapes of Distribution
   Statistical and Practical Significance
   Meta-Analysis and Effect Size
   The Interaction of Variables
   Situational Variables
Developmental Issues
   Cross-Sectional vs. Longitudinal Studies
Self-Fulfilling Prophecies
Evaluating Research Claims

THE NEED FOR RESEARCH

The first step in our quest to understand if, where, and when sex differences in cognitive abilities exist is an examination of the experimental and statistical procedures used to provide the answers. The kinds of questions we can ask and the answers we get depend on the experimental and statistical methods used in research on sex differences. The goal of this chapter is to consider the research issues that are important in evaluating the proliferating literature in the area of sex differences. Some of the issues are relevant to evaluating research claims in any area; others are unique to research that attempts to answer questions about sex differences. The issues range from the basic assumptions underlying hypothesis testing to methods of integrating results across multiple studies. Readers with little or no background in statistical and research methods may have difficulty grasping some of the more technical explanations in this chapter; however the general principles should be easily understandable to all readers. Reports of the actual research on sex differences will be presented in Chapter 3, and research and theories designed to explain why differences exist are presented in Chapters 4 and 5. As you will see in these chapters, not all of the research has employed the techniques that will be identified as desirable or necessary. The validity of the conclusions rest on the quality of the research from which they were generated.

Consider, for example, the following conclusion about men and women made in a research report by Landauer (1981): "This may well indicate that women have greater cognitive abilities" (p. 90). It is unlikely that you would simply nod your head and accept these results as *truth*. You'd want to know who the researcher used as subjects, how cognitive abilities were measured, what the relevant values are for each group, and how the investigator reached this conclusion. (In Landauer's research this dubious and overstated conclusion resulted from the finding that within a certain experimental paradigm, women made decisions faster than men did.) In fact, the experimental and statistical methods used may be more important in determining the answers we get to empirical questions than the underlying phenomenon being investigated. Although many people are distrustful of research results and, as discussed in Chapter 1, it is not value-free, the scientific method is the most objective, unbiased, and systematic approach available for finding answers to questions.

A number of years ago, I had a conversation about the nature of sex differences with a member of an Eastern fundamentalist religion. There were no unresolved questions for him. One of the tenets of his religion was that women are best suited for home and child care while men are best suited for the intellectual work needed to support a family. For him, any research on this question would have been superfluous since the answers were God given. Of course, not everyone shares his religious beliefs. I later learned that some members of his religious sect doubt his interpretation of the religious principles. For most of us, the many questions pertaining to sex differences require an empirical test. An empirical test requires collecting information in as an unbiased a manner as possible and then carefully scrutinizing it in accord with the rules of evidence to determine what, if any, conclusions can be drawn. Research methods provide the tools for understanding the relationships among variables, in this case, among sex (or gender) and the cognitive or intellectual abilities. The experimental method is a potentially objective method that allows researchers to confirm or disconfirm their hypotheses or beliefs. I have described the experimental method as potentially objective because it is impossible for research to ever be totally objective. The very questions researchers are interested in and the way they construct hypotheses and decide what variables to measure are contaminated by their beliefs, prejudices, and societal values.

There are several different ways of conducting research, each of which has advantages and disadvantages associated with it. Let's consider the way various experimental methods can influence the type of information they yield.

TYPES OF EXPERIMENTAL INVESTIGATIONS

Anecdotal Evidence and Surveys

Most people have strong beliefs about sex differences. Stop and ask almost anyone about sex differences with regard to a specific ability, math for example, and you're likely to get an answer like this one: "Of course, boys are better than girls in math. Both my sons did well in math, but my daughter just hated it." (Notice that this answer switched from performance in math to attitudes toward math.) Or, you might get an answer like this one: "Personally, I think that women are better at math than men. My husband always depends on me to balance the checkbook." There is a tendency for people to rely on and to prefer personal anecdotal answers to questions instead of general ones derived from large samples. This preference reflects a well-documented bias in favor of using one's own experiences in understanding human behavior.

There are many problems with anecdotal answers. First, our own experiences and those of our friends and family may not be typical of people in general. We may be generalizing to all or most males and females from atypical observations. Second, they are biased in predictable ways. Our memories are fallible and may be influenced by our beliefs and expectations. There is a wealth of evidence in the social psychological literature that shows that stereotypes are difficult to disconfirm because we select and remember information from our environment which is consistent with our beliefs (e.g., Halpern, 1985). Third, anecdotal evidence lacks precision. You might remember that your brother got higher grades in math than you did, but you might not remember how much higher. Most importantly, such evidence can rarely be used to determine cause. Did your sister perform poorly because she lacked ability or was she discouraged from performing well? Despite the typical reliance upon personal experience to formulate general laws of human behavior, only systematic investigations of large samples of data that are representative of the population we want to know about (in this case, all men and all women) can provide answers to questions relating to sex differences.

Another weak type of evidence for understanding the nature of sex differences comes from survey data. Surveys can take many forms. Sometimes, surveys ask what skilled activities you perform well or poorly. If more women than men were to report that they write poetry well, would you be willing to consider this finding as support for the notion that women have better poetry or language skills than men? I hope not because differences in self-reports may not reflect differences in actual abilities. The unreliability of self-report data is well established across many fields of study. It is possible that more women report that they write poetry well because it is a more socially acceptable trait for women. It is possible that comparable numbers of men also write poetry equally well, but they are unwilling to admit it.

Sometimes, surveys involve simple head counts of the number of women and men in a selected category. For example, virtually every such survey finds that there are many more men than women in math-related occupations such as accounting, mathematics, and physics. Head count surveys may provide interesting information about "how many" and "how much," but they can never tell us why each sex has disproportional representation in certain occupations. Are there more male mathematicians because men have greater math ability or only because it is more difficult in our society for women to gain access to certain occupations? Although anecdotes and surveys may seem intuitively appealing, they are limited in the type of research question for which they can provide answers.

On the other hand, one advantage of surveys is that the results can be used to suggest topics for future research. Fennema and Sherman (1977, 1978) for example, have conducted extensive surveys on attitudes towards mathematics among high school girls and boys. They found that girls perceive mathematics to be less useful than boys do and, in general, maintain less favorable attitudes toward the study of advanced mathematics. Sherman (1980) used these results as a springboard for further studies. She found that among equally able girls, perceived usefulness of mathematics and confidence in learning mathematics was a significant factor in determining their enrollment in mathematics courses.

Correlational Approaches with Nonrandom Assignment of Subjects

In a correlational approach, the researcher examines the relationship between changes in two or more variables. Consider, for example, an article on the relationship between marijuana use and scholastic aptitude that was recently published by a national newspaper. It argued that marijuana has a deleterious effect on scholastic aptitude based on the finding that Scholastic Aptitude Test (SAT) scores declined during the years that marijuana was in heaviest use, and SAT scores increased when marijuana use declined. This argument is based on the negative relationship between SAT scores and marijuana use; when marijuana use increased, SAT scores declined and when marijuana use decreased, SAT scores increased. Let's suppose that the data in support of this claim are correct. Can you find anything wrong with this line of reasoning? What is missing is the causal link. It is incorrect to infer that marijuana use was responsible for the rise and fall in SAT scores. It is possible that a third factor, for example, changes in the economy, was responsible for the increase in marijuana use and the decrease in SAT scores. (Perhaps when the economy is tight, students take school more seriously and have less money to spend on drugs with the reverse occurring in a booming economy.) It is also possible that changes in SAT scores caused the changes in marijuana use. Maybe when students perform poorly on the SAT, they smoke more marijuana and as their scores improve, they smoke less marijuana. The problem being raised here is commonly known as "causal arrow ambiguity." The coincidence of changes in two variables does not provide support for the notion that one variable is responsible for the concomitant changes in the second variable. In order to determine if marijuana smoking *caused* changes in SAT scores, students would have to be assigned at random to either smoke or not smoke marijuana for a predetermined period or time. If we found that the group who smoked marijuana scored, on the average, significantly lower on the SAT than the group that didn't smoke marijuana, then we could conclude that marijuana smoking is deleterious to SAT performance. Unless subjects are randomly assigned to conditions, it is likely that students who voluntarily smoke marijuana differ in many ways from those who don't (e.g., differences in socieconomic status, attitudes toward illegal drugs, etc.). It is possible that any or all of the other differences are responsible for the decline and subsequent increase in SAT scores.

Most of the research on sex differences does not employ the random assignment of subjects to conditions because it usually is not possible to intervene in people's lives and change their life experiences. Sex differences research often involves studying males and females "the way they are," that is, without experimental manipulations. For example, suppose an investigator reports that the ability to visualize objects in space is positively correlated with the amount of male hormones present during prenatal development. Such a result constitutes only weak evidence for the hypothesis that the prenatal concentration of male hormones causes good visual spatial ability because of the problem of causal arrow ambiguity. It is possible that many children with high levels of prenatal male hormones also had different home environments or different socioeconomic backgrounds than children with low levels of prenatal male hormones. Or, more likely, males not only have prenatal "male" hormones, but also have life experiences that encourage the development of spatial skills. How can we determine if it is the life experiences or the prenatal hormones or both that are responsible for the good spatial ability? Alternative explanations are possible whenever subjects are not randomly assigned to experimental conditions. All research based on naturally occurring events without experimental manipulations are necessarily confounded (i.e., more than one variable changes at the same time, in this case, the biological determinants of an individual's sex varies along with certain life experiences) and cannot provide causal information.

Correlational data with nonrandom assignment can provide a stronger case for causation if the results are in accord with a highly plausible theory. Suppose, for example, there is reason to believe that if male hormones are high during fetal development, then the neurons in the area of the brain specialized for vision show a more complex pattern of dendritic growth with more interconnections with other neurons. If this theory were true, then the finding that high concentrations of prenatal male hormones are positively correlated with the ability to visualize spatial objects would provide corroborative evidence that these hormones underlie spatial visualization abilities. This is a totally fictitious theory that I devised to make the point that research conducted with nonrandom assignment of subjects in conjunction with a strong theory provides better evidence for causation than the research alone. In this case, data involving nonrandom assignment of subjects would serve to corroborate other empirical sources of support for the theory. In fact, any report of sex differences without a theoretical underpinning to explain why the differences occurred should be viewed with skepticism. Like survey results, serendipitous findings can be valuable if they are used as an impetus for additional research and if they can be incorporated in a testable theory.

All research results are necessarily probabilistic, which means that sometimes sex differences will occur in experiments by chance. If all of the human research conducted tested for sex differences, many spurious reports of sex differences would clutter the literature. It is prudent to consider any atheoretical reports of sex differences as chance findings until they are replicated and cast in a theoretical framework.

If correlational data can be used to support a "highly plausible theory," the problem remains of determining what makes a theory "highly plausible." The mere existence of a theory is not sufficient. A theory needs to be supported empirically with research conducted in multiple settings, using different samples of subjects, and different measurement techniques before it gains the status of *highly plausible*. It also needs to fit within an existing framework of facts and beliefs. There are many theories about sex differences in male and female brains, for example. Yet, these theories are surprisingly mute on the mechanisms that underlie these differences. Like the proverbial chain, a theoretical network is only as strong as its weakest link. A strong theory can explain and predict the causes, correlates, and consequences of cognitive sex differences.

Observational Techniques

With observational techniques, researchers literally "look" at behaviors, usually in "real world" situations. Suppose that you were interested in knowing if young girls really differ from young boys with respect to aggression. You could observe the playground behavior of young children, keeping a tally of the number of aggressive acts committed by boys and girls. One of the advantages of this technique is that you would be actually observing *real* behavior rather than relying on some secondary technique like asking girls and boys about how aggressive they are. However, this technique has many of the same problems associated with it as noted in previous sections. Even if you found that boys (or girls) committed more aggressive acts, observation can never provide an answer as to why these sex differences occur. There are also other drawbacks to this technique. Observations are never really objective because we tend to see what we expect to see. If a girl pushes a child on the playground, it may appear less aggressive to an experimenter than when the same push is done by a boy. It is also likely that children will behave differently if they know that they are being observed. Thus, by observing the behavior, the researcher may actually have changed it. The choice of where to observe behavior also becomes important. A researcher may find sex differences on the playground, but not in the classroom or on the soccer field.

True Experiments

Most researchers consider the experiment as the method of choice for determining cause. In a ''true'' experiment, the researcher has greater control over the variables because subjects are assigned at random to experimental and control groups. Consider the hypothetical example cited above on the relationship between prenatal hormones and spatial visualization ability. In a true experiment, the researcher would select the subjects, in this case the unborn children (fetuses), assign them at random to either high-hormone or low-hormone conditions by administering drugs to their mothers, and measure their spatial visualization abilities later in life. The underlying assumption is that large groups of subjects selected at random will be more or less equivalent with respect to the variable of interest, in this case spatial visualization ability. If we systematically vary only one aspect of their lives (prenatal hormones) so that overall the two or more groups differ only in this way, we can attribute any major differences between groups to this ''treatment.'' Presumably, there would be rich and poor, smart and dull, tall and short, etc. children in each group, but the only consistent between-group difference would be the nature of the variable the researcher has manipulated.

The major difference between a true experiment and the correlational approach discussed earlier is the random assignment of subjects to manipulated conditions. Random assignment allows the experimenter to control the variable of interest so that any systematic differences between the groups are attributable to the manipulated variable. The underlying rationale is that people differ from each other in many ways. If we assign people to different treatment groups at random, then preexisting group differences would be unlikely since people of all sorts should be found in each of the groups. It then becomes more likely that any difference between the groups is due to the treatment. Thus, only a true experiment that randomly assigns subjects to conditions allows the experimenter to infer cause.

Very few "true" experiments are conducted in the area of sex differences. Obviously, we cannot vary the concentration of selected hormones that certain fetuses will be exposed to before birth. Such interventions would be unethical and unconscionable. Instead, we must take people "as they come" and lose the control that is needed to understanding causal links. A paradox in sex differences research is that the major variable of interest—being male or female—is never assigned at random. If we find that women perform a task, on the average better or worse than men, we still can't answer the question, "why?" There are many variables that covary or go along with biological indicators of sex in our society, such as hormone concentrations, social expectations, power, status, childbirth experiences, and learning histories to name a few. Given that so many variables are confounded with sex, and sex is never randomly assigned, causal attributions for any between-sex difference will be difficult to support. This is an important point because all sex difference research is basically correlational in nature. Researchers can never be certain if any between sex differences are due to the biological aspects of sex, psychosocial concomitants of sex, or some third unidentified factor.

The fact that biological sex creates very different environments for males and females from the moment of birth means that differences in biological sex are always associated with different environmental experiences. Distinguishing between nature or nurture as the more probable cause of sex differences is so difficult because of the confounding of nature and nurture. This is particularly germane to the controversies surrounding cognitive abilities. I return to this theme in several places throughout this book because it is critical in understanding the etiology of sex differences.

Factor Analytic Approaches

Traditionally, a common method of studying human cognitive or intellectual abilities has been the factor analytic approach (e.g., Thurstone & Thurstone, 1941). The underlying rationale for this approach is that cognition is not a single homogeneous concept. Most psychologists believe that there are several cognitive abilities and that individuals can be skilled or unskilled in one, some, or all of them. One of the most common theoretical distinctions is between verbal and spatial abilities. One way to test this hypothesis is to give a large number of women and men several tests of verbal abilities (e.g., vocabulary comprehension, verbal analogies) and spatial abilities (e.g., using maps, solving jigsaw puzzles). If these four tests are really measures of two different abilities, then through the statistical technique known as factor analysis, two factors or underlying dimensions will result from the data analysis. The first factor, which we believe represents verbal ability, will be created from the vocabulary comprehension and verbal analogies test scores, and the second factor, which we believe represents spatial ability, will be created from the using maps and solving jigsaw puzzles test scores. (The actual mathematical principles and procedures involved are not germane to the purpose of this discussion and therefore, are not described. The interested reader is referred to Kerlinger, 1979, for a lucid discussion.) If we obtained the same two factors for both our sample of women and our sample of men, then we would conclude that women's and men's cognitive abilities have similar factor analytic structures. Suppose, by contrast, that we found that only one factor emerged for our sample of women. This would mean that these four tests had a single underlying dimension for women. (Another way of thinking about this hypothetical result is that the four tests were all measuring the same unitary construct.) If our sample of men yielded two factors from these tests, and our sample of women yielded only one factor, then we would conclude that there are sex differences in cognitive structures.

Only a handful of studies have actually used factor analytic techniques to compare the cognitive structures of men and women. This is an important approach because it poses the more fundamental question of sex differences in the organization and structure of cognitive abilities as opposed to asking which sex is better at a given ability.

UNDERSTANDING RESEARCH RESULTS

The Logic of Hypothesis Testing

A researcher searching for sex differences is really considering two mutually exclusive hypotheses. The first hypothesis is that there really are no differences between males and females with respect to the variable being studied and, therefore, any differences found between the two groups are due to random error or chance differences in the samples selected. This hypothesis is called the null hypothesis. The competing or alternative hypothesis is that there really are differences between women and men and these differences are reflected in the sample of males and females. The researcher uses statistical tests to decide if any between-group differences are likely to have occurred by chance. If the tests show that the differences between the samples of women and men probably were not due to chance factors, then the experimenter can reject the null hypothesis and accept the alternative hypothesis. Thus, we formulate conclusions in a somewhat backward fashion. We conclude that the alternative hypothesis is probably true by deciding that the null hypothesis is probably false. In hypothesis testing, demonstrations of sex differences rely on a clear cut set of procedures which involve deciding that the null hypothesis (the one that states that there are no sex differences) is probably wrong, and therefore the competing hypothesis that sex differences exist is probably right.

What about failures to reject the null hypothesis? Any serious sex differences researcher is also concerned about sex similarities. How can she or he conclude that there are no sex differences? This is a much more difficult problem and one that is particularly troublesome for research in the area of sex differences. Unfortunately, we can never accept the null hypothesis. The best we can do is fail to reject it. The strongest statements that can be made from failures to reject the null hypothesis is that the data don't support the notion that sex differences exist. We cannot conclude that differences don't exist. There are two reasons why failures to find differences can't lead to the conclusion that there are no differences: statistical (the alternative hypothesis is not precise enough to permit the computation of the probabilities needed to reject it), and logical. (A more detailed explanation of the statistical reasons is beyond the scope of this book. Readers who have not had a course in statistics or experimental methods will have to take it on faith that there are mathematical reasons why claims of no sex differences can't be accepted statistically. Interested readers are referred to Adair, 1973; Christensen, 1985; and Leedy, 1981.)

Consider a simple example which should help to clarify this point. Suppose you formulate the null hypothesis that no one has more than or less than one head. You could collect a large sample of people, count the number of heads per person, and presumably find that each has only one. However, you haven't *proved* the null hypothesis since only one exception, that is only one person with more or less than one head, can disprove it, and it is possible that you failed to include this person in your sample. Similarly, even large amounts of negative evidence cannot be used to prove that sex differences don't exist. Thus, in the logic of hypothesis testing, we can never directly prove a null hypothesis. We can only disprove or reject the null hypothesis (the one that states that there are no sex differences) which, in turn, allows us to accept a mutually exclusive alternative hypothesis (the one that states that there are sex differences). (See Rozeboom, 1960, for a discussion about the failure to reject the null hypothesis.)

Most sex differences researchers are as interested in discovering similarities between females and males as they are in differences, yet, it is axiomatic that they can never conclude that differences don't exist. The logic of hypothesis testing is the backbone of the experimental method, and it does not permit a similarities conclusion.

Rosenthal and Rubin (1985) have recently distinguished between the use of the experimental method to establish facts versus its use to summarize research. They argue that it is virtually impossible to establish facts with any single study. Facts are established only through replicated findings across many studies. In their view, a research report is publishable "if it contributes important evidence on an important scientific question" (p. 527). I believe that their point is especially relevant to research into the nature of sex differences. While it may not be possible to *prove* that sex differences in a particular area don't exist because of the strict logic of hypothesis testing, it is important to know if large numbers of researchers fail to find sex differences. If, for example, we knew that 95 out of every 100 investigations of mathematical sex differences failed to find differences, this information would certainly cause us to alter our conclusions about this area.

Sampling Issues

There are several sampling pitfalls that are exacerbated in or unique to sex differences research. Five of these issues are considered here: comparable between-sex samples; sample size; inappropriate generalizations; age by sex interactions; and replication samples.

Comparable Between-Sex Samples

Sex differences research is concerned with ways in which women and men, on the average, differ. While we may want to know about all women and men in the United States or in the world, we can only collect data from a sample or subset of the population in which we're interested. The people we actually use in our study must be representative of the population we want to know about if our generalizations are to be accurate. Consider the issue of mathematical ability. One common approach to the question of whether males or females exceed in mathematical ability is to administer mathematical aptitude tests to males and females who have attained a given level of mathematical training. For example, a researcher might give an aptitude test to all students in a high school calculus course and then compare the scores obtained by the girls and boys. The major problem with this sample is that there may already have been considerable self-selection of subjects before entry into the calculus class. If mathematical ability is possessed by more boys than girls, then the attrition rate in mathematics courses should be higher for girls than boys with the result that fewer girls persist in mathematics courses. A study of high school calculus students would then be sampling only an extreme group of mathematically gifted or persistent girls (e.g., perhaps the top 10% of all girls) and a less extreme group of boys (e.g., perhaps the top 25% of all boys). Reiterating a point made earlier, studies like this one will not permit any causal statements because the subjects are not assigned at random to math classes. It is impossible to know why sex differences that might emerge from this study exist. They could be due to some factor or factors inherent in the biology of maleness or femaleness, due to societal expectations, or due to a host of other possibilities.

There is no single satisfactory way to resolve the problem of how to sample the sexes so that bias is eliminated. The logical alternative to sampling girls and boys with an equivalent number of mathematics courses is to sample the sexes without regard to the number or type of mathematics courses they have taken in school. The obvious disadvantage to this plan is that any differences that might be found are most likely attributable to the differences in mathematics education. Similar sampling issues arise with other cognitive abilities as well. One partial solution is to utilize statistical control in the form of partial correlations and analysis of covariance procedures. These techniques allow the experimenter to *hold constant* the effect of a variable, like the number of mathematics courses taken by each subject. These procedures statistically allow the researcher to ask a question like, "If boys and girls had taken the same number of mathematics courses, would we still find differences in mathematical ability?" Although these statistical approaches represent an improvement in the way we find answers to sex differences questions, they are also flawed. The use of analysis of covariance, for example, requires certain mathematical properties that are rarely true of any data set (e.g., linear effects across all groups, covariate unaffected by the treatment, homogeneity of between and within groups regression. Readers with an advanced background in statistics are referred to Evans and Anastasio, 1968, and Harris, Bisbee, and Evans, 1971, for a discussion of the use and misuse of analysis of covariance.)

Statistical techniques that control for sampling differences do provide some useful information. They could, for example, show that sex differences in mathematical ability tests could or could not be explained on the basis of course taking alone. Despite these advantages, research that utilizes statistical control procedures still begs the basic question of why there are differences in mathematical achievement tests and in the number of mathematics courses taken by boys and girls. It's like asking if poor people would vote like rich people if they weren't poor. Even if the researcher found that they would, this result would be of little immediate value because the poor people are still poor, and therefore will continue to vote for issues that concern the poor, despite the statistical control we've gained over our data with this technique.

Becker and Hedges (1984) recently focused on the importance of sampling issues in their review of the inconsistencies in the results obtained from research on cognitive sex differences. They concluded that "essentially all of the variability in the sex differences reported can be explained as a function of the publication date and the selectivity of the sampling plan used in the studies" (p. 583). Quite simply, the results you obtain from your study depend on whom you select as subjects. It is important to keep this in mind when interpreting research results.

Sample Size

A second sampling problem in sex differences concerns sample size or the number of subjects we need to include in an experiment. In general, large samples yield good estimates of population parameters (true values in the population). One of the major factors concerning sample size is the amount of variability in the population from which the sample is drawn. If the population has little variability (i.e., there is very little spread among the scores) then a small sample will provide a good estimate of the population parameters while a population with considerable variability (i.e., scores are spread out and do not cluster tightly around a mean value) will require a larger sample size in order to obtain stable estimates of its parameters. One theory in the sex differences literature is that male performance is more variable than female performance. (This hypothesis is discussed in more detail in Chapter 3.) If this hypothesis were true, then we would have to sample more males than females in order to obtain the same level of confidence in our statistics. This is virtually never done in practice, nor have I ever seen it addressed as a sampling issue.

The number of subjects selected for a study has important implications for the conclusions we can draw. Although large samples are desirable because they yield good estimates of population parameters, they also virtually insure that statistically significant sex differences will be found. For mathematical reasons, small samples are less likely to provide evidence of sex differences than large ones. The experimenter who is honestly seeking answers to sex differences questions will have to be concerned with sample size. Far too frequently, the issue of sample size is ignored or resolved on the basis of hunch or intuition. Ideally, all sex differences research (and other research) should begin with an estimate of the size of the sex difference effect that would be important to detect. For example, a researcher studying sex differences in intelligence might decide that a sex difference of less than two IQ points would not be important in understanding differences in cognition. The two point difference would then be converted into an "effect size" (discussed in more detail later in this chapter). It is then a simple procedure to solve a mathematical equation for determining how many subjects should be included in the experiment. Details of this procedure are presented in Cohen and Cohen's (1983) statistical text. Unfortunately, this method of determining sample size is rarely used.

Inappropriate Generalizations

A third issue in sampling concerns the use of atypical populations. Very frequently, researchers sample from abnormal populations to formulate conclusions about normal women and men. This approach is most commonly used in research that examines the effect of chromosomes and hormones on the cognitive abilities of normal women and men. The reasoning behind this approach is that by examining what happens when something goes wrong (e.g., extremely high concentrations of male hormones on developing fetuses), we can understand the role of the variable being investigated under normal circumstances (e.g., the effect of normal levels of male hormones on developing fetuses). There is an obvious flaw in this approach. First, abnormal populations differ from normals in many ways. An infant exposed to abnormal concentrations of prenatal hormones may develop a masculine body type or may receive specialized medical care or unusual treatment by family members. The secondary effects of the hormone anomaly may affect the variable under investigation and these effects could be mistakenly attributed to the hormone rather than the experiential factor. Thus, it is not possible to isolate the influence of hormones per se. In addition, abnormal hormone levels (or chromosome patterns or any other variable that is atypical) may have effects that are unrelated to the effect of normal hormone levels (or chromosome patterns).

Often, researchers concerned about understanding human sex differences conduct their research with other animal species. The major difficulty is generalizing from rats or monkeys to humans. We know that hormones, for example, play a greater role in the behavior of nonhuman species than they do in humans, while cognitive and social variables are more important in determining human behavior. Generalizing from animal research to humans is also difficult because contradictory results are obtained with different species and different breeds within a species. Thus, while animal research can provide information that is interesting in its own right, extreme caution is urged when extrapolating the results to humans.

Age by Sex Interactions

Another issue in selecting subjects is age. It is likely that some sex differences change over the life span and in different ways for each sex. A difference may be nonexistent in childhood, emerge during puberty, and disappear again into old age. Some abilities decline at different rates for elderly men and women. The ways we answer the sex differences questions will probably be age dependent. Research that utilizes only young adults in college (the favorite subject pool of academics) will undoubtedly fail to capture the age dependent nature of any differences that exist.

One of the main criticisms of Maccoby and Jacklin's (1974) major review of the sex differences literature was their extensive use of research utilizing young children to formulate general conclusions about sex differences. In general, researchers have tended to ignore the developmental nature of adult age differences in cognition. Because our cognitive abilities do not remain static throughout the life span, generalizations about sex differences that may be true at adolescence may be false for mid-life or older adults. The elderly remain one of the most understudied populations for cognitive sex differences, despite the fact that understanding sex-related developmental differences is crucial in an aging society.

Replication Samples

Because all research is necessarily probabilistic, sometimes spurious reports of sex differences will be found in the literature. The ultimate test of whether a report of a sex difference is real is whether it replicates, that is, does it reliably appear in other experiments? Good researchers are aware of this test and plan replications of their own work before they publish sex differences results. A replication sample is a second or third sample of subjects who are similar to those used in an original study. These subjects receive essentially the same treatment (if there is one) and have the same measurements taken as those in the original sample. If sex differences are also found in the second or third sample, then we

progress IN science

Copyright Richard Cline, 1985.

can accept the results with greater confidence than if they were only found in one sample. Although replication samples are always a good idea, they are especially important in research that doesn't employ the random assignment of subjects to conditions because research of this sort provides weaker evidence than true experiments. Unfortunately, few reports of sex differences are based on research with replication samples. Later in this book, I describe in detail a research report by Harshman, Hampson, and Berenbaum (1983) that I consider to be pivotal in determining the involvement of biological variables. One of the strengths of this study is the use of three separate samples, which means that we can be more confident that the results are not due to chance factors than we would be if only one sample had been used.

Measurement

Measurement is defined as the assignment of numbers according to rules. The way we measure or assign numbers directly influences the kinds of results we obtain. One of the major measurement issues with which sex differences researchers need to be concerned is how sex should be measured. This may seem like a surprising question if you are not familiar with the problem. Usually, sex is measured is a dichotomous (two choice) variable with every subject being either male or female. However, there are many times when it is desirable to measure the degree of maleness or femaleness. For most of us, the usual indicators of sex are in agreement. Our chromosomes, hormones, genitals, gonads, sex of rearing, and self-definitions all agree that we are either male or female. However, this is not always true. Consider the anomolous case in which chromosomes may indicate maleness, but genitals and sex of rearing are female. Is this person somehow "less male" and "less female" than the typical male or female?

Part of the measurement problem is that it is not always clear what researchers mean by *sex*. Sometimes sex is used to refer to biological differences with the term *gender* used for referring to the social construction of sex. The components of biological sex are usually, but not always, consistent, but components of gender (gender identity, sexual preference, gender role) are very often inconsistent with each other and with biological sex. These variations of sex make it difficult to think of sex as a single variable.

A more common dilemma with regard to dichotomous versus continuous measurement concerns sex-role orientation. This concept refers to the extent to which an individual's behavior conforms to the female or male sex role as defined in a given society. That is, does one conform to sex-typed expectations or stereotypes? The question of whether sex-role orientation should be dichotomous (i.e., men and women could be either masculine or feminine in sex-role orientation) or discrete with three or four possibilities (masculine or feminine or androgynous or undifferentiated) or continuous (more or less masculine or feminine) has been the subject of heated debate. Humphreys (1978) has argued that masculinity/femininity requires continuous measurement and Baucom and Welsh (1978) argue that dichotomous (extreme groups) level of measurement is appropriate. Continuous measurement generally provides more information and may be preferred when measuring variables like handedness in which one can be more or less right or left handed instead of dichotomously right or left handed. However, both levels of measurement are useful in assessing sex differences. It may be that the extremely masculine individual is qualitatively, not just quantitatively, different from a feminine individual. It seems that both dichotomous and continuous measurement can be used depending on the nature of the question being asked.

Multivariate Indicators

An examination of sex-related differences in several cognitive abilities will require that both sex and cognitive abilities be measured. In most research with normal populations, sex is measured by self-report. Virtually all people define themselves as either male or female reflecting sex or gender identity. The measurement of cognitive abilities is more problematic. If you want to investigate spatial ability, for example, how can you measure it in a meaningful way? A clear definition of what constitutes spatial ability is needed. There is often disagreement among researchers, each of whom tends to work with a somewhat different definition. There are literally hundreds of tests that can be used to measure spatial ability, and, as you can imagine, they do not all yield the same results. Some of the tests commonly employed include the performance section of the Weschler Adult Intelligence Scale (WAIS), finding simple figures that are embedded in larger ones, imagining how a figure will look if it is rotated in the depth plane, figuring out how the surfaces of a cube would fit together if a flat diagram were assembled, tracing a route on a real or imaginary map, and assembling a model from written instructions.

The problem for the researcher is to decide which of these tests will yield a *true* measure of spatial ability. It is usually possible to eliminate some tests on an a priori basis because they fail to meet certain criteria. Some of these tests may actually rely heavily on verbal skills or be inconsistent with working definitions of spatial abilities. There is probably no single ideal test. If a researcher wants to demonstrate sex differences in spatial ability, then several tests of spatial abilities should be employed in the same experiment.

Multiple indicators of cognitive abilities are desirable for several reasons. If sex differences in the same direction are consistently found on four different tests of spatial ability, then a more convincing claim that differences exist can be made than if differences are found on one test. Second, if sex differences are found on some tests of spatial ability, but not others, the experimenter can examine ways in which these two types of tests differ, yielding a more fine-grained analysis of the nature of sex differences. A hypothetical example of the way several tests could be used to isolate the nature of the sex difference is the finding that the sexes differ on tests that require short-term memory of spatial information, but not on other tests of spatial ability. These results would suggest that the locus of spatial ability differences is in spatial memory and not the ability to utilize spatial information per se.

Sometimes researchers use multiple indicators and then inappropriately use univariate data analytic techniques. For example, a researcher might use ten different tests of spatial ability, then analyze each test separately to determine if sex differences exist. The use of multiple univariate analyses increases the probability that a researcher will find sex differences that are due to chance sampling differences. Multivariate statistical techniques (e.g., MANOVA) are always needed when multiple indicators are used.

Variability and Shapes of Distributions

In order to understand if a sex difference exists with respect to a particular variable, the investigator needs to be concerned with the distribution of scores for women and men because the relative number of each sex that obtains a particular score on a test has important implications for the way we interpret the data. There are many ways distributions can differ. Consider the six hypothetical distributions of scores in Fig. 2.1.

The hypothetical distributions in Fig. 2.1 depict some possible outcomes for men and women on a test of musical ability. Figure 2.1A represents the case in which men and women obtain an identical distribution of scores, with most subjects obtaining a score of 50 on this test (the mean or average), and few obtaining scores as extreme as 0 or 100. The finding that both sexes have the same distribution of musical ability is seen by the overlapping identical curves. Both curves show the same peak (corresponding to the mean of the distribution in normal distributions) and the same bell-shaped curve (indicating that they have the same variability or "spread-outness" of scores).

Figure 2.1B shows a somewhat different distribution of female and male scores. In this case, the sexes have the same mean score (the *average* for both women and men is 50), but the sexes differ in variability. The male scores are more closely clustered around the mean, indicating less variability for men than for women. Thus, any man selected at random would be expected to be near the

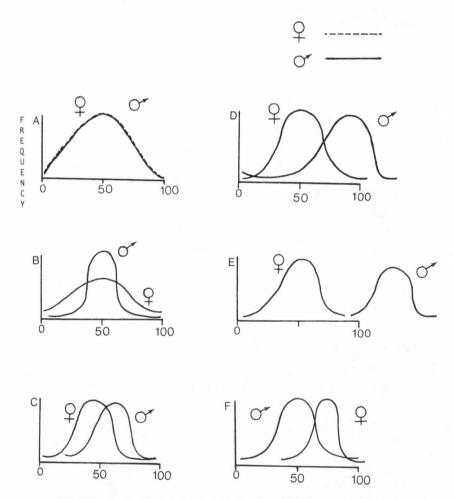

FIG. 2.1.   Six hypothetical distributions of male and female scores on a test of musical ability.

mean value in musical ability while any women selected at random would be expeced to be farther from the mean (either lower or higher) than her male counterpart.

Figures 2.1 C, D and E all depict situations in which the means between the sexes differ (in this case with males, on the average, outperforming females), but the variability remains the same. There is much overlap between the sexes in Fig. 2.1C, an intermediate amount of overlap in Fig. 2.1D and virtually no overlap in Fig. 2.1E. While each of these scenarios represents a case in which a researcher could legitimately conclude that males scored higher in musical ability than females, each figure tells a different story about the distribution of musical ability by sex. If Fig. 2.1E depicted the true results for males and females, then we would expect the most tone deaf males to have more musical ability than the most musically talented females. On the other hand, if Fig. 2.1C represented the true distribution, then we might expect only slight differences in the percentage of women and men at every level of musical ability.

Figure 2.1F represents another possibility. In this figure the female and male distributions have both different means and different variances. In this hypothetical example, females scored higher than males and showed less variability. If Fig. 2.1F were a true representation of these distributions, then we could expect more females to score well on this test and to score close to the female mean while men would be more variable with some obtaining low scores and others high scores. It is important to consider the shape of the distribution of scores when exploring sex differences. Research reports of sex differences that don't provide information about the relative shapes and amount of overlap between distributions provide only a small part of the information needed to understand the data.

Most of the research on sex differences reports mean group differences between women and men. Very few consider sex differences in the shape of the distribution of scores for the variable being measured and the extent to which they overlap. Percentiles of males and females at every ability level should also be provided. A report that women excel at verbal reasoning tasks is less meaningful than one that also indicates, for example, that 75% of women and 70% of men scored at or beyond a given score on the test. The additional information presents a clearer picture of the distribution of this ability between the sexes and allows a more meaningful comparison.

A related issue is the way researchers report measures of central tendency. Most report group means (averages) as a single number summary of the scores obtained by each sex. While this is useful, and possibly essential, in understanding what the data represent, mean values should also be reported along with confidence intervals, which are a range of scores that probably contains the true population mean. It is more meaningful to know that the population mean for women in a statistical aptitude test is probably between 85 and 115 while the comparable confidence interval for men is 87 to 117 than it is to know that the sample mean for women is 100 and the sample mean for men is 102. (In a more statistical vein, confidence intervals are computed for selected confidence levels, such as 95%, and can be interpreted as meaning that if the experiment were repeated 100 times, 95% of the intervals computed would contain the true population mean.)

Statistical and Practical Significance

In order to understand research results, the reader must consider both the statistical and practical significance of any mean difference between males and females. Let's begin with an example to clarify this point.

Suppose that a researcher wants to know if boys or girls watch more television. He carefully samples children within a given age range, socioeconomic status, etc., and then tallies the number of hours of television watched by each child in a week. He then computes the mean (average) number of hours of television watched by the boys and girls in the sample. Suppose that he finds that boys watch an average of 25 hours of television a week and girls watch an average of 25.4 hours a week. Obviously he can't simply look at these two mean values and conclude that the sexes differ with respect to average amount of television viewing. These differences could be due to chance factors (sampling error). Conclusions based on simply *eyeballing* the data are humorously called "binocular tests of significance." All serious researchers require a statistical test of significance.

Since research in sex differences always involves samples of males and females and since people are variable, there is always some chance or probability that conclusions based on the research are incorrect. There is very little in life, and especially in sex differences research, that is known with absolute certainty. It is important to keep in mind the probabilistic nature of research results. Suppose that 100 studies are conducted comparing the number of hours of television watched by boys and girls. If we set $p < .05$, then by chance alone, even if boys and girls watch television the same number of hours each week, 5 of these studies would find sex differences. Furthermore, if only studies finding sex differences appear in the published literature, then it is easy to see how incorrect conclusions are reached. There is no simple remedy for this dilemma. Tests of statistical significance constitute the backbone of research. They are essential in interpreting research results; however, they should really be considered as a first step in making sense from the results.

When research results are statistically significant, it is correct to conclude that there probably are differences between the sexes, especially if the results can be interpreted in a theoretical framework and have been replicated with different samples. Given these results, a second question should be, "Is the difference large enough to have any practical significance?" In other words, are the results meaningful or useful? Considering the current example, the researcher and reader need to ask if the finding that girls watch, on the average, .4 of an hour more television each week than boys has any practical significance. Clearly it would be incorrect to construe this difference as implying that girls are glued to television sets while boys are off doing other things. The obtained mean difference translates into an additional 24 minutes a week or 3.4 minutes a day! Even if such a result is statistically significant, it tells us very little of any practical importance about boy/girl differences in television watching.

Meta-Analysis and Effect Size

The literature on sex differences is enormous. How can anyone sift through thousands, perhaps even tens of thousands, of research reports to determine which of the reported differences is *real?* No single experiment can ever provide the answer to sex differences questions. In an area as complex as this, researchers need to consider the preponderance of results before stating a conclusion. One of the best known attempts to synthesize the literature on sex differences was undertaken over a decade ago by Maccoby and Jacklin (1974). They tallied all of the studies investigating sex differences that had been published in recent American journals. They set as a criterion that sex differences existed only when a large number of studies found sex differences in the same direction for a given variable. While this was the first major attempt to synthesize the sex differences literature, their procedure has been criticized as the "voting method." (See Block, 1976, for a criticism of their methodology.)

A more sophisticated technique of integrating research findings is meta-analysis which, as its name implies, is the analysis of analyses, or an analysis of many individual research results. It provides a measure of the strength or importance of a relationship between two variables. The need for meta-analysis is obvious in a research area in which the size of the literature can be measured in linear feet or pounds of paper generated. Meaningful integrations of research findings are the best way to interpret the voluminous literature. The purpose of meta-analysis is not only to determine how many studies obtained sex differences results in the predicted direction, but also how large the differences between women and men were.

Meta-analyses allows us to take a broad overview in summarizing research results. It is important that the research that is analyzed with meta-analytic techniques be representative of the research in the field. A major problem is finding representative research. The most logical place to find research is the journals and books found in libraries; however, due to publication practices, there is a bias to publish only studies that have found evidence of sex differences. Suppose that 100 researchers investigated sex differences in cognitive styles and that 90 of them found no differences. Suppose further that of the 10 that found differences, two found differences that favored men and eight found differences that favored women. Given the current publication practices, it is likely that only the ten studies that found sex differences would ever get published. Suppose further that a researcher who is eager to understand the nature of sex differences in this area attempts to perform a meta-analysis. She would most likely use only the published studies in her analysis. After all, how would she even know about the unpublished studies which could have been conducted in universities and other settings around the world? If the eight studies supporting female superiority found even moderately large sex differences, meta-analysis statistics would support the conclusion that females have better cognitive styles than males, a conclusion that may be unwarranted in light of the 90 studies that found no sex differences. Fortunately, there are a few sources that allow access to unpublished research reports. Doctoral dissertations are usually available through *Dissertation Abstracts*. Education related research that appeared as paper presentations at conferences or other unpublished presentations are available in ERIC (an educational information retrieval service). Anyone who is contemplating a meta-analytic review of an area should be sure to search these sources for research so that unpublished experiments are included. While inclusion of these sources of data will help to ameliorate some of the bias associated with publication practices, it is also true that papers that report significant group differences are more likely to be accepted for presentation at a conference than research reports that fail to find differences. There is probably no truly unbiased data source.

Meta-analysis has been criticized for its use of unpublished research on the grounds that unpublished research tends to be poorer in quality than published research that has undergone the peer review process. Glass, McGaw, and Smith (1981) defend the practice of giving equal weight to published and unpublished research on empirical grounds. They found small differences in effect size between studies judged as "high validity" (good) and "low validity" (poor). Although several meta-analyses have been conducted in the area of sex differences in cognition, few have made a conscious effort to seek and include unpublished research, thus biasing the results obtained.

Two statistics that are used to determine the importance or size of the experimental effect are ω^2 (omega squared) and d. Each has a somewhat different meaning and use, although both are used in understanding how much the sexes differ with respect to a given variable. Each of these two measures is described separately below.

ω^2

In order to understand the meaning of ω^2, we need to reconsider variance, the measure of the variability in a set of data. As previously described, variance is a measure of how disperse or spread out the individual scores in a data set are. If the scores are very spread out, variance will be large; if the scores are closely clustered, variance will be small. ω^2 is a measure of the proportion of total variance in a data set that can be explained by a particular variable, in this case, sex (Hays, 1981).

Consider the following hypothetical example. If we asked a sample of young and old women and young and old men to respond as quickly as possible to a set of stimuli, we'd usually find that the older subjects took longer to respond than the younger ones. We might also find sex differences, depending on the type of stimuli we employed. Suppose that in this hypothetical study we also found that men responded more quickly overall than women. The first test of the data would be to determine if the differences between age groups and sexes are likely to have occurred by chance. If we found that the results we obtained would have occurred by chance alone less than five times in one hundred, then we'd conclude that the results were unlikely to be due to chance; therefore, real differences probably exist between the age groups and sexes. This type of test is a test of statistical significance. Virtually every research report includes a test of significance. Finding statistically significant results should constitute the first step, not the final step, in data analysis.

In the hypothetical example being considered, some of the variability is due to the fact that two age groups of subjects were used. If the differences in the age groups accounts for most of the variability in the data, then the proportion of total variability due to age will be large. Conversely, if there are large differences in the scores obtained by women and men, then ω^2 will be large for the sex variable. If ω^2 for sex is large, then if we know an individual's sex we could use this knowledge to predict his or her ability to perform the task. If ω^2 for sex is small, then knowing an individual's sex will yield poor predictions about her or his ability on the task. When two or more variables are investigated in the same experiment, the ω^2 associated with each variable can be compared to determine, for example, whether sex or age is more important with respect to the ability being investigated.

In a meta-analysis, ω^2 is computed for each of several experiments investigating the same ability. An average (median) ω^2 is computed from the values obtained in each of the studies. In this way, research results from many experiments on the same topic can be summarized with a single measure of the average effect size.

Despite the fact that effect size statistics have been available in the literature for decades (e.g., Hays, 1963), it is still unusual to find them reported. This failure to report effect size statistics is probably because they are often small, indicating that the variable being investigated was not an important determinant of the ability being measured. Effect size statistics are extremely important in understanding the extent to which sex plays a role in cognitive abilities. A major limitation in interpreting ω^2 or any proportion of explained variance statistic is that the value obtained depends on the other variables investigated in the experiment. ω^2 for sex in an experiment that investigated sex and age variables will not be comparable to the ω^2 for sex in an experiment that investigated sex and socioeconomic variables. Because ω^2 depends on the other variables in the experiment, across-experiment comparisons can only be made when the same set of variables are investigated in different studies.

d

Another statistic used in meta-analysis is "d." It is a measure of the magnitude of the difference between two groups. "d" is a standard unitless mode of expressing the difference between two group means. It is computed by calculating the difference between means on a given variable for women and men and then dividing by the standard deviation. (A standard deviation is a measure of variability. It is equal to the square root of the variance.) Mathematically, $d = \dfrac{M_{\female} - M_{\male}}{S.D.}$. One problem in using "d" is that the standard deviations for women and men are assumed to be equal when computing its value. As discussed earlier, equal variability cannot always be assumed, thus the actual value of "d" may be somewhat off, although this is not likely to be a major concern.

The value of "d" will be large when the difference between means is large and the variability within each group is small; it will be small when the difference between means is small and variability within each group is large. Unlike ω^2, d provides a measure of the direction of an effect. Thus, if we compare "d" from several different studies, a positive value will indicate that females scored higher than males and a negative value will indicate that males scored higher than females as long as the male mean is always subtracted from the female mean. Both ω^2 and "d" allow for comparisons of results across studies. In general, large values indicate large sex differences, and small values indicate small sex differences. For a more advanced discussion of meta-analysis, see Orwin and Cordray (1985).

The Interaction of Variables

One of the main themes of this book is that finding answers to sex differences questions won't be easy, nor will the answers be simple. The cognitive abilities women and men develop depend on many variables. It seems likely that our abilities are influenced by age, birth order, cultural background, socioeconomic status, sex role orientation, learning histories, etc., in addition to the simple fact that we were born either female or male. In reality, these variables work together in their effect on cognitive abilities. It is possible, for example, that wealthy females who are firstborn tend to develop excellent verbal ability, whereas lower-middle class females who are second or third born don't tend to develop these same excellent abilities. In this example, the influence of sex depends on the levels of other variables. A host of sociodemographic (e.g., age, place of residence), psychological (e.g., motivation), biological (e.g., health status), and life history (e.g., level of education) variables operate in conjunction with sex to determine the level of each cognitive ability that an individual obtains. The term *interaction* is used to denote the fact that the effect of sex differs depending on the value of other variables (e.g., low, middle, or high socioeconomic status).

It is important to consider any research on sex differences in light of the other variables that could be influencing the results. Understanding the manner in which sex interacts with other variables will provide a richer and more meaningful interpretation of the way maleness and femaleness influence cognitive development than merely considering the main effect of sex alone.

Situational Variables

It is important to keep in mind that all behavior occurs in a context. Most everyone will agree that people often respond in different ways in different situations. This may be especially true of sex-related differences. Suppose, for example, that you are interested in sex differences in assertive behavior. Furthermore, you are aware that results obtained in laboratory settings may not generalize to the real world. So, you decide to examine assertiveness in a public place. Suppose, further, that you choose to study sex differences in assertiveness at the movies. You carefully note that in mixed sex dyads the male usually drives to the movies, purchases the movie tickets, hands them to the ticket taker, and yes, even makes the important popcorn decisions (buttered or unbuttered). Based on this naturalistic observation, you would conclude that males are more assertive than females. However, you would have failed to study other situations in which women tend to be assertive, such as dealing with a child's angry teacher, returning defective merchandise, handling an emergency at the office, or negotiating the sale of a residence as a real estate broker. You probably recognize each of these scenarios as stereotypically female, yet, you may never have realized that each requires assertiveness, a stereotypically male trait.

Experiments conducted in laboratory settings often involve artificial situations. Because so much of our behavior is situation dependent, it is important to consider ways in which the experimental situation may have biased the results. This is an important point in understanding sex-related cognitive differences. Men, for example, may not perform as well on tasks that are viewed in our society as feminine (e.g., embroidery) when they are being observed as they do when performing the same tasks in private. Sex and race of experimenter are important situational variables which are often overlooked despite the power of their effects. Subjects respond differently to same-sex and other-sex experimenters as well as to experimenters whose race may be different from their own.

DEVELOPMENTAL ISSUES

Cognitive abilities, like physical abilities, do not remain static across the life span. Different activities follow their own developmental course, reflecting the influences of age-dependent biological and sociological changes. Sex differences may appear and disappear depending on the age of the subject. The welter of contradictory evidence in the literature makes it clear that there can be no useful answer about sex differences in any cognitive ability without reference to the ages of the subjects.

Cross-Sectional vs. Longitudinal Studies

If cognitive abilities wax and wane across the lifespan, developmental studies will be needed to understand the phenomena involved. Developmental studies are usually either cross-sectional (sampling at random from different subjects in several age groups) or longitudinal (repeatedly measuring the same individuals at several ages as they mature). Sometimes combinations of these techniques are employed when, for example, several age groups are measured repeatedly over 5- or more-year-periods.

A major problem with cross-sectional studies is the cohort or peer group effect. The cohort effect refers to the fact that people who are the same age also had similar age-dependent experiences. Consider, for example, the following problem: A researcher wants to know about age dependent changes in the ability to read maps. Using cross-sectional samples, he tests men and women in their early 20s, mid-40s and late-60s. Suppose he finds that there are no sex differences in the young group, small differences favoring males in the middle-aged group, and large differences favoring males in the oldest group. Could he conclude that sex differences favoring males develop throughout the adult years? He couldn't make this conclusion since experiences with reading maps of the oldest women are probably different from those of the middle-aged women, who in turn had different experiences than the young women. It seems likely that the oldest women have fewer years of driving experience—an activity that often requires map reading—while many of the middle-aged women and virtually all of the young women drive on a regular basis. By contrast, virtually all of the men in all three age groups drive regularly, thus having similar experiences with maps. The age-dependent sex difference in map reading is more likely due to cohort or generational experiences than it is to life span changes in abilities. It may be that the young women will maintain their map reading skills into old age so that when they are in their late 60s they will perform in a manner comparable to their male counterparts.

Cohort effects, which are always possible in cross-sectional developmental research, are especially likely to contaminate developmental data in sex differences. Women's roles are changing rapidly and it is therefore difficult to control experiential factors across generations. Generational differences in the experiences of women and men will make any determination of why the differences exist very difficult.

Longitudinal research also has drawbacks associated with it. When subjects are measured repeatedly throughout their lifespan, it is always possible that earlier testing experiences influence later ones. There is also the problem of subject loss due to death, moving out of the area, refusal to continue, and other reasons. It is likely that the lost subjects differ from those who continue in subtle ways (e.g., they may be less able). Finally, longitudinal research will take years to provide answers. If you want to study changes that occur from birth into old age, your children or grandchildren will have to collect the last of the data since the study would extend beyond a single lifetime.

SELF-FULFILLING PROPHECIES

It would be naive to believe that researchers approach their work without any bias or prejudice about the expected outcome. We are all committed in varying degrees to either proving or disproving the notion that females and males have comparable cognitive abilities.

A large body of literature exists to document the finding that experimenter expectancies often influence research results. One of the pioneers in this area was Robert Rosenthal who is famous for his work in the area of self-fulfilling prophecies. This term refers to the concept that experimenters and others will often act in ways that influence results so that the outcome is in accord with their beliefs. In a classic study (Rosenthal, 1966), elementary school teachers were told that some of their pupils had obtained high scores on a special test designed to measure intellectual development. Intelligence tests given later in the school year showed that the ''bloomers'' had made greater gains in IQ points than the ''nonbloomers.'' The teacher reported that the bloomers were more interested, more curious, and happier than the other children. What is remarkable about these results is the fact that the children identified as ''bloomers'' had been picked at random and, therefore; did not differ from the other children. Somehow, the teachers had communicated their expectations to the children, who in turn responded to these expectations.

Sex differences research is particularly vulnerable to experimenter and subject expectations. If an experimenter believes that females will outperform males on a particular test, he or she may unknowingly act friendlier toward the females or provide them with a little more encouragement or allow a little extra time in completing the test. Subject expectations also influence results. If, for example, girls believe that mathematical ability is unfeminine, it is likely that they will reflect this belief in their performance. The girls could give up easily on the more difficult problems because they don't believe that they could solve them, or even deliberately select wrong answers in order to maintain a feminine self-concept.

In reading research reports, it is difficult to detect ways that either experimenter or subject expectancies biased the results. One way to circumvent this problem is by having the data collected by researchers who are *blind* to or uninformed about the hypothesis being investigated. Subjects should also be unaware of the fact that sex differences are being examined. Experiments in which the sex of the subject is unknown to the experimenter will also eliminate the effects of sex-related experimenter expectancies. This is possible, however, only in research with young children and research that doesn't require face-to-face interaction between the researcher and subject. (Young children could dress in standard smocks or jeans that don't provide the experimenter with clues as to the child's sex.)

Research in the area of sex differences is particularly vulnerable to self-fulfilling prophecies. It is not necessarily true that simply because someone maintains a philosophical position (e.g., feminist, misogynist, defender of status quo) that he or she is unable to conduct research or formulate conclusions in a fair manner. Readers, regardless of their personal beliefs about the issues discussed in the following chapters, are asked to maintain an open mind and to consider carefully the evidence on both sides of the issues.

EVALUATING RESEARCH CLAIMS

The purpose of this chapter was to raise issues that are important in evaluating research claims about sex differences. In evaluating conflicting claims or strong statements, keep in mind the following issues:

1. Who were the subjects and how were they selected? Is the sample size appropriate for the question being examined (keeping in mind that large samples virtually insure significant differences and small samples yield unstable estimates of population parameters)? Are results from abnormal populations or other species being generalized to all women and men?

2. Are studies that employed neither random assignment of subjects to conditions nor manipulation of any variables inferring causal information?

3. Is the measurement appropriate? Have multiple indicators of abilities been used, and if so, were the data analyzed with multivariate statistical techniques?

4. Are the results both statistically significant and practically significant? How large is the effect size?

5. Has detailed information about the distribution of scores within each sex been provided? Are the results logical and understandable?

6. Has the way sex interacts with other variables in determining the results been investigated? What alternative explanations are plausible?

7. How might the results vary across the life span? Have cohort effects been included as a possible explanation of the results?

8. Are the results reported consistent with the prior literature and/or a theory of sex differences? If not, why not?

9. How could the results have been influenced by experimenter and subject expectations?

The literature on sex differences has been proliferating in recent years. Although much of it is thoughtful and high in quality, some of it is not. The goal of finding answers to the broad, complex, and socially and politically sensitive question of sex differences is of profound importance. The informed reader will have to evaluate the research with an open mind and an awareness of what constitutes good research.

3 Empirical Evidence for Cognitive Sex Differences

CONTENTS

Intelligence
Verbal Abilities
Visual-Spatial Abilities
  Cognitive Styles
  Chess and Music
Quantitative Abilities
Relationship Between Visual-Spatial Abilities and
  Quantitative Abilities
Magnitude of the Differences
  Effect Size for Verbal Abilities
  Effect Size for Visual-Spatial Abilities
  Effect Size for Quantitative Abilities
  Effect Size for Cognitive Abilities Overall
Sex Differences in Factor Structures
Chapter Summary

INTELLIGENCE

The first question most people ask about sex-related cognitive differences is which is the smarter sex—males or females? It might seem that a logical way to answer this question is to obtain large random samples of women and men, give them a psychometrically sound intelligence test (one with good mathematical properties), and compare the scores for women and men. The sex with the higher average score would be the smarter sex. Although this may seem like a logical, straightforward approach to answering the question of sex differences in intelligence, in fact, it won't work. Intelligence tests are carefully written so that there will be no average overall difference between men and women. During the construction of intelligence tests, any question that tends to be answered differently by males and females is either thrown out or balanced with a question that favors the other sex. Therefore, average scores on intelligence tests cannot provide an answer to the sex differences question because of the way the tests are constructed.

A second way to decide whether men or women are, on the average, smarter might be to look at who performs the more intelligent jobs in society. Of course, one would have to decide which jobs require greater intelligence. Suppose that we could agree in principle that jobs like government leader, architect, lawyer, physician, professor, mathematician, physicist, and engineer all require a high degree of intelligence. An examination of who performs these jobs reveals that the overwhelming majority of these jobs are held by men. Does this mean that men are, in general, more intelligent? Looking at the types of jobs typically performed by men and women in society can't provide an answer to the intelligence question because of differential sex roles for women and men. Many professions were formally or informally closed to women until recent years. Similarly, there are few male nurses, secretaries, and child care workers because of the constraints imposed by the male sex role. There are still considerable differences between the sexes in background experiences, types of encouragement, amount and type of education, and social expectations for success. We don't know if the differences in the numbers of men and women in the various job classifications is related to overall intelligence differences or to differential socialization practices or to some combination of the two. This issue is discussed in greater depth in the chapter on psychosocial hypotheses (Chapter 5).

A third way of answering the intelligence question is to look at school achievement. Which sex, on the average, gets better grades in school? It seems that females get better grades than males in school (Johnson & Gormly, 1972). Paradoxically, girls get better grades than boys even in "traditionally male" content areas such as mathematics in which boys score higher on ability tests (Hyde, 1985). Once again, however, this does not prove that there is a smarter sex because alternative explanations are possible. Being a good student is more consistent with the female sex role than it is with the male sex role. Our schools tend to reward quiet, neat students who do as they are told. These are characteristics that are seen as more appropriate for girls than for boys in our society. Thus, school achievement cannot be used to decide if males or females are smarter. In fact, we have not yet discovered a satisfactory way to answer this question.

A more fruitful approach to the cognitive sex differences question is to examine specific abilities, especially in light of the fact that intelligence is not a unitary concept. It is theoretically more useful to think of multiple "intelligences" than to consider intelligence as a single homogeneous mental ability. The question then becomes, "What are the sex differences in cognitive abilities?" Although intelligence tests are constructed so that there will be no overall sex difference in intelligence, the tests do differ in the pattern of intellectual abilities for the two sexes. Surprisingly, in an area as controversial as this one, there is little disagreement about which of the cognitive abilities differ by sex. As you will see, the most heated debates revolve around whether the differences are large enough to be important and why these differences exist.

In 1974, Maccoby and Jacklin published a text that has become a classic in psychology. In their text, they reviewed over a thousand research reports on sex differences in contemporary American society. Although their synthesis and review of the literature is now over a decade old and has been severely criticized on methodological grounds, it has provided a foundation for much of the research that has followed. They identified three cognitive abilities and one personality variable in·which sex differences are "fairly well established" (p. 351). The sex differences literature has burgeoned in the last decade and has, in general, confirmed their conclusions. The three cognitive abilities that have been identified as the loci of sex differences are verbal, quantitative, and visual-spatial ability. Each of these abilities is discussed in turn below. Aggression was identified as the personality variable that differs by sex. The possibility that aggression mediates or influences cognitive abilities is discussed in the next chapter (Biological Hypotheses). It is important to keep in mind that while the preponderance of the data support these conclusions, there is also conflicting evidence in each of these areas, and no single sex difference is unanimously supported in the literature.

VERBAL ABILITIES

Evidence from a variety of sources supports the finding that, on the average, females have better verbal abilities than males. The term "verbal abilities" applies to all components of language usage: word fluency, grammar, spelling, reading, verbal analogies, vocabulary, and oral comprehension. Of all of the cognitive sex differences, it is probably the first to appear. Females aged 1- to 5-years are more proficient in language skills than their male counterparts (McGuiness, 1976). There is also some evidence that girls may talk at an earlier age, and produce longer utterances than boys (e.g., Moore, 1967), although this finding has not always been replicated in recent investigations. In general, the evidence for female superiority in verbal ability tends to support the idea that females are more verbally precocious than males.

Female superiority on verbal tasks may seem reminiscent of the stereotype that females talk more than males, but it is important to keep in mind that it is the quality of the speech produced and the ability to comprehend or decode language that is being assessed, not merely the quantity.

Although verbal sex differences favoring girls in early childhood may be somewhat tenuous, they emerge clearly at adolescence and continue into old age. There are numerous studies documenting sex-related verbal differences beginning at age 11. One of the earliest and best documented reports was established by Wechsler (1955), the author of the Wechsler Intelligence Scale for Children (WISC) and Wechsler Adult Intelligence Scale (WAIS). The WISC and WAIS yield three scores of intelligence: an overall IQ score which does not show sex differences, a verbal subscore comprised of scores on verbal subtests, and a performance subscore comprised of scores on performance or spatial subtests.

Wechsler found that during the middle childhood years (ages 6 to 11) there were no consistent sex differences in the verbal subscores; however, women aged 16 to 64 obtained higher mean scores on the verbal subtests of the WAIS than similarly aged males. These results have been replicated many times since they were first reported in 1955. Sex differences in verbal ability are commonly found in the American College Tests (ACT) and Scholastic Aptitude Tests (SAT) used for college admission (e.g., Burnett, Lane, & Dratt, 1979).

There are numerous other indicators of sex differences in verbal abilities. Young boys are more likely to stutter when producing speech and more likely to have difficulty in learning to read (Corballis & Beale, 1983). There are also sex differences in the ability to regain language following strokes and brain surgery, with males suffering more language impairment and recovering language ability more slowly than females (Witelson, 1976). The research evidence from a variety of sources favors female superiority on verbal tasks. Despite the finding that females score higher on most tests of verbal ability, the overwhelming majority of critically acclaimed writers are male. There are several possible reasons for this discrepancy. It is possible that women are not using their talents as frequently as men, or the tests are not measuring high level creative ability, or differential criteria are being used to judge women's and men's writing. Another likely reason for the lack of critically acclaimed female writers is the fact that until recently women were not educated and, even when educated, had little time to write. It is interesting to note that several outstanding women writers such as Dickinson and Brontes were single women with other means of support. If ability is only a small part of eminence, then the lack of eminent female writers is unsurprising.

VISUAL-SPATIAL ABILITIES

The term "visual-spatial abilities" probably does not convey much meaning to anyone except cognitive psychologists. In fact, it is not an easy term to define because it is not a unitary concept. Generally, it refers to the ability to imagine what an irregular figure would look like if it were rotated in space or the ability to discern the relationship among shapes and objects. The ability to utilize spatial relationships is an important aspect of human thought. It seems likely that visual-spatial skills are used extensively in engineering, architecture, chemistry, and the building trades. Tests of visual-spatial ability have been used to predict success in first year engineering courses (Poole & Stanley, 1972).

Early factor analytic studies that sought to delineate the structure of intelligence found that verbal tests and visual-spatial ability tests formed two distinct factors. The distinction between verbal and visual-spatial abilities as separate components of intelligence has been replicated many times. There is also the possibility that visual-spatial ability differs as a function of ethnicity or race. In a review of the literature on race differences in perceptual functioning, Mandler and Stein (1977) concluded: "From the existing data, we conclude that there *may* be a visualization factor involving rotations or transformations of shapes that differs among ethnic groups" (p. 189). While this possibility is intriguing, there are no well-controlled studies to document this possibility. (See Loehlin, Lindzey, & Spuhler, 1975, for a dissenting review.)

More recently, tests of visual-spatial abilities have been analyzed and two separate factors have emerged (McGee, 1979). It seems that visual-spatial abilities are comprised of:

1. a visualization factor which includes the ability to imagine how objects will appear when they are rotated or how a flat object will appear if it is folded or how a solid object will appear if it is unfolded, and

2. an orientation factor which includes the ability to detect relationships between different stimuli and the ability to perceive spatial patterns accurately.

Figure 3.1 depicts test items similar to the kinds used to measure visualization and orientation abilities.

A large variety of tests has been used to measure visual-spatial ability, and sex differences with regard to test results seem to depend on the type of test used. As stated earlier, visualization and orientation factors both underlie visual-spatial ability; however, these components are not always highly correlated (Kagan, 1982). This means that some individuals are good at visualization and not orientation or vice versa, and are not necessarily good or poor at both types of tasks. Given the multidimensional complexity of visual-spatial abilities, you could probably predict that this is an area replete with contradictory findings.

In a recent review of the spatial abilities literature, Caplan, MacPherson, and Tobin (1985) questioned the legitimacy of the assumption that the construct "spatial abilities" exists. They believe that the entire notion suffers from a "definitional dilemma." As noted in a response to Caplan, MacPherson, and Tobin (Halpern, in press), much of the confusion in this area is attributable to the types of spatial ability tests used. Although some researchers have failed to find sex differences (e.g., Fennema & Sherman, 1978, using the Spatial Relations Test), sex differences that favor males are consistently found with spatial visualization tests which require subjects to imagine the appearance of irregular three-dimensional objects that are rotated in space (Bouchard & McGee, 1977; Sanders, Soares, & D'Aquila, 1982). In his comprehensive review of sex differences in visual-spatial abilities, McGee (1979) concluded, "male superiority on tasks requiring these abilities is among the most persistent of individual differences in all the abilities literature" (p. 41).

One curious problem with sex differences in visual-spatial abilities concerns the variability of test scores. Most major reviews of the literature have concluded that males are more variable in their visual-spatial performance than females

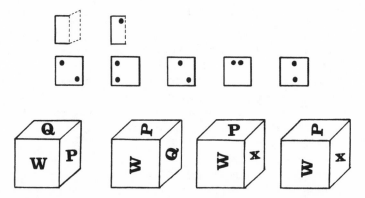

FIG. 3.1.   Sample test items similar to those used to measure visualization and orientation spatial abilities. *Visualization* (top figure) - Imagine folding and unfolding a piece of paper. The figure at the top represents a square piece of paper being folded. After being folded, a hole is punched through all of the thicknesses. Which figure is correct when the paper is unfolded? *Orientation* (bottom figure) - Compare the three cubes on the right with the one on the left. No letter appears on more than one face of a given cube. Which of the three cubes on the right could be a different view of the cube on the left?

(e.g., Maccoby & Jacklin, 1974); however, some researchers report opposite results. Kail, Carter, & Pelligrino (1979), for example, concluded that, "it appears that the important difference is not the average level of ability, but in the variability within each sex" (p. 186). They found that female performance was more variable than male performance. One of the most interesting reports of sex differences in variability in spatial tests was reported by Burnett, Lane, and Dratt (1979) who found that with the same sample of college students the men were significantly more variable on one spatial test (Guilford-Zimmerman Spatial Visualization Test) and the women were significantly more variable on another test (Identical Blocks Test).

One of the implications of group differences in variability is that predicting any individual's performance becomes more difficult. Differences in variability also support the notion that there may be differences in the way men and women perform spatial tasks. Suppose, for example, that the women in the group sampled use different strategies. Perhaps some try to visualize an answer and others try to use verbal labels. These different approaches could result in increasing the variability in the women's scores. If men, on the other hand, tended to use a similar strategy, visualization for example, then their group might be expected to show less variability. It is difficult to say at this time why there are variability differences (with men's performance more variable in some studies and women's performance more variable in others), but the differences are probably not due to chance and suggest some differences in the way females and males solve visual-spatial problems. One possible explanation of the inconsistent and contradictory findings with respect to sex differences in variability on visual-spatial tests is that the differences among the results can be attributed to the nature of the tests. It is possible that women are more variable on certain visual-spatial tasks (perhaps those involving visualization), and men are more variable on other types of visual-spatial tasks (perhaps those involving orientation). Understanding the inconsistent and contradictory findings in variability on tests of visual-spatial ability is a fruitful area for further research.

Petersen and Crockett (1985) reported sex differences on two-dimensional mental rotation tests (described below) among children in elementary school. In contrast, earlier reviews of the literature (Maccoby & Jacklin, 1974) concluded that spatial ability sex differences didn't emerge until adolescence. There is still some confusion about the youngest age at which this effect is found. It seems clear that for some tests, sex differences do appear in childhood. It is possible that sex differences emerge earlier for some spatial abilities than for others. Sex differences are consistently reported from adolescence into old age. In addition to sex differences, there are also age-related differences in verbal and visual-spatial abilities. It is well established that both males and females maintain their verbal abilities into old age, while visual-spatial abilities (especially when measured with speeded performance tests) begin to decline considerably earlier. The decline in old age of visual-spatial abilities is so well established that it is often referred to as "the classic aging pattern" (Winograd & Simon, 1980). In recent applied research on this question, Halpern (1984b) found that older drivers took significantly longer to respond to common symbolic or pictograph traffic signs (e.g., a red slash through an arrow pointing to the right) than to their verbal analogues (e.g., the words "No Right Turn"), while young adult drivers were equally fast at responding to both types of traffic signs. Furthermore, there is some evidence of a sex and age interaction with the finding that visual-spatial abilities may decline more in older women than older men (Elias & Kinsbourne, 1974), although there is insufficient evidence to provide strong support for this contention.

A common experimental paradigm for assessing visual spatial abilities is the mental rotation task devised by Shepard and Metzler (1971). An example of a mental rotation task is presented in Fig. 3.2. In this paradigm, subjects are required to make a comparison between a rotated figure and its standard form and to decide whether the rotated figure is the same as its standard or the mirror image. A recent experiment by Clarkson-Smith and Halpern (1983) found that both the time to respond and number of errors in a mental rotation task increased as a function of age; however, when their subjects, all of whom were women, were encouraged to use verbal strategies in this task, errors decreased significantly for the oldest group. It seems that verbal mediation strategies can attenuate the sex and age-related deficits in visual-spatial abilities.

While some tests of visual-spatial ability do not reveal sex differences, others yield reliable differences. One test that is sensitive to sex differences is the

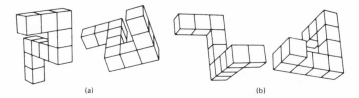

FIG. 3.2.   Examples of a mental rotation task. Can the pairs of three dimensional objects be made congruent by rotation?

"Water Level Test" originally devised by Piaget and Inhelder (1956). In one version of this test, the subject is shown a bottle partially filled with water and is told to notice the way the water fills the bottle. The subject is then asked to predict where the water will be when the bottle is tipped. Piaget and Inhelder believed that the knowledge that water level remains horizontal would be attained at an average age of 12 years. It seems that girls know this principle at a later age than boys. In fact, it has been estimated that 50% of college women don't know the principle that water level remains horizontal. This is a surprising result that has been replicated several times. It is difficult to understand why this should be such a formidable task for college women. (See Harris, 1978, for a review of the research in this area.) One possible version of the Water Level Test is shown in Fig. 3.3.

In an attempt to understand the nature of sex differences with respect to the water level task, Harris (1975) used a multiple choice format to determine if there were sex differences in the ability to recognize the correct answer. He gave this test to a sample of boys and girls in first through fourth grade. Harris found that while the percentage of boys selecting the correct answer exceeded the percentage of girls at every grade level, the differences obtained statistical significance only at the fourth grade. For boys, the percentage selecting the correct answer from first to fourth grade ranged from 25% to 52%, while the corresponding figures for girls ranged from 22% to 28%. The Water Level Test, like mental rotation, is a test in which sex differences are found in childhood.

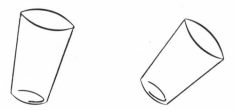

FIG. 3.3.   One version of the Water Level Test. Assume that these bottles are half filled with water. Draw a line to indicate the top of the water line.

Cognitive Styles

There has been considerable interest in recent years in the notion that males and females may have different cognitive styles. The term "cognitive styles" does not have an intuitive meaning. In general, it refers to individual differences in modes of perceiving, remembering, and thinking (Kogan, 1973). It is used by some psychologists in conjunction with the concept of psychological differentiation (Witkin, Dyke, Faterson, Goodenough, Karp, 1962). An individual who is highly differentiated can separate herself or himself from the environment and can separate items from each other in the environment. According to the theory of psychological differentiation, we all differ in terms of how well we can separate items in the environment. There are several dimensions or aspects of psychological differentiation. One dimension along which the sexes are said to differ is in field-articulation or "field-dependence and independence." These terms were coined by Witkin and have been used to characterize the degree to which subjects are influenced by objects in their visual field.

One way of assessing field-dependence and independence is with the "Rod and Frame Test." In this test, subjects are seated in a darkened room and are presented with a luminous rectangle (the frame) that has a luminous rod positioned inside of it. The rectangle is rotated to different orientations by the experimenter. The task for the subject is to position the rod so that it is vertical. Figure 3.4 shows a schematic drawing of some rod and frame combinations that subjects could be presented with. Some subjects' judgments of true vertical for the rod are influenced by the tilt of the frame surrounding the rod. They are labeled "field-dependent." Other subjects' judgments of true vertical for the rod are not influenced by the tilt of the frame surrounding the rod. They are labeled

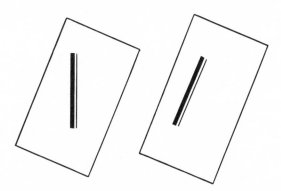

FIG. 3.4. A schematic diagram of the Rod and Frame Test. Subjects are required to position a rod to the vertical position within a tilted rectangular frame. Correct vertical alignment is shown in the left-hand figure. The rod is incorrectly positioned in the right-hand figure.

"field-independent." In general, sex and age differences are found with the Rod and Frame Test (although differences are not unanimously reported). The usual findings are that children are more field dependent than adults, and females are more field dependent than males.

Measures of field-dependence and independence obtained with the Rod and Frame Test are highly correlated with measures obtained with a test known as the Embedded Figures Test. In the Embedded Figures Test, subjects are shown a simple geometric form and then must maintain it in memory and pick it out from a more complex form. Sample items similar to those found in the Embedded Figures Test are shown in Fig. 3.5.

Both the Embedded Figures Test and Rod and Frame Test require the subject to segregate a geometric form from its context, and in both tests females are more influenced by the context than males. Field dependence has been hypothesized to reflect personalities that are conforming, submissive to authority, into comfortable ruts, and passive (Elliot, 1961). Women's field-dependence has been described as "accepting the field more passively than men" (Sherman, 1967, p. 290). On the basis of these test results, women's cognitive style has been described as "global," "conforming," and "child-like." According to Witkin, it is similar to the undifferentiated thought processes found in "primitive" cultures. The field independence associated with male performance has been described, by contrast, as reflecting a cognitive style that is "analytic" and "self-reliant." (The value laden bias in these descriptive terms is too obvious to require comment.) Witkin et al. (1962) believe that because women are unable to

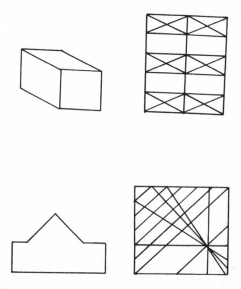

FIG. 3.5.   Sample items similar to those found in the Embedded Figures Test. Subjects have to find the shape on the left outlined in the shape on the right.

maintain a "sense of separate identity" (p. 218), they are less skilled at certain types of problem solving, more likely to conform to group pressure, and more concerned with the facial expressions of others. Thus, different cognitive styles have been ascribed to men and women on the basis of their performance on these two tests.

Several researchers have argued that sex differences in field independence are an artifact of sex differences in visual-spatial ability because both the Rod and Frame Test and the Embedded Figures Test have a strong spatial component (Sherman, 1967). What about other measures of field-dependence and independence that don't rely on spatial abilities? None of the nonspatial tests (e.g., tests that require subjects to match the brightness of a rotating disk) that measure field-dependence and independence yield sex differences. In a test of the hypothesis that sex differences in the Rod and Frame Test and Embedded Figures Test merely reflect differences in visual-spatial ability, Hyde, Geiringer, and Yen (1975) administered a series of tests to a sample of college women and men. The tests included the Rod and Frame Test, Embedded Figures Test, a spatial ability test, arithmetic test, vocabulary test, and word fluency test. All between-sex results were in the predicted direction with males performing better on the test of spatial ability, Rod and Frame Test, Embedded Figures Test, and arithmetic test, and females performing better on the vocabulary test and word fluency test. When they reanalyzed their data statistically controlling for differences in spatial ability, the results changed dramatically. Sex differences in the Rod and Frame Test, Embedded Figures Test, and arithmetic test became nonsignificant. A similar analysis in which they statistically controlled for differences in vocabulary ability had little effect on the two tests of field independence. It would appear that the two spatial tests of field dependence and independence are not indicative of cognitive styles, notwithstanding the claims of Witkin (1950; Witkin et al., 1954) and others, but merely reflect sex differences in visual-spatial ability.

Developmental data support the notion that sex differences in field independence are really reflections of sex differences in visual-spatial ability. Several investigators have found that field independence declines in old age, so that older people of both sexes are generally more field dependent than comparable samples of younger adults (e.g., Crosson, 1984). As already stated, visual-spatial ability also shows a parallel decline in old age. This finding needs to be interpreted with caution because almost all of the research has employed cross-sectional sampling techniques and may represent generational effects rather than actual declines within individuals.

Chess and Music

Sex differences in visual-spatial abilities should be found in the everyday tasks and activities that utilize spatial skills. Two highly skilled activities that seem to have spatial components are chess and music. Is there any evidence of sex differences in these activities? This is not an easy question to answer, and research has not provided us with useful conclusions. Clearly, the vast majority of chess masters and master musicians are men, but, as discussed earlier, this does not mean that women have less ability.

In a careful study of chess masters, de Groot (1966) found that the ability to reproduce the positions of the pieces on the chess board after only a brief glimpse of a legitimate game in progress is what distinguished master players from novices. The masters could quickly code and utilize information from actual "plays," but were no better than the novices when the pieces were placed randomly on the board. This finding suggests that the master players have a highly developed visual memory for the spatial array of meaningful chess boards, but not for other visual-spatial arrays. These results support the conclusion that an extraordinary memory for a visual-spatial array is not a distinguishing characteristic of chess masters. The special ability of chess masters seems to lie in their knowledge of the rules of chess and their ability to organize the displays in terms of the rules. If these inferences from the research are correct, then superior visual-spatial ability is not needed for success in chess, and the most likely reason that women are underrepresented in high level chess tournaments is psychosocial. This is a difficult hypothesis to test experimentally. Although we know that fewer women participate in chess tournaments, we don't know if this is due to actual ability differences or societal pressures to eschew tasks that are typically considered to be "masculine."

Music is another ability that is, at least partially, spatial in nature. High and low notes are placed in different spatial locations on the staff, and melodies and tunes have a definable shape or contour. In addition, the right hemisphere of the brain which is specialized for visual-spatial tasks also underlies musical ability (Springer & Deutsch, 1981). If sex differences in visual-spatial abilities are real, then you would expect similar differences in musical ability. For a variety of reasons, these have been under-studied areas. If reliable sex differences favoring males were found, then we would have convergent validity for sex difference in visual-spatial ability. The only reliable finding of sex differences in musical ability is that females exceed males on tests of dynamic interpretations, which includes the ability to distinguish subtle changes in volume and musical "phrasing" (McGuiness, 1976). Music, like chess, is a very complex activity which probably involves both verbal and spatial abilities. Karma (1979, 1980, cited in Shuter-Dyson & Gabriel, 1982) hypothesized that musical ability is more highly associated with spatial ability than with verbal ability, and that females might process musical stimuli verbally while males might process it spatially. Although his earlier research tended to support his hypothesis, he later concluded that the essential difference in how people process musical stimuli is the amount of experience with music one has and not the sex of the subject.

In Shuter-Dyson and Gabriel's (1982) review of the psychology of music, they conclude that sex differences in most tests of musical ability are small enough to disregard. Currently, there is no good reason to believe that there are sex differences in musical ability, despite the tremendous disparity in sex ratios among society's most accomplished and recognized musicians. A recent literature search for experimental studies showed that this is an underinvestigated area. Given the paucity of research in this area and findings that are sometimes opposite to those predicted, this is another area ripe for additional research. It is hoped that future researchers will include tests of chess and musical abilities in their investigations of sex differences because information about these areas of ability will help to advance our understanding of the interrelationship among several visual-spatial variables.

QUANTITATIVE ABILITIES

Plake, Loyd, and Hoover (1981) recently summarized findings of sex-related differences in quantitative (mathematical) ability: "There is little doubt that females score differently from males on mathematical tests" (p. 780). As you can probably guess, "differently" is a euphemism for poorer, but does this necessarily mean that males have more quantitative ability?

The finding that males outperform females in tests of quantitative or mathematical ability is robust. Consistent sex differences have been found in many large-scale studies. Males tend to outscore females on the quantitative portion of the Scholastic Aptitude Test. The male advantage on this highly standardized test which is administered nationally to college bound high school seniors in the United States is approximately 50 points (Burnett, Lane, & Dratt, 1979; Gersh & Gersh, 1981). Developmentally, sex differences in quantitative ability are sometimes reported in children, with reliable differences emerging somewhere between 13- and 16-years-of-age and persisting throughout adulthood (e.g., Badger, 1981). The developmental nature of quantitative sex differences was examined in a recent study of over 5000 students aged 13 and 17. No sex differences were found for the 13-year-olds, whereas by age 17 the males were significantly outperforming the females with an average of 5% more correct answers (Jones, 1984). There is also evidence that sex differences in quantitative abilities emerge earlier for boys and girls pursuing an academic curriculum than for students in a nonacademic course of study. A longitudinal study conducted by the Educational Testing Service found that sex differences emerged in 7th grade for a group of college-bound students, but did not appear until 11th grade for their peers who were not college bound (Hilton & Berglund, 1974). These results are consistent with a hypothesis presented later in this chapter that suggests that sex differences will be greatest among the most gifted group of females and males.

Quantitative skills are a prerequisite for entry into jobs requiring scientific and technical skills. Sells (1980) has described mathematics as a "critical filter" which allows only some to pass into the higher paying prestigious jobs. One major problem with reports of sex differences in quantitative ability is the failure to take into account the fact that the sexes are disproportionately represented in advanced mathematics courses. The single best prediction of scores on tests of mathematics is the number of mathematics courses an individual has taken (Jones, 1984). Meece et al. (1982) reported that when the data are adjusted to take into account the number of prior mathematics courses, sex differences are substantially reduced, but not eliminated. Thus, a major portion of the difference can be attributed to mathematical background, but not all of it.

It seems that quantitative ability, like spatial ability, is not a unitary concept. There are several different aspects of quantitative ability, and there is at least some evidence that sex differences may not be manifested in all of them. Stones, Beckmann, and Stephens (1982) examined this question with students at ten different colleges. The students, who obviously are not representative of all females and males because they had already met college admissions requirements, were given tests in ten different mathematical categories. No significant overall sex differences were found using multivariate procedures that allowed the experimenters to consider all ten test scores at once. Sex differences were found, however, on the individual subtests. Females scored significantly higher than males on the tests of mathematical sentences and mathematical reasoning, perhaps reflecting the use of verbal strategies in solving these problems. Males scored significantly higher than females in geometry, measurement, and probability and statistics, perhaps reflecting the use of visual-spatial strategies in these areas.

Sex differences have been reported among mathematically gifted boys and girls. Johns Hopkins University has been involved in a nationwide talent search to identify boys and girls that are exceptionally talented in mathematics (Benbow & Stanley, 1980, 1981, 1983). One finding was that there are substantial sex differences in the number of girls and boys identified as "mathematically precocious." They reported that among 7th and 8th grade youth identified as mathematically talented, the male to female ratio on the College Board's Scholastic Aptitude Test (SAT-M) were as follows: 2:1 at >500, 5:1 at >600, and 17:1 at >700 (Stanley & Benbow, 1982). Furthermore, they reported that this ratio has remained stable over eight different talent searches. This is a considerable sex difference that has generated heated controversy. The fact that these differences emerged from very large samples and have been replicated at least eight times lends credibility to these results. Do these differences reflect actual ability differences or are they artifacts of the way the students were identified? Benbow and Stanley believe that students were selected in an unbiased manner while their detractors argue that girls will always be underrepresented in fields that are defined by society as masculine. These two possibilities are considered in the next two chapters.

Rossi (1983) believes that even if these number reflect genuine sex differences at the upper end of ability, the way they are presented is misleading. He has argued that by reporting sex differences in terms of ratios instead of an effect size statistic such as "d" or ω^2, the actual group differences are exaggerated. (See Chapter 2 for a discussion of these statistics.) Only 5% of Stanley and Benbow's sample scored above 599 on the mathematics portion of the SAT. For the other 95%, the actual sex differences were negligible (.44 for d and .044 for ω^2). While these distinctions may seem highly technical to a reader without an extensive background in statistics, they are important in understanding the size and nature of sex differences in mathematical ability. In summary, the differences seem large when considering only the most highly gifted youth and much smaller when considering moderately gifted youth.

RELATIONSHIP BETWEEN VISUAL-SPATIAL ABILITIES AND QUANTITATIVE ABILITIES

Several researchers have suggested that sex differences in quantitative abilities, like those in field-dependence and independence, are a secondary consequence of differences in visual-spatial ability. There are a number of logical and empirical reasons to support this causal link. If you think for a minute about the nature of advanced topics in mathematics—geometry, topology, trigonometry, and calculus—you'll realize that they all require spatial skills. Ancillary support for this relationship comes from the developmental pattern of sex differences which is similar in both areas. In addition, a National Science Foundation study of women mathematicians found that they were more likely to select algebra and statistics as an area of specialization than other mathematics specialties in which spatial perception is central (Luchins, 1979). Empirical evidence for this relationship comes from a variety of studies. Spatial ability and quantitative ability are highly correlated. Fennema and Sherman (1977) found a significant positive relationship between scores on a spatial relations test and achievement in mathematics ($r = .50$) (although they did not find this relationship in later studies). Scores on tests of spatial visualization and spatial orientation are correlated with performance in college mathematics courses ($r = .23$ and $r = .22$, respectively) (Hills, 1957). Additionally, when spatial ability was statistically controlled, sex differences in quantitative ability became nonsignificant (Burnett, Lane, & Dratt, 1979; Hyde, Geiringer, & Yen, 1975). Maccoby and Jacklin's (1974) conclusion that the magnitude of sex differences in quantitative abilities is probably not as large as in spatial abilities is also in accord with the hypothesis that much of the difference in quantitative abilities is attributable to sex differences in visual-spatial abilities.

A recent factor analytic study of skills conducted with college undergraduates also supports the relationship between visual-spatial and mathematical skills. Hunt (1985) found that three distinct ability factors or dimensions emerged when his subjects were given a variety of cognitive tests. The first factor was a verbal ability factor comprised of reading comprehension and vocabulary tests. The second factor was a quantitative/spatial factor comprised of tests of visual-spatial ability and mathematics tests. The third factor was identified as "mechanical reasoning." The fact that quantitative and spatial skills loaded on one factor suggest that there is a single underlying dimension that is responsible for performance on both types of tasks.

MAGNITUDE OF THE DIFFERENCES

While the preponderance of the experimental evidence points to sex differences in verbal, visual-spatial, and quantitative ability, the question of the size or magnitude of these differences has not been easy to resolve. Are the differences trivial and of no practical significance or do they represent meaningful ability differences between the sexes? Even if we were to conclude that there are large between-sex differences with respect to a cognitive ability, I'd like to warn readers, once again, that most research analyzes group average results that cannot be directly applied to any individual.

All of the cognitive sex differences have been replicated numerous times and are statistically significant, which means that they are unlikely to have occurred by chance, but are they of any practical significance? Can they be used to explain why we have so few female mathematicians or engineers? Can they help us predict a male's or female's ability to perform a task? Can they be used to justify discrimination? Are they merely curiosities whose only good is to keep psychologists busy? Answers to these questions are hotly debated with important implications for modern society.

On an intuitive level, effect size is a quantification of the size of the average between-sex difference on a particular test or set of tests. Unfortunately, the numbers we use to express effect size are not intuitive. Differences like the finding that men tend to outscore women an average of 50 points on the quantitative portion of the SAT's have an immediate meaning to anyone who is familiar with the scoring system for the SAT's. Unfortunately, sex differences in abilities are measured with many different tests and a common measure of the average difference is needed to make comparisons across many studies. The effect size statistic is used to convey the size of the differences when many different tests are used. (Readers for whom this is a new concept are referred back to Chapter 2 where statistical concepts are discussed in more depth. It is also possible to follow the gist of the following discussion without understanding the fine points of some of the statistical concepts that are discussed.)

There are few guidelines for determining if the size of a sex difference with respect to a cognitive ability is large enough to be important. Cohen (1962, 1965) provided an arbitrary statistical definition of small, medium and large effect sizes using standard deviation units (.25 s.d. is small, .50 s.d. is medium, and .80 to 1.00 s.d. is large). There is, however, no good reason to accept his effect size markers except for the fact that they provide a common ruler for comparing differences. It is also important to realize that effect size should not be confused with importance. A small effect could still be important, depending on how importance is defined and who defines it. Percentage of explained variance statistics (omega-squared, R^2, eta squared) are useful in this regard, but they still leave us with the question of how much explained variance is large enough to be important. If sex explained 5% of the variance in the data, is this a large or small number? In another context, like medicine, 5% of explained variance attributable to a treatment could mean many lives would be saved. Thus, the question of whether 1% or 5% or 50% of explained variance is important depends on both the context and value judgments. Value judgments never lend themselves to statistical analysis, and thus, precise answers to the question of how large does a difference have to be to be important will remain debatable.

Williams (1983) and others (Gelman et al., 1981; Hyde, 1981) have concluded that looking at the ways large numbers of women and men differ, on the *average,* is misleading because the magnitude of the differences is quite small. "This means that when we look at measures of such behavior we invariably find that differences within a sex category, for example, differences *among* women, are greater than differences *between* women and men" (Williams, 1983, p. 115). While this statement focuses the finding that there is considerable variability among women, it does not necessarily imply that the between-sex differences are small or unimportant.

Effect Size for Verbal Abilities

The magnitude of the sex difference for verbal ability is probably the smallest among the cognitive sex differences. In their review of the literature published before 1974, Maccoby and Jacklin found that the female advantage on verbal tests ranged from .1 to .5 standard deviation units with the usual difference approximately .25 standard deviation units. In other words, the mean of the female distribution of scores was one fourth of a standard deviation above the mean of the male distribution. For those for whom it is easier to think in terms of actual point differences on the SAT's, this translates to an average 25 point difference on the verbal portion of the SAT's. Reiterating a point raised earlier, differences need to be reported in terms of standard deviation units because the way verbal abilities are measured varies among the studies. Using Cohen's heuristic for judging effect size, this is a small effect.

More recent analyses of the verbal ability effect size have confirmed Maccoby and Jacklin's calculations. Plomin and Foch (1981), for example, computed the average difference to be .18 standard deviation units. Calculations of the percentage of variance explained by sex also yielded small values. Hyde (1981) reported that the median ω^2 computed from 27 studies of verbal abilities was only 1%. Although this is a small effect size, it may or may not be important depending upon one's criterion for importance. Although none of the meta-analyses considered effect sizes at various ages, it is possible that sex accounts for a much greater percentage of the variance in verbal ability among young children and possibly among older adults than these figures would lead us to believe.

Effect Size for Visual-Spatial Abilities

As stated earlier, findings of sex differences in visual-spatial ability are the most robust of the cognitive sex differences. It also appears that the largest sex differences are found here.

Although Hyde (1981) reported that the difference between the means on tests of visual-spatial abilities for females and males was only .45 standard deviation units, accounting for only 4.3% of the variance, data from other researchers suggest that these values underestimate the population effect size. A substantial effect size was reported by Sanders, Soares, and D'Aquila (1982). They gave 672 college women and 359 men two tests of visual-spatial ability and got very different results for each test. Although the men scored, on the average, higher on both tests, the magnitude of the difference varied substantially between the tests. For one test, a card rotations test, the means were .29 standard deviation units apart with sex accounting for a mere 2% of the variance. The other test, however, was a mental rotation test with group means .83 standard deviation units apart and 16% of the variance accounted for by sex. In Cohen's (1965) cogent discussion of effect size, he describes effects that are of this magnitude as being so large that no statistical analysis is needed to document the between-sex difference. In order to make the magnitude of this difference understandable, Sanders, Soares, and D'Aquila claim that it is as large as the difference in IQ scores between Ph.D's and typical college freshmen or as large as the difference in heights between 13- and 18-year-old-girls. Other tests that require the mental rotation of objects in space yield similar effect sizes. Petersen and Crockett (1985), for example, found a sex effect of one standard deviation on a three-dimensional mental rotation test, while the effect size on another spatial ability test (Primary Mental Abilities Space Subtest) and other two-dimensional rotation tests were only ⅓ of a standard deviation. The magnitude of the sex effect seems to depend on the test used to measure spatial ability.

The finding that magnitude of the sex difference in visual-spatial ability depends on the type of visual-spatial test used helps to explain some of the discrepancies in the literature. This result is consistent with the notion that visual-spatial ability is not a homogeneous construct and sex differences may depend on which component of visual-spatial ability is being measured. Sanders, Soares, and D'Aquila do suggest that the female advantage with verbal tasks might be as large as the male advantage with visual-spatial tasks, if we found the right test to tap into the sex-related verbal difference.

Another way of understanding the size of the sex-related difference is to compare the percentage of females and males exceeding a given score on a test.

To underscore the size of the sex difference on a mental rotation test, Bouchard and McGee (1977) reported that only 20% of the females in the 200 families they tested scored above the median (50%) for males. A number of other researchers found similar male–female disparities (Harris, 1978). In fact, the Differential Aptitude Tests are separately normed for each sex because of these differences. At grade 12, for example, a girl who scores at the 80th percentile has a test score that is equal to that of a boy at the 70th percentile.

Effect Size for Quantitative Abilities

The magnitude of the effect size for sex differences in quantitative ability is medium, placing it somewhere between the small effect associated with verbal ability and the large effect associated with visual-spatial abilities. Hyde (1981) reviewed 16 studies that examined sex differences in quantitative ability and found that the median between-sex difference was .45 standard deviation units with approximately 1% of the variance accounted for by sex. This means that 99% of the variance was due to sampling error and/or variables that were not investigated in the study. These values agree with those reported by other investigators (Burnett, Lane, & Dratt, 1979). Gelman et al. (1981) interpret these values as "rather small," but according to Cohen's guidelines they would be considered medium effect sizes.

When we examine quantitative sex differences among mathematically gifted preteens and teenagers, the sex effects appear to be much larger. In Benbow and Stanley's (1980, 1981) highly publicized report of the Johns Hopkins talent search for mathematically precocious youth, they reported several indices of sex differences. They identified 7th graders in the top 2nd, 3rd, and 5th percentile in the United States in a test of mathematical reasoning ability. The male:female ratio over several years remained stable at 57 boys for every 43 girls. The mean between sex difference on the mathematics portion of the Scholastic Aptitude Test (SAT-M) was 32 points. Among the highest scoring students, the differences were magnified to an even greater proportion. Boys outnumbered girls 2:1 among students who scored above 500. When they examined scores over 700, 23 boys and no girls were found in this extreme range. In effect size units, the boys' mean was .50 standard deviation above the girls' mean on the SAT-M.

It may seem strange that a medium effect size (.50 standard deviation units) is associated with such large sex differences in this mathematically gifted sample. In fact, small mean (average) differences often create large differences at the tails or extreme ends of distributions. To demonstrate this point, Hyde (1981) considered a hypothetical example in which group means were .40 standard deviation units apart. If we considered only the top 5% of scores we'd find that 7.35% of males and 3.22% of females would exceed this cut point. This is a 2:1 ratio, similar to that reported by Benbow and Stanley for students scoring above 500 on the SAT-M. Thus, if we are concerned with extremely gifted individuals, small average sex differences can create large sex differences in this highly elite group, and small or medium effect sizes become important.

Effect Size for Cognitive Abilities Overall

Some researchers assumed a broader view and studied the effect size for several cognitive abilities in the same study. Backman (1979), for example, studied the relationship among ethnicity, socioeconomic status (SES), and sex, and their joint influence on mental abilities. She administered tests of verbal knowledge, English language, grammar, mathematics, reasoning with spatial forms, perceptual speech, and memory to over 2,000 twelfth grade students. She accounted for over 90% of the total variance with the main effects and interactions of her variables, but the relative importance of these variables was surprising. "Differences between the patterns of mental abilities of males and females were more marked than were differences among the patterns of ethnic or SES groups. Sex accounted for 69% of the total variance, ethnicity 9% and SES 1%" (p. 264). It is difficult to know how to interpret the extremely large effect of sex in this study, given that it accounted for a very much smaller percentage of explained variance in the other studies of individual abilities. It seems that sex was a very important determinant of how well the students performed on these tests. It also seems that sex as a variable can explain a much greater proportion of the total variance when several sex-related cognitive abilities are considered simultaneously in a single experiment than when individual abilities are being studied.

In one of the most advanced analyses to date, Rosenthal and Rubin (1982) attempted to shed light on the question of how large an effect size must be in order to be of practical importance. Using a statistical test known as the Binomial Effect Size Display (BESD), they calculated that when sex explains only 4% of the variance in test scores, this translates into distributions in which 60% of the higher scoring sex is above the median and only 40% of the lower scoring sex is above the median. They argue that outcome rates of 60% versus 40% are important since they can be used to predict performance on ability tests in these areas. They also looked at the consistencies among effect sizes across twelve studies of verbal ability, seven studies of visual-spatial ability, seven studies of quantitative ability, and fourteen studies of field articulation (field independence and dependence). They concluded that effect sizes differed from study to study, supporting the idea that the magnitude of the sex difference in any area depends on the type of test used.

SEX DIFFERENCES IN FACTOR STRUCTURES

Terms like verbal, visual-spatial, and quantitative ability are hypothetical constructs that represent underlying unobservable variables that help to explain test results that presumably measure them. Terms like these have been called "convenient fictions" invented by psychologists who want to understand human intellect. One way to confirm or disconfirm our belief that tests of vocabulary, reading, and verbal analogies are all tapping the hypothetical entity we've labeled "verbal ability" is to subject scores on these tests from many individuals to a statistical procedure known as factor analysis. Kerlinger (1979) describes factor analysis as a way of explaining phenomena by describing the way variables are related to each other. If the vocabulary, reading, and verbal analogies tests are all tapping the same ability, then they will be highly related to each other, and a single factor will emerge from the factor analysis. By examining the number of factors and the extent to which each test is associated with each factor, we can assess the structure or architecture of the human intellect.

A few researchers have attempted to address the question of sex differences in the factor structure of these abilities. With a factor analytic approach, the experimental question is no longer whether there are sex differences on any particular test (there is already ample evidence that reliable sex differences will emerge on certain tests), but whether both sexes use similar abilities in how they solve different problems. The scanty evidence we have to date suggests that there are few, if any, major differences between the sexes in the factor structure of their cognitive abilities.

In an attempt to examine the possibility that there are qualitative differences in cognitive abilities, Hertzog and Carter (1982) administered ten different cognitive ability tests (e.g., vocabulary, spatial reasoning, arithmetic) to two generations of women and men. They compared the way the ten tests were related to Spatial Abilities and Verbal Abilities factors for each sex and generation group using a sophisticated statistical technique known as structural equation modeling. Hertzog and Carter concluded that women and men in both generations had similar intellectual factor structures. In other words, cognitive abilities are organized in similar ways for both sexes in both generation groups. Thus, while there are quantitative differences (males better in spatial abilities and females better in verbal abilities), there do not appear to be any qualitative between-sex differences in the structure or organization of cognitive abilities.

In a similar investigation, Hyde, Geiringer, and Yen (1975) gave nine different tests to male and female college students: spatial ability; Rod and Frame Test; Embedded Figures Test; mental arithmetic; vocabulary; word fluency; alternate uses (creativity); femininity, and achievement motivation. These tests were chosen to allow them to investigate the relationship among spatial ability, two tests of field articulation (Rod and Frame and Embedded Figures) and arithmetic for each sex separately and for the entire sample as a whole. One hypothesis that was considered earlier in this chapter was that sex differences in field articulation and mathematics are really artifacts of sex differences in spatial ability. If this hypothesis is correct, then these four tests should emerge on a single factor while the verbal tests should emerge on a separate factor. (The reasoning behind the inclusion of tests of creativity, femininity, and achievement motivation is not considered at this time.) They found typical sex differences on each of these tests verifying the well known sex differences in these abilities (males outscoring females in spatial ability and arithmetic and appearing more field independent on the Rod and Frame Test and Embedded Figures Test, and females outscoring males on the vocabulary and word fluency tests). In general, factor structures were similar for both sexes; however, spatial ability seemed less related to the factor composed of the Rod and Frame Test, Embedded Figures Test, and mental arithmetic for the women than for the men. Thus, it is possible that women use different approaches in solving spatial problems than men. One possibility, for example, is that women rely on verbal strategies whereas men tend to use spatial ones to solve the same problems. Additional support for this claim comes from the finding reported earlier of male and female differences in variability on spatial tests.

CHAPTER SUMMARY

Although sex differences have not been found in general intelligence, they have been reported reliably with a female advantage in verbal abilities and a male advantage in visual-spatial and quantitative abilities. A popular hypothesis points to the differences in visual-spatial ability as the underlying cause of the sex differences in quantitative ability. Empirical evidence of this relationship is sometimes, but not always, found.

In general, verbal ability differences are small in magnitude, visual-spatial ability differences are large, and quantitative ability differences are intermediate. It was noted, however, that even small differences can be important if we are concerned with extremely gifted individuals. The few studies that examined the underlying factor structure of these abilities found structures to be essentially similar for women and men with the possible exception that visual-spatial abilities may be associated with different factors for each sex.

4 Biological Hypotheses

CONTENTS
The Notion of Biological Determination
Genetic Theories
   Sex-Linked versus Sex-Limited
   Heritability of Spatial Skills
   Heritability of Verbal Skills
   Heritability of Mathematical Skills
   Arguing from Abnormalities
Sex-Related Brain Differences
   Size, Weight, and Complexity
   Sexual Dimorphism in Hemispheric Specialization
   Some Tentative Conclusions about Sex-Related Brain Differences
Sex Hormones
   Prenatal Hormones
   Childhood and Puberty
   Adulthood and Old Age
Critique of Biological Hypotheses
   Biological and Environmental Interactions
   The Notion of Optimal Cerebral Organization, Optimal Hormone Balance, and Optimal
     Genetic Configuration
   Intervening Variables
   Differences and Deficiencies
Chapter Summary

Perhaps this chapter should come with a warning similar to the ones found on cigarette advertisements: Readers are warned that some of the research and theories described in this chapter may be disturbing to their basic belief systems. I have taught this material many times, and there have always been students who have found the possibility that even a small portion of the sex differences in cognitive abilities may be attributable to biological factors to be profoundly disturbing. When reading this chapter, it is important to keep in mind that even if we were to conclude that biological variables are partial determinants of sex differences in cognitive abilities, the importance of psychosocial factors is not necessarily diminished. Biological and psychosocial variables interact in their influence on the development of individuals, and although biological and psychosocial hypotheses are presented in separate chapters, this organization is not meant to imply that they are diametrically opposed or independent concepts.

THE NOTION OF BIOLOGICAL DETERMINATION

The concept of "biological determination" can take either a strong or weak form. A proponent of the strong form was Sigmund Freud who is well known for his oft quoted aphorism, "Biology is destiny." This quote represents the strong form of biological determination or determinism because it implies that, for each of us, our destiny is unavoidably preplanned by biological forces beyond our control. A proponent of the weaker form of biological determinism would maintain that while biology may underlie some tendencies or make certain experiences more probable, we are not inevitably the products of the biological systems that comprise our bodies. An analogy from health science may help to explain this point. Some people may be born with a biological tendency to develop "hardening of the arteries"; however, with proper exercise and diet they can avoid or postpone this destiny. Similarly, a weak form of biological determinism allows for the possibility that females and males may, by self-determination or some other means, overcome sex-related biologically based predilections or tendencies to develop certain cognitive abilities; the weak form of biological determinism considers the impact of environmental influences on male and female human existence.

Of course, there are numerous and obvious biological differences between women and men. If we were concerned with sex differences in reproduction instead of cognition, there would be few unresolved issues. The different roles that men and women play in reproduction are incontrovertible. But, when the issue is cognition, the questions and answers become more difficult. Are the sex-related differences in cognitive ability inherent in the biology of femaleness and maleness? Or, are the biological factors that make you male or female unrelated to the types of cognitive abilities that you develop?

There are three possible biological systems that could be responsible for cognitive sex differences: (1) chromosomal or genetic determinants of sex; (2) neuroanatomical differences in the structure, organization, and/or function of the brain; and (3) differences in the sex hormones secreted from the endocrine glands. Theory and research on the biological determinants of sex-related cognitive differences have centered on these three biological systems. One of the major difficulties in understanding the contribution of each of these biological systems is that in normal individuals they are confounded. Chromosomes determine the type of sex hormones that are secreted, and these hormones influence brain development. Sex hormones also direct the development of the internal reproductive organs and external genitals. Thus, for most people, all of the biological indications of sex are congruent. The question for research psychologists is whether any or all of these biological sex differences underlie cognitive sex differences.

GENETIC THEORIES

Fetal development proceeds under the direction of the genetic information coded on the genes. Whether you were born male or female with black or white skin and blue or brown eyes was determined by the chromosomes and genes that are responsible for your very existence. Every trait which you have inherited from your ancestors was transmitted via your genes. Genetic information constitutes the "genotype" of an individual, while traits that are expressed are called the "phenotype." Phenotype depends on the interaction of genes with environmental influences. The term "gene-environment transaction" is sometimes used to emphasize the fact that any trait that is expressed depends on the mutual effect of genetic and environmental influences.

Researchers use observable characteristics (phenotypes) to infer genetic information (genotypes). There are four research strategies commonly used to study the influence of genetic information on cognition (Eliot & Fralley, 1976):

1. Examine a large number of people to determine, for example, the proportion of women and men who exhibit good spatial or verbal abilities.

2. Look at the heritability pattern of abilities across generations to determine the "pedigree" of cognitive abilities. Researchers utilizing this approach might examine siblings or parents and children to ascertain whether good mathematical or verbal ability tends to run in families.

3. Utilize individuals with genetic abnormalities to infer the effect of genetic information in normal individuals. An example of this approach would be to discover if individuals who are genetically male, but appear female, show typical "male" patterns of cognitive abilities.

4. Examine monozygotic and dizygotic twins to determine the extent to which cognitive abilities are under genetic control. If monozygotic ("identical") twins are more similar than dizygotic ("fraternal") twins, then these results would provide some support for genetic influences on cognitive abilities.

All of these strategies have been used to understand the role of sex-related genetic factors in the development of cognitive abilities.

Sex-Linked Versus Sex-Limited

One of the major differences between males and females is the pair of sex chromosomes that differ markedly from each other in size and shape. Females have two X chromosomes—one is contributed by the father and the other by the mother during fertilization. The male sex chromosome pair is designated XY. The X is contributed by the mother and the Y is contributed by the father. The Y chromosome is very small and contains little genetic information except for determining sex (Carter, 1972). In contrast, the X chromosome is relatively large and contains a great deal of genetic information. Characteristics (like whether an individual develops ovaries or testes) that are determined by genes on the sex chromosomes are called "sex-linked characteristics." Such characteristics are inextricably tied to the fact that we are born either male or female because they are carried on the chromosomes that determine sex.

In addition to the pair of sex chromosomes, humans have 22 pairs of other chromosomes known as autosomes. Sometimes a characteristic that is coded on an autosome appears predominantly in one sex or the other. Such characteristics are called "sex-limited," and appear predominantly in one sex because of a multiplicity of genetic influences. Baldness, for example, occurs primarily in men and is inherited through genetic information on an autosomal pair of chromosomes. Such characteristics are less intimately tied to genetic determinants of sex than sex-linked characteristics.

Heritability of Spatial Skills

There has been considerable interest in recent years in the hypothesis that spatial ability is inherited. The whole question of the extent to which intelligence is inherited has been hotly debated throughout the history of psychology and seems no closer to being resolved today than it was over a century ago. Despite the lack of agreement on the question of how much intelligence is inherited, even staunch environmentalists will agree that it is, at least, partially inherited. Similarly, there seems to be a heritability component to the cognitive abilities that comprise intelligence. Vandenberg (1969), for example, administered a test of spatial abilities to a sample of twins, reasoning that the greater the percentage of genes shared by two people, the greater the similarity you would expect in their ability scores if the ability is inherited. The test included measures of the ability to visualize and mentally rotate figures in space. High correlations between twin pairs led Vandenberg to conclude that these abilities are partially determined by heredity factors. However, simply knowing that some cognitive abilities may be inherited doesn't explain sex differences in these abilities.

Sex-Linked Recessive Gene Theory

Any genetic explanation of sex differences in visual-spatial ability would need to posit an inheritance mechanism that is differentiated by sex. A major genetic theory of cognitive sex differences is based on the assumption that high spatial ability is a sex-linked recessive trait that is carried on the X chromosome. (A recessive trait is one that will be expressed, that is, it will appear in a person's phenotype, only if the corresponding gene on the other member of the chromosome pair also carries the recessive trait.) If this theory were true, then females would have a double dose of the genes that determine spatial ability because they have two X chromosomes; whereas, males have only one dose and that one always comes from the mother who contributes the X chromosome to her son. For males, the other member of the sex chromosome pair is the very small Y chromosome which does not carry any genetic information about spatial ability. According to this theory, the high spatial ability gene is recessive; therefore, this trait will occur more frequently in males than in females because males have no other gene to mask the effects of the recessive gene. Since females would have to have the genetic information on both X chromosomes and males only need to have it on one, males are therefore more likely to demonstrate good spatial ability. Table 4.1 depicts which individuals would be predicted to demonstrate good spatial ability as a function of their genotype if the sex-linked recessive theory were true.

The beauty of this theory is the explicit quantitative nature of the predictions derived from it. One of the predictions generated from the sex-linked recessive gene theory concerns the total proportion of men and women who would be expected to show good spatial ability. Bock and Kolakowski (1973) estimated that a recessive spatial ability gene should appear among American Caucasians with a frequency of approximately 50%. (Estimates for other racial groups were not given.) If this were true, then approximately 50% of all Caucasian men and

TABLE 4.1
Predictions Derived From the X-Linked Recessive
Gene Theory of Spatial Ability

Good spatial ability would be found in:

1. Hemizygous recessive males
   (Gene for good spatial ability is
   carried on the X chromosome) $\male\ X^r Y$

2. Homozygous recessive females
   (Gene for good spatial ability is
   carried on both X chromosomes) $\female\ X^r X^r$

Good spatial ability would <u>not</u> be found in:

1. Hemizygous dominant males
   (Gene for poor spatial ability is
   carried on the X chromosome) $\male\ X^D Y$

2. Heterozygous females
   (Gene for poor spatial ability is
   carried on one X chromosome, gene
   for good spatial ability is carried
   on the other X chromosome) $\female\ X^D X^r$
                                      or
                                     $\female\ X^r X^D$

3. Homozygous dominant females

   (Gene for poor spatial ability is
   carried on both X chromosomes) $\female\ X^D X^D$

Note. r = recessive, D = dominant

approximately 25% of all Caucasian women would be expected to show this trait phenotypically. This prediction can be seen in the male genetic configurations shown in Table 4.1. There are two equally likely male genetic patterns, one of which would be associated with good spatial ability. The 25% prediction for females can also be seen in Table 4.1. There are four equally probable female configurations, only one of which would be associated with good spatial ability. The data, however, do not conform to these proportions. The prediction that half of all males and one-fourth of all females would show this trait phenotypically has not been supported (DeFries, Vandenberg, & McClearn, 1976).

Another prediction derived from the sex-linked theory of spatial ability is an explicit pattern of relationships among parents, children, and siblings (Boles, 1980). One of the hypothesized relationships is that sons' spatial abilities should resemble their mothers' more than their fathers'. The reasoning behind this hypothesis is that males have a single X chromosome that they inherited from their mothers. If a spatial ability gene is carried on this chromosome, then, on the average, a son should be more similar to his mother in spatial ability than he would be to his father. Daughters, on the other hand, should tend to be more similar to their fathers in terms of their spatial ability than they would be to their mothers. The reasoning behind this relationship is somewhat more complex. Mother-daughter pairs have a total of four X chromosomes, two each from the mother and daughter. Two of these four are held in "common" because the daughter receives one of her X chromosomes from her mother. Daughter-father pairs have a total of three X chromosomes, two of which are jointly held because daughters receive one of their X chromosomes from their fathers. According to this logic, daughters share a larger proportion of their total daughter-parent X chromosome pool with their fathers than with their mothers. The prediction that sons' spatial abilities should resemble their mothers' more than their fathers' and that daughters should resemble their fathers' more than their mothers' is opposite from any predictions made from psychosocial theories. Thus, if this pattern of relationships was empirically supported, this would constitute strong support for genetic determination.

Early studies with small samples provided weak support for this hypothesis. Stafford (1961, 1963) found the pattern of relationships among daughters and fathers, daughters and mothers, sons and mothers, and sons and fathers in the order predicted by this theory, but only for one of the ten tests he used to measure spatial abilities, and even that one failed to obtain statistical significance. Later studies with larger samples failed to replicate this pattern (Bouchard & McGee, 1977; Loehlin, Sharan, & Jacoby, 1978).

Additional fine-grained predictions are also derivable from this theory. For example, if a father doesn't have the gene responsible for good spatial ability, then none of his daughters will have this trait, but his sons could have it if they received the trait from their mother. If a father does have the gene for good spatial ability, then his sons and daughters could show this ability, depending on whether their mother is heterozygous (one X chromosome carries the gene and the other one doesn't) or homozygous (both X chromosomes carry the gene).

Despite early support for the sex-linked recessive hypothesis, it now seems clear that its validity is unfounded. Thomas (1983) recently suggested that the basic assumptions of this model were wrong, and all of the studies that reported correlation orderings as evidence for this model were using incorrect assumptions about the mathematical properties of inheritance. Perhaps one of the biggest problems is with the notion that a complex multidimensional variable like visual-spatial ability would have a single genetic determinant. As described in Chapter 3, spatial ability is comprised of visualization ability and spatial orientation ability. These two components are not necessarily closely related. Genetic theories that fail to make distinctions between these two components of spatial ability will never be able to describe adequately the phenomenon. All of the sex differentiated cognitive abilities are composed of multiple components, and it is unlikely that there is a single gene that controls the expression of any of these abilities. In addition, visual-spatial ability is a characteristic that we all exhibit to some degree, a fact that cannot be explained with a single genetic code.

Heritability of Verbal Skills

There is very little support for the notion that verbal skills are highly heritable. In Vandenberg's (1968) study of the verbal and spatial abilities of twins, he made two conclusions: (1) both abilities have heritability components, and (2) verbal abilities are more influenced by environmental events than spatial abilities. In a review of Vandenberg's study, Rohrbaugh (1979) questioned his first conclusion concerning the heritability of verbal skills, and agreed with his second conclusion that environmental factors are of primary importance in the development of verbal skills. Vandenberg's conclusions were based on the similarity between twins on verbal tests. Monozygotic or identical twins who share 100% of their genetic make-up were more similar than dizygotic or fraternal twins. Nontwin siblings showed the least similarity. A major problem in inferring the heritability of any cognitive ability from twin data results from the fact that twins are also more likely to be similar to each other than other pairs of nontwin siblings in terms of their social and learning histories. It is just as likely that the similarity in environmental factors could be responsible for the similarity in their scores as the hypothesis that the degree of genetic information that they shared is responsible.

An X-linked recessive trait theory for verbal ability, similar to that proposed for visual-spatial ability, was proposed by Lehrke (1974). Lehrke's hypothesis was based on the inheritance pattern or pedigree of certain mental deficiencies involving verbal abilities. Although it remains possible that some mental deficiencies are transmitted via X-linked recessive genes, there is no evidence for an X-linked gene for verbal ability among individuals within the normal range of intelligence.

Heritability of Mathematical Skills

Stafford (1972) offered a pattern of family intercorrelational data in support of the notion that mathematical skills are inherited via the now familiar X-linked recessive gene. Sherman (1978) provided a cogent criticism of these data which not only failed to fit the proposed model, but were substantially divergent from those predicted by the model. There is no support for a sex-differentiated mode for the inheritance of mathematical skills.

Arguing From Abnormalities

In normal individuals, genetic information and concentrations of sex hormones are confounded. Individuals whose sex chromosomes are XX also appear female, are raised as females, and secrete sex hormones associated with being female. The reverse is, of course, true for males with XY sex chromosome pairs. The problem is isolating the effect of any one of these variables on the cognitive abilities that are differentiated by sex. In order to decide if the finding that men and women tend to excel in different types of intellectual tasks is due to genetic programming, the influence of genetic information needs to be disentangled from that of hormones and other life experiences that vary with sex. One way of examining genetic effects is to study people with genetic abnormalities such that the sex hormones and/or external genitals are not consistent with genetic sex.

There have been several studies of people with genetic abnormalities on their sex chromosomes. Rovet and Netley (1979) for example, studied five females with a genetic anomaly known as Turner's Syndrome. Instead of the usual pair of X chromosomes, females with Turner's Syndrome have a single X chromosome. This syndrome is designated as 45XO to indicate the fact that they have 45 chromosomes instead of the usual 46 and only one X chromosome. The second X chromosome is missing. Individuals with Turner's Syndrome are clearly female in appearance. Perhaps their major distinguishing feature is that they tend to be short and will usually require treatment with female hormones in order to exhibit the female secondary sex characteristics at puberty. According to the X-linked recessive gene theory, Turner's Women, as they are sometimes called, should display the male pattern of cognitive abilities, that is, on the average, they should score higher on visual-spatial performance tests than verbal ones. The reasoning behind this prediction is straightforward. Like men, they have a single X chromosome, and thus should be more likely to show a recessive X-linked characteristic since there is no other gene to carry the dominant trait. Rovet and Netley found results opposite to those predicted from this theory. All five of the females they tested had higher verbal scores than visual-spatial performance scores.

In the same study, Rovet and Netley (1979) also tested three individuals who were phenotypically male (appeared to be male), with a 46XX genotype (female gene pattern). If the sex-linked recessive gene pattern were correct, then these males should show a "female pattern of cognitive abilities," with higher verbal skills than visual-spatial performance skills. The reasoning behind this prediction is that if the sex chromosomes are important determinants of cognitive ability, then any group of individuals with female sex chromosomes should, on the average, tend to show the pattern of abilities associated with being female. Again this theory was not confirmed. Contrary to predictions, all three of the phenotypical males scored higher on the visual-spatial performance tests than on the verbal tests. Although this study used only a small number of subjects, these results are compelling and have been confirmed by other researchers (Money & Ehrhardt, 1972). It seems clear from these studies that cognitive abilities conform to phenotypic rather than genotypic sex. Currently, there is little support for the notion that sex differences in cognitive abilities are due to inherent differences in male and female genetic codes.

SEX-RELATED BRAIN DIFFERENCES

A second biological hypothesis that has been proposed to explain cognitive sex differences concerns brain differences. The human brain resembles, in appearance, a giant mushy walnut with two halves or hemispheres that control higher mental functioning. Sex differences researchers have been concerned with the question of whether there are differences in male and female brains, and, if so, whether these differences can be used to explain sex-related cognitive differences.

If we were to examine brains taken from females and males there would be no gross differences that could be used to identify the sex of their owner. Microscopic examinations of the structure of the nerve cells and nerve tissues that comprise the brain would show that the cells are morphologically identical except for visible X chromosomes (known as Barr bodies) in many of the nerve cells in women's brains and Y chromosomes in the men's nerve cells (Gersh & Gersh, 1981).

Although there are no gross anatomical differences in female and male brains, it is clear that there are some sex-related brain differences. Menstruation, for example, begins as a brain event with a hormone feedback loop involving the pituitary and hypothalamus, which are brain structures. Certain between-sex synapse differences are visible microscopically in the hypothalamus, presumably reflecting the role of the hypothalamus in menstruation. Thus, there are sex-related brain differences that reflect the fact that women menstruate and men don't. The picture becomes somewhat more complicated when we also consider that there are cortical hormones that function as sex hormones, indicating some between-sex cortical hormone differences (Keeton, 1967). Despite these well-documented differences in female and male brains, the brain structures and systems involved in menstruation are not thought to be important in influencing intellectual abilities. There is no reason to believe that the portions of the brain that regulate menstruation in females and sexual behavior in males and females are also involved in the higher cognitive functions we've been considering. A picture of a normal human brain is shown in Fig. 4.1. Notice its convoluted exterior and the apparent symmetry between the two hemispheres.

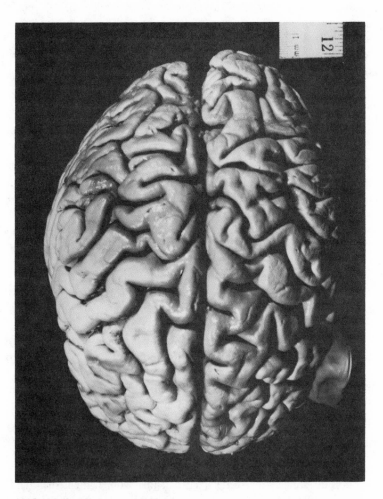

FIG. 4.1.   A normal human brain. Can we ever fully understand how all of human experience is processed and stored in a complex web of neurons and neurotransmitters? Photo courtesy of Dr. John Allman, California Institute of Technology, Pasadena, California.

Size, Weight, and Complexity

Early reports of differences between female and male brains parallel findings of black and white race differences. According to earlier theorizing, the supposedly inferior race and the supposedly inferior sex had similar brain deficiencies. Nineteenth century physicians warned that the female nervous system was delicate and not well suited for intellectual work. According to Burnham (1977) these physicians claimed that both women and blacks had "smaller brains with less capacity" (p. 10). One of the arguments for denying women the right to vote was their purportedly inferior biology. Presumably, their smaller and less complex brains couldn't handle the complex decisions required of informed voters. The "theory" went even further in suggesting that intellectual endeavors would be bad for women's health because the increased blood flow to the brain would drain the blood normally needed for menstruation. The fact is that women's brains are somewhat smaller than men's brains, but this in no way supports the ludicrous position that they are inferior. Brain size and weight are positively correlated with body size. Because men, on the average, tend to be larger than women, they also tend to have larger brains. There is no evidence that larger brains are, in any way, better than smaller brains (within normal limits). If this hypothesis were true, then people with the largest hat sizes (reflecting greater brain sizes) would be the smartest, a "prediction" which is obviously untrue. Furthermore, there is no evidence that male or female brains differ in complexity. Similar earlier reports that blacks have smaller brains than whites are totally unfounded and merely reflect racism (Gould, 1978).

Sexual Dimorphism in Hemispheric Specialization

A large body of research has revealed that the two hemispheres or halves of the brain are, to some extent, specialized or dominant for different cognitive functions. Laboratory tests have been conducted with both clinical and normal populations. Clinical populations have included people who have had their corpus callosum (the thick bundle of nerve fibers that connects the two halves of the brain) split to alleviate the symptoms of epilepsy, individuals with damage to one area of the brain, post mortem examinations of corpses, and patients undergoing laboratory tests such as direct electrical stimulation of selected brain regions. Normal populations include people who have had EEG activity and evoked potentials recorded off their scalp, their blood flow monitored with radioactive isotopes, and CAT scans to identify brain anomalies. Both populations have shown a distinct distribution of abilities between the two hemispheres.

Approximately 95% of all right handed people maintain speech and language control in their left hemisphere. Actual percentage estimates vary somewhat for the proportion of left handed people who maintain the same lateralization pattern as right handed people. Levy and Reid, 1978, have estimated that among the left handed population 60% maintain language functions in the left hemisphere with the remaining 40% having the reversed pattern. Springer and Deutsch (1981) have estimated that among left handed people, 70% have speech and language control in their left hemisphere, with approximately 15% maintaining verbal control in their right hemisphere, and the remaining 15% with control in both hemispheres. Small variations in these estimates are of no practical concern for the purposes of this review; however, the fact that a much larger proportion of left handers than right handers have right hemisphere language specialization is important in understanding hypotheses about the relationship between sex and cerebral lateralization.

What does it mean to say that one hemisphere is dominant with respect to a cognitive ability? According to Geschwind (1974), "One hemisphere may be said to be dominant for a given function when it is more important for the performance of that function than the other hemisphere" (p. 9). Hemisphere dominance does not mean an either/or division of tasks. It means instead that one half of the brain is more or less specialized or proficient in its ability to process certain types of stimuli.

Laboratory investigations of hemispheric dominance rely on the fact that most of the nerves from one side of the body connect to the contralateral (opposite) hemisphere. Consider audition (or hearing) for example. A majority of the nerves in the auditory track that connect to the right ear send their impulses to the left hemisphere, with the reverse innervation for the left ear. In a classic experimental paradigm, the researcher will present different sorts of stimuli to each ear. The subject would be required to respond to a stimulus in some way such as classifying it as a letter or word or responding with a key press as quickly as possible to certain types of stimuli. The usual finding is that right handed subjects respond more accurately to linguistic stimuli (letters or words) when they are presented to the right ear than when they are presented to the left ear, suggesting that the left hemisphere is dominant or specialized for linguistic tasks. Stimuli that are difficult to verbalize (random sound sequences or noises that are not readily identifiable) are usually responded to better by right handed subjects when they are presented to the left ear than the right, suggesting that the right hemisphere is specialized or dominant for nonlinguistic tasks for right handed subjects.

Research similar to that described with hearing is also conducted with vision, although the pattern of innervation, or the way the neurons connect, is somewhat more complicated. Nerve fibers from the left half of each eye connect to the left hemisphere and nerve fibers from the right half of each eye connect to the right hemisphere. Researchers can determine which hemisphere is receiving visual information by presenting visual stimuli very briefly (a fraction of a second) to the right or left of a subject's fixation point. A fixation point is the point an individual is looking directly at when she or he is looking straight ahead. Any stimuli presented to the left of the fixation point, an area known as the left visual field, are, initially, represented in the right hemisphere. Similarly, any stimuli presented to the right of the fixation point, an area known as the right visual field are, initially, represented in the left cerebral hemisphere (Kitterle & Kaye, 1985). A schematic diagram of this experimental paradigm is presented in Fig. 4.2. Results with visual stimuli support those found with audition: the right hemisphere is primarily important in visual-spatial skills (depth perception, detecting the orientation of a line, visual point location) and the left hemisphere is primarily important in verbal skills (naming concrete nouns and the recognition of words and digits) (Geschwind, 1974).

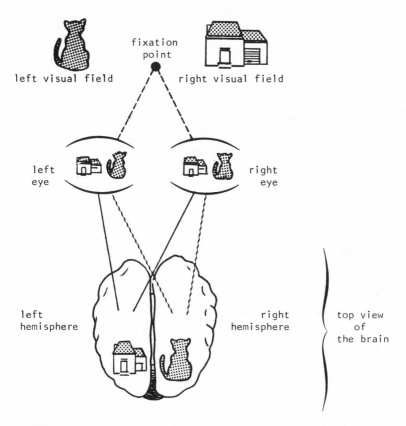

FIG. 4.2.   Schematic drawing of the images projected to the right and left half of each eye when a subject is looking at a fixation point that is straight ahead. Notice that the cat in the left visual field is projected onto the right half of both eyes and then is represented in the right hemisphere. The opposite pattern occurs for the house shown in the right visual field.

Theories of Sex Differentiated Asymmetries

All of the major theories of sex differences in cerebral organization began with a simple analogy. Given that the types of abilities that differ by hemisphere of specialization are the same ones that differ by sex, it seemed to many psychologists only a short leap to suggest that the sexes differ in the way their hemispheres specialize these abilities. The logic behind this reasoning is that since sex differences are primarily found with verbal and visual-spatial tasks and that hemisperic specialization differs with respect to these two abilities, then it is plausible that there are sex differences in cerebral lateralization. In 1972, two major theories were proposed based on this theorizing. Unfortunately, the two theories began with opposite assumptions about the way the brains of each sex were lateralized and with different predictions about the consequences. Not surprisingly, most psychologists rejected both of these theories because of the confusion generated by their inconsistencies. A brief review of each of these theories should provide a framework for understanding the research designed to investigate the question of sex differences in cerebral lateralization that has been conducted in the intervening years since 1972.

Buffery and Gray's Hypothesis

Buffery and Gray hypothesized that verbal skills would develop best in individuals who are strongly lateralized for verbal ability, that is in individuals for whom one hemisphere is specialized for language tasks. On the other hand, spatial skills benefit from bilateral representation which involves both hemispheres about equally. They go on to hypothesize that females are more strongly lateralized for both verbal and spatial tasks, a neural organization that facilitates verbal performance, but is detrimental to performance on spatial tasks. According to Buffery and Gray, male brains are less lateralized, a pattern that is consistent with the finding that males tend to be poorer on verbal and better on spatial tasks.

Buffery and Gray's neuropsychological theory of sex differences is based on the notion that cerebral lateralization for language occurs earlier in girls than in boys. Girls do mature earlier than boys throughout childhood and adolescence, so they argued that lateralization is just another index of maturation, and thus, would also occur at an accelerated rate in girls relative to their male counterparts. It seemed to them that if lateralization occurs at an earlier age for girls than for boys, then it also occurred more completely so that, overall, girls tended to rely on one hemisphere (left for verbal tasks and right for spatial tasks) more than boys. This pattern, they presumed, continued into adulthood.

Levy's Hypothesis

Levy (1976, Levy & Nagylaki, 1972; Levy-Agresti & Sperry, 1968) has hypothesized, at least in her earlier work, that spatial performance is optimized when spatial ability is strongly lateralized in one hemisphere. Thus, unlike

Buffery and Gray, she begins with the assumption that lateralization is the best neural organization for spatial tasks. According to Levy (1976), when verbal and spatial processes are confined to single and separate sides of the brain, the underlying neural connections are optimal for each of these functions. However, if lateralization is incomplete or weak, then the two hemispheres will compete when an individual is performing a task. This aspect of her hypothesis has come to be known as the "competition hypothesis." Task performance is impaired under these conditions. Levy goes on to suggest that because verbal skills are so important to the human species, spatial ability is more likely to suffer when verbal and spatial processes compete in the same hemisphere.

In explaining sex differences in cognitive abilities, she posits that females are less lateralized than males because of sex-related biological differences in the rate and pattern of development, and, therefore, they are more likely to have bilateral representation of verbal abilities. Bilateral representation of verbal abilities will be an advantage to verbal skills because more "cortical space" is devoted to language functions. On the other hand, bilateral representation of verbal skills impairs the ability to perform spatial tasks because there is less cortical space devoted to spatial function due to the "crowding out" of spatial representation by the bilateral cortical representation of language. In other words, females are more likely to involve both hemispheres when solving spatial tasks than males. One implication of this brain organization is that females may use a verbal cognitive style when solving spatial problems, a point that I return to later in this chapter. Since bilateral representation is not an optimal neural organization for spatial tasks, women show impaired performance on spatial tasks.

Levy has also suggested that women's patterns of cognitive abilities should be similar to that of left handed males. Handedness (whether an individual is right or left handed) is often used as a rough index of lateralization. Because approximately 95% of all right handed people maintain language control primarily in their left hemisphere and spatial control in their right hemisphere, and only about 60% to 70% or fewer of left handed people have this pattern of neural organization, as a group left handed people are more likely to have bilateral representation of language functions. According to Levy's hypothesis, women, as a group, are also more likely to maintain bilateral representation. Thus, left handed men and women in general should have weaker lateralization or specialization of cognitive skills, especially language skills, than right handed men. Both groups would be expected to have better verbal skills than spatial skills, if this theory were true. Later in this chapter, I return to the theme that cognitive abilities depend on both sex and handedness (a laterality indicator).

Empirical Evidence for Sex Differences in Lateralization

These theories are confusing and contradictory. To make matters even more difficult, Levy's theoretical positions have shifted somewhat over the last 15 years. In explaining sex differences in spatial ability, Levy claims that females are more *weakly* lateralized and Buffery and Gray claim that females are more *strongly* lateralized. The complexities in the research and in relating the research to theory often seem overwhelming. It is little wonder that most psychologists have concluded that this area is too filled with inconsistencies to support any conclusion about sex differences in cerebral asymmetries.

Neuropsychologists and other brain researchers have substantially advanced our understanding of the human brain in the years since 1972 when these two theories were originally proposed. Although neither theory has received unanimous support in the research literature, and this remains an area filled with controversial and often discrepant findings, the majority of the results favors Levy's hypothesis which has undergone several revisions and refinements in the years since it was originally proposed. A summary of some of the research results supporting the components of her hypothesis is presented below.

1. In general, male's brains are more strongly lateralized than female's brains, possibly because of high levels of fetal hormones (Levy & Gur, 1980; Levy & Reid, 1978, Waber, 1977).

2. Left hemisphere lateralization for verbal abilities develops earlier for girls than for boys, and in general, females rely more on bilateral representation for both verbal and visual-spatial abilities (Ray, Georgiou, & Ravizza, 1979).

3. Sex differences in brain lateralization are related to sex differences in physical maturation rate (Ray, Newcombe, Semon, & Cole, 1981, Waber, 1977).

4. There is limited support for the prediction that strong lateralization is associated with high spatial performance (Levy & Reid, 1978; Waber, 1976).

The first point, that male brains are more strongly lateralized than female brains, is probably the most important because it begins with the conclusion that there are sex differentiated asymmetries in the organization of the human brain. Support for this conclusion comes from a variety of sources: In dichotic listening tasks there is a stronger right ear advantage for verbal stimuli for males than for females (Lake & Bryden, 1976); When stimuli are presented visually for brief periods with a tachistoscope, males show greater right visual field superiority for verbal materials (Day, 1977), and greater left visual field superiority for spatial stimuli (Kimura, 1969, Kimura & Durnford, 1974); Dimond & Beaumont (1974) reported a consistent right hemisphere superiority for males with spatial tasks, but could only demonstrate this result with females under limited and specified conditions; Males with high spatial ability showed EEG patterns of right hemisphere activity that were associated with successful spatial performance with an opposite hemisphere pattern for males with low spatial ability, whereas, no consistent hemispheric activity pattern was found for high- and low-spatial-ability females (Ray, Newcombe, Semon, & Cole, 1981). Clinical investigations of the recovery of cognitive functions following unilateral brain damage also differ by sex such that males show more impairment on verbal tests following left hemisphere damage and more impairment on spatial tests following right hemisphere damage than females (Inglis & Lawson, 1981).

Four recent reviews of the literature have also arrived at similar conclusions. Kimura (1983) has said, "It is now widely agreed that males and females probably differ in brain organization for intellectual or problem solving behaviours" (p. 19). Springer and Deutsch (1981) concluded that overall, girls, "show more bilateral representation for both types of functions" (p. 127). McGlone (1980) stated, "There is an impressive accumulation of evidence suggesting that the male brain may be more asymmetrically organized than the female brain both for verbal and nonverbal functions" (p. 215). Further support for this conclusion was provided by Seward and Seward (1980), who stated, "Subject to future developments, the bulk of the evidence suggests that women's hemispheres are probably more symmetrical than men's" (p. 64). It is important to keep in mind, however, that these quotes do *not* represent the unanimous opinion of researchers in the field. There are many researchers who failed to replicate these results. What is most compelling is that when they are found, they are almost always in the same direction—females less lateralized than males. If these were spurious findings, then you would expect the results to go in either direction about equally often.

The next two summary statements are based on the idea that the cerebral hemispheres lateralize or mature at different rates for females and males. It is widely documented that girls begin puberty earlier than boys. Girls in sixth and seventh grade not only tend to be taller than their male classmates, but also tend to exhibit secondary sex characteristics at an earlier age and develop reproductive capabilities earlier (Faust, 1977). One of the leading proponents of the maturation rate hypothesis is Waber (1976) who speculated that sex differences in lateralization were due to differences in maturation rate. To test her hypothesis, she compared early and late maturers of both sexes ranging in age from 10- to 16-years-old. All subjects participated in a dichotic listening task to ascertain hemispheric specialization for speech perception and took three tests each of verbal and spatial skill. The results provided strong support for her theory.

Early maturers of both sexes were better at the verbal tests than the spatial ones; late maturers of both sexes showed the reverse pattern of results. This difference in performance, however, was almost entirely due to the considerable superiority of the late maturers on the spatial tests. Second, there were no statistically significant sex differences in the verbal and spatial tests when the sexes were equated for maturation rate. A final result was the finding that the dichotic listening task showed the strongest lateralization among the older subjects who were late maturers, regardless of sex. Taken together, these results suggest that late maturation is associated with good spatial skills and strong lateralization for both sexes, and early physical maturation is favorable to the development of good verbal abilities and weaker lateralization. Since, in general, girls mature earlier than boys, they would be expected to show less lateralization, better verbal ability, and poorer spatial ability.

Partial confirmation of Waber's maturation rate hypothesis was provided by Ray, Newcombe, Semon, and Cole (1981). They found a positive correlation between age at puberty and performance on the Guilford-Zimmerman test of spatial orientation with later maturing individuals solving more problems correctly than those who experienced puberty at an earlier age. Petersen and Crockett (1985) also found a timing of puberty effect in their study of 135 postpubertal adolescents. Late maturers out performed early maturers on the Embedded Figures Test. However, a timing of puberty effect was not found with a mental rotations test—a test that usually shows large sex differences prior to adolescence. Thus, the notion that the biological substrates that are responsible for the onset of puberty also affect spatial ability has been replicated, but only with selected spatial ability tests.

Additional support for the maturation rate hypothesis was provided by Witelson (1976). Witelson used a tactile perception task in which 200 children ranging in age from 6 to 13 were required to match a meaningless shape that they manipulated with either their right or left hand to a visual display. She found that the boys performed this task more accurately when the shapes were presented to their left hand than when they were presented to their right hand, presumably reflecting a right hemisphere advantage in dealing with spatial information. There were no significant hand differences for the girls. It is important to note, however, in interpreting these results that there were no overall sex differences in accuracy, so that while there were no hand (or hemisphere) differences for the girls, they were, on the average, as good at this task as the boys.

If the maturation rate hypothesis is correct and females rely more upon both hemispheres in processing verbal and spatial information than males, then we should expect a lower incidence of language and spatial disorders for females since they can rely on both hemispheres and would be less impaired by local brain injury or trauma. This is true. Females have fewer reading disabilities including dyslexia, fewer speech disorders including aphasia, dysphasia, and stuttering, and a lower incidence of autism (McGlone, 1980; Witelson, 1976).

Recordings of the electrical events in the brain with electroencephalograms (EEG's) show sex differences in the underlying neural activity. The patterns of electrical activity suggest that boys tend to use their right hemispheres when performing spatial tasks while girls use their left hemispheres for both spatial tasks and verbal tasks (Levy, 1976). While these results support the idea that boys are more lateralized than girls, it is also possible that they reflect strategy differences between the sexes with girls using verbal strategies to solve spatial problems.

The notion that males develop right hemisphere specialization sooner than females was supported in a study that examined the ability of normal sighted children to learn how to read Braille. Braille is an alphabet system developed for the blind in which letters are presented as a pattern of raised points in a matrix. Rudel, Denckla, & Spalten (1973) found a left hand (right hemisphere) advantage for 13- and 14-year-old-boys, but not for girls on this task. They concluded that these results support the hypothesis that boys develop right hemisphere superiority for spatial tasks earlier and/or more completely than girls.

Sex, Lateralization, and Cognitive Abilities

It would probably be useful at this point to recapitulate two main points in Levy's hypothesis concerning the relationship among sex, lateralization, and cognitive abilities:

1. Women are more likely to have language functions represented in both hemispheres; this means that there is less "room" for spatial abilities to develop in their nondominant hemisphere.
2. Men are more lateralized for language; this means that their nondominant hemisphere is more specialized for spatial tasks.

A critical, but weak link in the argument that sex differences in brain organization underlies cognitive sex differences is that strong lateralization (a "male" organization) be related to high spatial performance. Thus, while data in support of the claim that there are sex differences in lateralization which vary as a function of maturation rate are interesting, the relationship between degree of lateralization and cognitive ability must be demonstrated before we can accept Levy's hypothesis. The data in support of this relationship are not strong. Levy and Reid (1978) found partial support for this hypothesized relationship using spatial performance tests with a sample of male subjects, but they used an atypical sample of extremely high functioning subjects. Their experiment was weak for several reasons: First, the males in their study surpassed the females in the verbal test, a highly unusual result that would not be predicted from this theory. Second, the verbal test results collected from their female subjects failed to confirm the predictions derived from their model. (The actual research results are quite complex, involving hand posture in writing as a variable. Readers interested in the details of this research are referred to Levy and Reid's report.) Thus, the prediction that strong lateralization would be related to good spatial ability and weak lateralization would be related to good verbal ability has received only weak confirmation.

Disconfirming Evidence

As you probably guessed, all of the research does not support the conclusions about sex differences in lateralization that were listed earlier. In an area as complex as understanding the human brain, there are inconsistent and contradictory data. The twin foundations of Levy's theory are that females are better in verbal skills because of their bilateral representation of language and males are better in spatial skills because they are more strongly lateralized. McKeever and Van Deventer (1977), for example, systematically examined the effects of handedness, sex, and hemispheric dominance in right and left handed university students. They obtained the usual finding that males outperformed females on spatial tasks in all handedness and cerebral dominance groups; however, contrary to Levy's hypothesis they failed to obtain any significant effects for handedness or dominance for either the verbal or spatial tasks. "It is concluded that the hypothesis of verbal-spatial processing incompatibility within the same hemisphere is not supported" (p. 321).

Although many of the research results support the notion of sex differences in cerebral asymmetries that are related to differences in physical maturation rate, it is difficult to understand why some researchers report contradictory results. Of course there are always differences in procedures, samples, and materials that could account for empirical differences. Berenbaum and Harshman (1980) have pointed out a number of methodological weaknesses that could be responsible for some of the negative findings in this area. It is also possible that females and males rely on different underlying processes and strategies to perform the same task. If, for example, women use verbal strategies in a spatial task, they could perform the task quite well by compensating for weaker spatial abilities with superior verbal abilities.

Another possible locus for the inconsistencies reported in the literature concerns the way laterality is measured. In the usual paradigm, verbal or spatial (nonverbal) information is initially presented to either cerebral hemisphere via different auditory presentations to the right and left ear (dichotic listening) or by presenting visual stimuli to the right or left visual field. Lateralization is then measured by analyzing for right or left ear or right or left visual field advantages. For example, if a subject reports more verbal stimuli correctly when they are presented to the right ear (left hemisphere) than when they are presented to the left ear (right hemisphere), we would conclude that the subject has left hemisphere dominance for verbal information. Identical logic is used for determining cerebral dominance or lateralization for nonverbal stimuli or for visual field presentations. Group differences with respect to lateralization report percentage of subjects with a particular pattern of correct answers (e.g., 78% reported more verbal stimuli correctly when thet were presented to the right ear) or the mean difference in correct responses between right and left ears (Richardson, 1976). Teng (1981) has expressed numerous concerns about the reliability and validity of these methods of measurement. While Teng's reservations about the measurement of lateralization are too technical for review here, readers should be aware that measurement problems could be responsible for some of the inconsistencies reported in this area. It seems clear that there will be no simple answers to the many questions of cognitive sex differences and additional unexplored variables including the technical aspects of measurement and method of stimulus presentation will need to be considered to resolve the inconsistencies.

Cognitive Similarities Between Left Handed Men and Women

Perhaps one of the more controversial aspects of Levy's hypothesis is the notion that if an individual maintains a bilateral representation of verbal skills, then there will be less room left (or fewer neural structures) for spatial abilities in the right hemisphere, and therefore, spatial abilities will suffer. In addition, left handers and women should, in general, have more bilateral representation of verbal ability and thus should have poorer spatial skills. Levy verified this prediction in her early work at California Institute of Technology, where she found that left handed graduate students had lower performance subscales on a standardized intelligence test than their right handed counterparts, with no difference between the groups on the verbal subscale (Levy, 1969). Despite Levy's own success in supporting her hypothesis, the majority of studies that have attempted to replicate this relationship have failed (e.g., Hardyck, Petrinovich, & Goldman, 1976; Sherman, 1979). Levy's earlier notion that left handed men are similar to women in terms of their cognitive abilities has proven to be too simple. As is seen later in this chapter, specific combinations of sex and handedness need to be considered before ability predictions can be made.

Recent research on the relationship between handedness and sex may have provided some of the missing puzzle pieces while also suggesting a locus for some of the inconsistencies in the earlier literature. Harshman, Hampson, and Berenbaum (1983) have provided the most convincing evidence to date to support the hypothesis that sex and handedness differences in cognitive ability are, at least in part, neurological in origin. To ensure the generalizability of their results and to control for spurious findings (Type I errors—concluding that differences exist when the results were really due to chance), they employed three separate large-scale samples and multiple measures of spatial ability, verbal ability, dichotic listening, and reasoning. A test of reasoning was included in the belief that intellectual or reasoning ability could be mediating the sex and handedness effect on spatial ability.

Harshman, Hampson, and Berenbaum's results were clear cut: Among subjects who scored high on the reasoning test, males outperformed females on 14 of the 15 spatial tests, as expected; however, the most interesting results were obtained with the sex by handedness interactions. Across all three samples and all 15 spatial tests, left handed males performed worse than right handed males, while on 12 of the 15 spatial tests left handed females performed better than right handed females. Among subjects who scored low on the reasoning test, males again outscored females on 14 of the 15 spatial tests with a somewhat inconsistent pattern of sex by handedness interactions.

When reasoning ability is used as a mediator in verbal ability, the results are the mirror image of those found with spatial ability. Among subjects high in reasoning ability, left handed males performed better than right handed males and left handed females performed worse than right handed females. Again, among the low reasoning ability subjects, the results were less consistent. These results are summarized in Table 4.2.

If, as these results suggest, sex and handedness differences in cognitive abilities depend on reasoning or intellectual ability, then contradictory and negative results would be expected if the researcher used either low-ability subjects or mixed high- and low-ability-subjects in a single experiment without controlling for ability level. The pattern of results for the "high reasoners" is in accord with predictions made by Levy and Gur (1980). Harshman, Hampson, and Berenbaum also provided converging evidence to support their conclusion that these results reflect neurological organization. (Cognitive differences were associated with familial sinistrality [family history of left handedness], hand posture during writing, and ear of asymmetry in the dichotic listening task. Further discussion about this ancillary evidence is beyond the scope of this chapter, but interested readers are referred to their research report.)

You may be wondering why reasoning or intellectual ability should be important in mediating these results. Harshman, Hampson, and Berenbaum believe that certain brain organizations promote high reasoning ability and that by dividing their data into reasoning ability subsets, they have produced homogeneous subsets that allow them to investigate "how sex and handedness differences in brain organization impose various hardware trade-offs which produce better performance on one type of task, at the cost of reduced performance on a different type of task" (p. 182). (For additional support of the sex by handedness interaction in cognition, see Gottfried & Bathurst, 1983).

TABLE 4.2
Summarization of Sex By Handedness By
Reasoning Ability Interactions
(Harshman, Hampson, & Berenbaum, 1983)

Spatial Ability

    Subjects with high reasoning ability
      males > females
      left-handed males < right-handed males
      left-handed females > right-handed females
    Subjects with low reasoning ability
      males > females
      no consistent sex by handedness effects

Verbal Ability

    Subjects with high reasoning ability
      females > males on selected tests
      left-handed males > right-handed males
      left-handed females < right-handed females
    Subjects with low reasoning ability
      no consistent sex by handedness effects

Note: > should read "better than"
     < should read "worse than"

These results suggest that Levy was correct in her belief that sex and handedness (as an index of laterality) would be important determinants of the pattern of cognitive abilities; however, she underestimated the complexity of the relationship in her earlier work. It is reasonable to assume that the California Institute of Technology graduate students that she employed as subjects in her 1969 study were high in reasoning/intellectual ability and thus showed the pattern of cognitive results Harshman, Hampson, and Berenbaum found in their high ability group. More recent work by Levy (Levy & Gur, 1980) corroborate these results with "high reasoners." It seems that answers to all of the important questions in psychology require a qualifying "it depends" or "sometimes." At least among those who are high in intellectual ability, left handed men seem to be poorer in spatial ability, a trait usually associated with women; however, these results suggest a cognitive tradeoff with the result that they may also be superior in verbal ability, thus demonstrating the "female cognitive pattern."

There have been numerous other studies that point to the importance of sex by handedness interactions in understanding the way cognitive abilities differ. Colley (1984), for example, found a significant interaction of sex and handedness on a spatial (bimanual thumb positioning) task. Other studies have examined familial sinistrality or family history of left handedness as an indicator of laterality and have found that sex by familial sinistrality or sex by familial sinistrality by handedness interactions are significant factors in cognitive ability (McKeever & Van Deventer, 1977; Piazza, 1980, for auditory tasks, but not for visual tasks; Tinkcom, Obrzut, & Poston, 1983, for nonverbal dichaptic tasks; Yeo & Cohen, 1983, for spatial tasks, but not verbal tasks). Two studies that addressed the relative importance of sex and handedness in predicting cognitive abilities concluded that handedness is the more important factor (Johnson & Harley, 1980; Nagae, 1985). Geschwind has noted that stuttering and dyslexia both occur in greater numbers in left handers and males. He believes that the high levels of testosterone that cause the prenatal sexual differentiation of the gonads so that they develop into testes are also responsible for some language disorders. While this theory is still speculative, it does represent an additional possible sex by handedness link.

Some Tentative Conclusions About Sex-Related Brain Differences

Although current researchers have made obvious progress in unraveling the tangle of brain and sex variables, there are still many knotty issues that have to be resolved before a strong theory of sex differentiated brain functioning is posited. A verifiable theory that can account for the diverse nature of the experimental results is still needed. Numerous questions still need to be answered. What are the principles of brain organization that can account for results that are only found among "high reasoning" subjects? Why are there so many glaring inconsistencies in the data? How does familial sinistrality fit into the cognitive sex differences literature? What is the role of genes in determining cerebral laterality? We know that left-handedness is, at least in part, genetically determined. The probability of a child developing left-handedness is .46 if both parents are left handed, .17 if one parent is left-handed, and only .02 if neither parent is left-handed (Springer & Deutsch, 1981). It seems, therefore, that cerebral lateralization is inherited, but we know little about sex differentiated patterns of inheritance of lateralization. Some researchers have reported a greater incidence of left-handedness among males, but this finding has not been replicated consistently. While it seems reasonable to conclude that sex related differences in cerebral lateralization influence the development of cognitive abilities, the exact nature of the influence is still unknown.

Although some general conclusions and a critique of biological theories in general can be found at the end of this chapter, some conclusions about sex-related brain differences are in order at this point. Based on current data, there are some differences in brain organization and structure that, on the average, vary by sex. This conclusion is in no way meant to imply that men can't write poetry or that women can't be architects or mathematicians because their brains aren't "wired" for these tasks. Obviously, there are outstanding male poets, and the number of women in the natural sciences and mathematics is increasing dramatically: these are facts that can't be explained on the basis of brain differences. Environmental and sex role influences on cognitive sex differences are discussed in the next chapter, and their importance in directing how we develop our cognitive abilities cannot be overestimated. It is possible that sex related lateralization patterns result from or are influenced by sex differentiated patterns of socialization, although I know of no empirical data that support this possibility. Despite the importance of environmental influences, there is no reason to believe that sex role pressures or other environmental pressures are different for right and left handed individuals. The fact that cognitive ability results depended on both sex and handedness is difficult to explain with a strictly environmental theory. The only plausible explanation of the sex by handedness interactions found by Harshman, Hampson, and Berenbaum and others is that they are reflective of underlying neurological differences. This is obviously an incendiary topic, and the possibility that these conclusions will be misused poses a serious concern to anyone who is concerned with prejudice and discrimination. The practical effect of sex differences in cerebral lateralization needs to be interpreted in a societal context in which skills and abilities are prized and encouraged in a sex differentiated manner.

Apparently, the notion that there are sex differences in human brain asymmetry is not a new one. McGlone (1980) began her review of this topic with an 1880 quote from Crichton-Browne: "It would appear that the tendency to symmetry in the two halves of the cerebrum is stronger in women than in men" (p. 215). Over a century later, we are still arriving at the same conclusion. Recent research by Kimura (1985) suggests that the notion that women's brains are more bilaterally organized than men's brains may depend on the task being investigated. She believes that some speech functions are organized in a sex differentiated manner *within* the left hemisphere. In other words, speech centers may be located in different places in the left hemisphere depending on sex.

It is important to note that not all reviewers agree with the conclusion that there are sex differences in brain organization and structure. For a dissenting view, the reader is referred to a commentary by Annett (1980) in which she argues that sex differences in laterality are not reliably found. Other recent reviews (Hyde, 1985) have concluded that the nature of brain differences in the functioning of the hemispheres is not yet well known. None of these reviews has considered the most recent research evidence that has helped to resolve some of the earlier contradictory research findings and has helped to provide a stronger theoretical framework for interpreting the results. I believe that the research reviewed in this chapter provides strong evidence for sex differentiated asymmetries in cerebral organization which may vary as a function of handedness and even family history of handedness. The practical significance of these differences and the relative importance of the other variables investigated still remain unknown.

SEX HORMONES

Mention sex differences with respect to almost any ability and someone is sure to say, "It's all in the hormones." Clearly, one of the major biological differences between females and males is the relative concentration of the *female* sex hormones, estrogen and progesterone, and *male* sex hormones or androgens, most notably testosterone. Sex hormones are powerful chemical messengers secreted by the ovaries in women, testes in men, and adrenal glands in both sexes. Because they circulate freely throughout the blood stream, sex hormones are able to affect distant target organs, including the brain.

Despite common misconceptions, it is not true that women have only female hormones and men have only male hormones. Both sexes have measurable quantities of estrogen, progesterone, and testosterone. The relative concentrations of each of these hormones vary by sex and throughout the life cycle.

Because of dramatic age-dependent fluctuations in hormone levels, it seems likely that the influence of these hormones would also vary with age. The age-dependent nature of hormone effects is examined in separate sections for each developmental stage beginning with prenatal influences and ending with adulthood and old age.

Prenatal Hormones

Prenatal hormones are critically important determinants of whether a developing fetus will grow into a male or female infant. The genetic configuration of the sex chromosomes (XX for female, XY for male) determines whether the undifferentiated developing gonads (sex glands) will become ovaries or testes. If they are developing according to a male program, they will begin to differentiate approximately 7 weeks after conception. The newly formed testes will secrete male hormones (primarily testosterone) which, in turn, directs the development of the internal male reproductive organs and external genitals. If, on the other hand, the genetic program is XX, the gonads will develop into ovaries and, in the *absence* of male hormones, internal female reproductive organs and external female genitals will develop. It is important to note that it is the absence of male hormones, not the presence of female hormones, that directs the growth of female organs since in the absence of hormones, or usable hormones, the sexual differentiation of the fetus will be female. A schematic diagram of prenatal development is presented in Fig. 4.3. It charts the development of female and male babies from conception until birth.

It seemed plausible to many researchers that the presence or absence of particuliar sex hormones during this critical stage of development could also play a role in the sexual differentiation of the developing brain. Much of the research in this area has been performed on lower mammals, especially rats. While there are numerous biological similarities between lower mammals and humans, one of the major differences is the extent to which hormones direct and control behavior. As we ascend the phylogenetic scale, hormones become less important in determining behavior. Thus, while results obtained with rats or other mammals may be suggestive of possible relationships for humans, they are not directly applicable. Extrapolation from animal data to humans can lead to erroneous conclusions.

For most people, the configuration of their sex chromosomes, prenatal and postnatal sex hormones, reproductive organs, genitals, sex role pressures, and sex of identification are the same. In order to understand the role that hormones play in shaping the other biological and psychological indices of sex, it is necessary to isolate experimentally and manipulate sex hormones independent of the other covariates of sex. Two general approaches are used to understand the effect of sex hormones. The quantity and type of sex hormone are manipulated in lower animals under careful laboratory conditions, and naturally occurring or drug induced human abnormalities are studied. There are strengths and weaknesses associated with each of these approaches.

Laboratory Investigations With Lower Animals

The majority of the work in this area has been conducted with rats, although other lower animals and primates have been used. Prenatal hormones are manipulated by either castrating the developing male, thereby depriving him of the testosterone secreted by the testes, administering male hormones (androgens) to developing females, or administering any hormone of interest to the pregnant mother who will pass the hormone onto the developing fetus. Timing of these manipulations is important because there appears to be a critical developmental

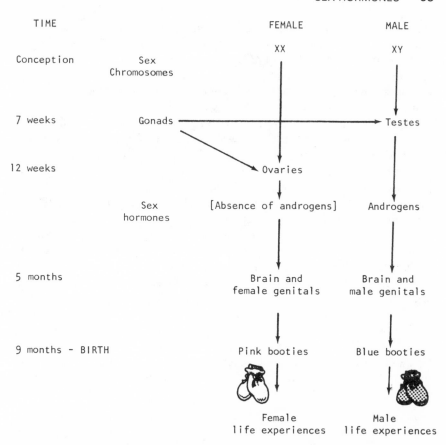

FIG. 4.3. Schematic diagram of sex differentiation during prenatal development.

period for brain differentiation. Recent research with rodents using these techniques has mapped hormone sensitive cells in the brain that respond differentially to prenatal sex hormones (McEwen, 1981). In their review of the literature, MacLusky and Naftolin (1981) cited a number of sex differences in brain morphology that depend on prenatal hormone exposure including volume differences in certain cell groups and differences in synaptic and dendrite organization. Diamond (cited in Kimura, 1985) found that testosterone can have asymmetrical affects on the developing brains of prenatal female and male rats. When additional testosterone was supplied, male rats showed increases in the thickness of their right hemispheres; whereas female rats showed increases in the thickness of their left hemispheres. While these results are of scientific interest, it is not possible to relate this directly to human brains or any aspect of human functioning. Extrapolations from other species to humans should be made cautiously, especially when considering hormone effects.

One well established effect of prenatal hormones is in the function and development of a tiny brain structure known as the hypothalamus. The hypothalamus influences reproductive behavior and controls the release of reproductive hormones from the pituitary gland. There is no reason to believe that the hypothalamus and pituitary are involved in the higher level cognitive abilities that vary by sex; however, other brain structures may be affected by prenatal hormones. Clear cut findings in lower mammals have led researchers to conclude that prenatal hormones influence sexual behavior, aggression, activity in open fields, and maze learning. In general, if male hormones are administered then typical male behavior results, and if male hormones are removed the typical female behavior results. Male rodent behaviors include male sexual posturing (mounting), increased open field activity, increased aggression, and faster maze learning. Female rodent behaviors include female sexual posturing (lordosis), decreased open field activity, decreased aggression, and slower maze learning.

The finding that sex differences in lower mammal and primate brains and sexual and aggressive behaviors are mediated by prenatal hormones is interesting in its own right, but there is ample reason to believe that for humans, sexual and aggressive behavior is shaped, to a greater extent, by social learning and other life experiences. Thus, human applications of these results are highly speculative and await replication in humans. Of course, such manipulations are unethical for human subjects. The closest we can come to examining hormone effects in humans is to examine "human accidents" or hormone abnormalities.

Prenatal Sex Hormone Abnormalities

Fetal Androgenization. What is the effect of high levels of male hormones on a developing fetus? This question has been answered with two different groups of subjects who were exposed to abnormally high levels of androgens during fetal development.

Since the early 1950s, millions of pregnant women have been treated with synthetic sex hormones to prevent miscarriage. Although a variety of hormones has been used in varying doses depending upon the individual situation and current medical practice, all have some androgenic or masculinizing effect. Research with lower animals has shown that aggressive behavior is hormonally mediated. Reinisch (1981) reasoned that if prenatal hormones have similar effects in humans, then individuals who had been exposed to high levels of masculine hormones before birth should also demonstrate an increased potential for aggressive behavior. She studied 17 female and 8 male subjects who had been exposed to synthetic hormones before birth. The measurement of aggression in humans poses a research problem because most people demonstrate aggressive impulses only under limited and threatening circumstances. For this reason, Reinisch utilized a paper and pencil measure of aggression. She used same-sex unexposed siblings as the control group in the belief that siblings offer a control for environmental and genetic influences. Both her subjects and their siblings had a mean age of 11 years at the time of testing.

As expected from all of the sex differences literature, Reinisch found that males had higher aggression scores than females. Reinisch also found that her subjects who had been exposed to synthetic hormones before birth reported higher physical aggression than their unexposed same-sex siblings. She interpreted these results as providing strong support for prenatal hormone mediation of human aggressive behavior. The implication of this research is that since, under normal conditions, males are exposed to more androgens before birth than females, sex differences in aggression are due to sex differences in prenatal hormonal milieu.

Other researchers have provided corroborative evidence that prenatal hormones contribute to aggression and/or general energy level. Ehrhardt and Meyer-Bahlburg (1979) reported that boys with congenital adrenal hyperplasia (CAH), a genetic condition that causes the adrenal glands to produce excessive amounts of sex hormones, had "higher energy expenditures" than their unaffected male siblings. While it is reasonable to conclude that at least under abnormally high concentrations, prenatal hormones affect human aggressive potential, what about their role in sex differentiated human cognitive abilities?

Hines (1982) examined the relationship between prenatal sex hormones and cognitive abilities using 16 females whose mothers had taken DES during their pregnancy to prevent miscarriage. (DES has recently been in the news as a probable cause of a rare form of genital cancer among girls and boys born from DES pregnancies.) DES, like the other synthetic prenatal hormones, has masculinizing effects on the developing fetus. If the synthetic hormones influence brain development in a masculine direction, then females would be expected to show a brain organization that is more similar to the masculine pattern than their unexposed sisters. Hines found that the DES females she tested were more strongly lateralized for verbal stimuli than their sibling control groups. Recall from the previous section on sex differences in cerebral asymmetries that males are, in general, more strongly lateralized than females, a result that may be linked to sex differences in verbal and spatial abilities. Hines' findings that DES exposed females have strongly lateralized brain functions supports the view that prenatal hormones are determinants of female and male brain organizations. Geschwind, a leading neuropsychologist in this area, also believes that high levels of prenatal testosterone partially determine left-handedness. All of this research suggests the same conclusion: prenatal sex hormones are partial determinants of sex-differentiated cerebral organizations.

In a direct test of the role of prenatal sex hormones on cognitive abilities, Dalton (1976), studied English children whose mothers had been given extremely high doses of sex hormones during pregnancy. Dalton reported that these children had significantly better "number ability," a result that would be predicted if these hormones also influence mathematical ability. However, Dalton's studies have been criticized on a number of statistical and methodological grounds including her failure to utilize a control group when evaluating number ability, thus considerably weakening the impact of these findings. Meyer-Bahlburg and Ehrhardt (1977) attempted to replicate these results using better controls and more rigorous research methods. They did not find any relationship between prenatal hormone exposure and number ability, although it must be pointed out that the synthetic hormone taken by Meyer-Baklburg and Ehrhardt's subjects' mothers was less potent than the one investigated by Dalton.

Androgen Insensitivity and Turner's Syndrome

All of the studies discussed in the previous section examined the effect of high levels of prenatal masculinizing hormones. Another experimental approach is to examine the effect of extremely low levels of masculinizing hormones. Will such individuals develop cognitive abilities and personality traits usually associated with being female?

Androgen insensitivity is the term used to describe genetic males whose bodies are unable to respond to male hormones. During fetal development their testes produce the appropriate male hormones, but for reasons not fully understood, their tissues are insensitive to these hormones and development proceeds as though no male hormones are present. These genetic males develop female genitals and are usually raised as girls. Ehrhardt and Meyer-Bahlburg (1979) reported "a significant, but modest, tendency toward verbal rather than space-form abilities" among genetic males with androgen insensitivity (p. 422). Even if these results were large, we would not know if they were due to prenatal hormone effects, postnatal hormone effects, or the fact that they were identified and raised as girls. Thus, these results cannot be used to understand hormone effects on cognition.

Another possible population for investigating prenatal hormone effects is women with Turner's syndrome. Recall that these women have a genetic abnormality such that their second sex chromosome is missing. They are genetically denoted as 45XO to signify that they have a total of 45 chromosomes, and only a single X sex chromosome. They usually have underdeveloped ovaries and very low levels of both female and male hormones. Hines (1982) found that while Turner's women have normal range IQ's, they tend to have specific deficits in visual-spatial functioning. Could these specific deficiencies be due to extremely low levels of male hormones? An indirect way of answering this question is by examining the extent to which Turner's women were lateralized for cognitive tasks. When Hines (1982) investigated this relationship, she found that Turner's women had reduced laterality for cognitive tasks. Although this result is consistent with a brain organization that may be detrimental to spatial tasks, the cause of this organization is not entirely clear. Postnatal hormones could also be contributing to these results. Turner's women also have certain physical characteristics that could be mediating these results. They tend to be short with a relatively unfeminine body type (small breasts, thick necks). If they respond to these external manifestations of their genotype, it is possible that they exaggerate female tendencies, including poorer visual-spatial abilities.

Taken together, research on the influence of prenatal sex hormones on cognitive abilities has not yet provided any definitive answers. Although it is possible that there are direct influences mediated through female and male patterns of brain lateralization, the currently available data are inconclusive. Even in those instances where positive effects have been reported, it is very difficult to tease out the contributions of genetic influences, postnatal hormones, and life experiences. Furthermore, abnormal hormone levels could produce results that are not associated with normal levels of the same hormones.

Childhood and Puberty

Throughout infancy and childhood, both girls and boys have very low levels of all sex hormones. In fact, in those instances where, for some medical reason, sex reassignment surgery is needed (e.g., ambiguous or deformed genitals), there is usually no need to begin hormone therapy until adolescence. The body shapes of young boys and girls are so similar that it is difficult to tell girls and boys apart unless they wear sex-typed clothing or hair styles. Sex hormones, however, become extremely important at puberty since they are necessary for the development of secondary sex characteristics in both sexes and the timing of menarche (first menstruation) in girls. Several researchers have investigated the possibility that hormone events at puberty are also implicated in the development of cognitive sex differences.

One of the major theories of sex differences in cerebral laterality posited that they were a by-product of sex differences in maturation rate at puberty. Waber (1976, 1977), a proponent of this theory, found that late maturing adolescents of both sexes were more lateralized for speech perception and exhibited better spatial skills than earlier maturing adolescents of the same age. (Waber measured maturation by the development of secondary sex characteristics during a well child physical examination conducted in a nurse's office.) She concluded that differences in cortical organization were related to one's rate of physical maturation. The fact that girls generally attain physical maturation earlier than boys could explain cognitive sex differences. Thus, according to this view, the same hormonal events that are responsible for the timing of puberty are also responsible for sex differentiated patterns of brain lateralization which, in turn, create sex related cognitive differences. In support of this theory, Petersen and Crockett (1985) also found that late maturing adolescents were better than their early maturing peers on the Embedded Figures Test.

Two other theories have been proposed to explain the relationship between sex hormones and cognitive abilities. Like Waber's theory, these other two also point to puberty as a critically important time in one's life for the development of these abilities.

Hier and Crowley (1982) have proposed that the amount of androgens available at puberty can be a determinant of visual spatial ability. They studied 19 men with androgen deficiencies at puberty. Compared to normal male adolescents, the androgen deficient males showed impaired spatial abilities. There were no differences between the groups with regard to verbal ability. Furthermore, they found a direct relationship between the severity of the androgen deficiency and the severity of the spatial impairment. That is, the men with the lowest amounts of androgen were also the poorest at spatial tasks and those whose androgen levels were closer to normal showed the least impairment. Hier and Crowley believe that puberty is a critical period for the development of spatial skills, and once spatial skills are established via sufficient levels of androgens at puberty, these skills are viable for a lifetime, even if androgen levels fall later in life. Conversely, if spatial abilities fail to develop in puberty because of low levels of androgens, this disability cannot be corrected later in life. They support their argument by noting that both Turner's women and genetic males with androgen insensitivity have poor spatial ability, and both groups have abnormally low levels of androgen (or, in the case of androgen insensitivity, usable androgen) at puberty.

Hier and Crowley admit that they don't understand the mechanism by which male hormones mediate the development of spatial ability. They hypothesize that testosterone, a major male hormone, has transient effects on the central nervous system. Their own conclusion is that, "Our results suggest that androgenization (presumably mediated by testosterone or one of its metabolites) is essential to the full development of spatial ability" (p. 1204).

It is important to keep in mind the fact that Hier and Crowley used a small sample of abnormal males to arrive at their conclusion. Even if it were true that a minimal level of male hormones is needed for the development of spatial ability, we have no idea what that minimal level is. Females have measurable quantities of male hormones in their bloodstream, most of it produced by their adrenal glands with a smaller quantity produced by the ovaries (Bleier, 1984). While males have more of these hormones, it has not been demonstrated that unusually high levels of androgens are correlated with exceptionally good spatial ability. Logical follow-ups to this study would examine: (1) what happens to these males if they are administered androgens during puberty, (2) the spatial abilities of females with malfunctioning adrenal glands, and (3) both males and females with high levels of male and female hormones during puberty.

A third theory about the relationship between the sex hormones available at puberty and the development of spatial skills is based on the idea that it is not the absolute quantity of androgens that is important; rather, it is the relative amounts of female and male hormones that determine spatial ability. In a test of this hypothesis, Petersen (1976) inferred the quantity of sex hormones available from the development of secondary sex characteristics in a sample of normal females and males at 13, 16, and 18 years. She found that for males, high levels of male hormones were associated with *low* spatial ability, while the reverse was true for females. For females, high levels of male hormones were associated with *high* spatial ability. In other words, superior spatial ability was associated with *more* male hormones for females and *less* male hormones for males. Taken together, these sex differentiated results point to an optimal balance of female and male hormones. Support for this position was provided by Maccoby (1966) who reported that boys with high spatial ability test scores were rated as less masculine by their peers than boys with low spatial ability test scores. Using the theoretical framework provided by Petersen's theory, Maccoby's results can be understood by reasoning that the boys who appeared less masculine probably had lower levels of androgens, a condition that Petersen believes is correlated with high spatial ability in males.

A major criticism of Petersen's study concerned the method she used to infer sex hormone levels (McGee, 1979). She rated photos of her subjects on the extent to which they had developed secondary sex characteristics. There is considerable room for inaccuracies with this measurement technique. Petersen's results need to be replicated with the more precise measurement of hormone levels that is possible with hormone assays (blood samples) collected from large samples of adolescents.

In summary, three theories have been proposed to explain the effect of sex hormones available during puberty on the development of cognitive abilities: (1) The "maturation rate" theory posits that physical maturation under the direct control of sex hormones during adolescence directs brain organization such that early maturers are less lateralized than late maturers. In general, girls mature earlier than boys; therefore, they are less lateralized. (2) The "androgen at puberty theory" maintains that a minimal level of androgen must be present at puberty for spatial abilities to develop, thus it is the male hormones that are critical for the development of good spatial skills. (3) The "optimal female-male hormone balance" theory states that the relative amount of male and female hormones is the critical element for the development of spatial abilities. Smaller amounts of male hormones are associated with good spatial ability in males, and larger amounts of male hormones are associated with good spatial ability in females. Of these three theories, only the maturation rate theory can explain both female superiority on verbal tasks and male superiority on spatial tasks. The last two theories are only concerned with explaining sex differences in spatial ability.

In deciding which of these three theoretical positions accounts best for the data, it is important to keep in mind that these three theories are not mutually exclusive. It is possible that all three are correct to some extent. Possibly, a minimal level of male hormones is needed for spatial ability to develop, and beyond the minimal level relative amounts of both types of hormones become critical. Maturation rate could direct brain lateralization as well as require minimal quantities of selected hormones. Research that has addressed the question of the relationship between sex hormones and cognitive abilities seems to suggest that there is some relationship, but the nature and strength of the relationship is unknown. It probably depends on many other variables that have not yet been identified or investigated. Although adolescence is the time in the life cycle when sex-related cognitive differences clearly emerge as well as the time when dramatic changes in sex hormone levels begin, the coincidence of these two events may be secondary to other salient life changes that occur at the same time, such as the adoption of adult sex roles and different expectations of adolescents with mature bodies.

One problem with all of these theories is that they cannot explain the sex differences that are found in childhood. While cognitive differences are found more reliably at adolescence, there are reports in the literature of differences emerging earlier, most notably for verbal skills and selected tests of spatial ability (mental rotation and the Water Level Test). The nature and validity of cognitive sex differences in childhood is likely to be an active area of research during the next several years. If future researchers can document childhood and toddler differences, then theories that focus on adolescence as the critical period for the development of these cognitive abilities will have to be revised.

Adulthood and Old Age

Sex hormones throughout adulthood and old age follow very different patterns for women and men. For women, the female hormones follow a monthly (approximately) cycle in which they ebb and flow while the concentrations of male hormones remain relatively constant. At menopause, the amount of the female hormones diminishes substantially with little change in the levels of male hormones. For men, the concentrations of sex hormones remain fairly constant throughout the adult years, with a gradual decline into old age. In recent years, there has been considerable interest in the notion that male hormones fluctuate in a cyclic fashion throughout the month, but there has been too little research on this topic to warrant a conclusion (Doering et al., 1974).

A hormone-based theory devised to explain cognitive sex differences was proposed by Broverman, Klaiber, Kobayashi, and Vogel (1968). They began with the premise that sex hormones activate the central nervous system in a manner that facilitates the performance of simple, overlearned, repetitive tasks and interferes with tasks that require inhibition of an initial response. Their second supposition is that female hormones are more "powerful" than male hormones with the result that women are superior on "simple, overlearned, perceptual motor tasks" such as those found in "clerical aptitude tests." Males, on the other hand, are naturally better at "more complex tasks requiring inhibition of immediate responses." Broverman et al.'s theory has been criticized on a number of grounds (Singer & Montgomery, 1969). One major problem concerns the way they classified their tasks. Verbal skills, including language comprehension and usage, are neither simple nor overlearned, yet these are the tasks at which females usually excel. Their initial assumptions about the effects of estrogens and androgens on the central nervous system are incorrect on physiological grounds. There is little supporting evidence and considerable contradictory evidence for the hypothesis of Broverman et al. that neural processes respond in the ways they propose.

Because the major female hormones vary in a cyclical fashion throughout the month in adult women, it would seem that cognitive abilities should also vary in a similar cycle if these hormones mediate cognitive processes. For most healthy adult women, both estrogen and progesterone, the major female hormones, are available only in small quantities during the premenstrual, menstrual, and immediately postmenstrual portion of their cycle. Both hormones increase to a peak quantity at approximately midcycle and then decline to premenstrual levels. Is there any evidence that women's cognitive or intellectual abilities decline during the portion of the cycle when these hormones are low? In response to this question, Tiger (1970) wrote:

> An American girl writing her Graduate Record Examinations over a two-day period or a week-long set of finals during the premenstruum begins with a disadvantage which almost certainly condemns her to no higher than a second class grade. A whole career in the educational system can be unfairly jeopardized because of this phenomenon.

If Tiger is correct, then we would have to schedule individual final exam dates for women so as to avoid the premenstrual and menstrual phase of their cycles. There might also be good reasons to exclude women from high government offices and any responsible position because of periodic deficits in their intellectual abilities. Research on this question has clearly shown that Tiger is wrong. Golub (1976) conducted a careful study of whether there are differences in women's cognitive functioning over the menstrual cycle. Her results with 13 different cognitive tests administered to 50 women aged 30 to 45 showed no significant menstrual cycle effect. Even though some women reported mood changes between the premenstrual and menstrual phases of their cycle, apparently these changes were not large enough to affect their ability to perform cognitive tasks. There is no evidence to support the notion that cognitive abilities fluctuate in a cyclical fashion.

Several researchers have sought to explain the cognitive sex differences that occur at the end of the life span. There is a well documented decline in the ability to utilize and retain spatial information relative to the ability to utilize and retain verbal information among the elderly (Clarkson-Smith & Halpern, 1983; Halpern, 1984b). Parallel to the decline in spatial abilities is a decline in both female and male sex hormones in both women and men. While it is possible that there is a cause and effect relationship between these two events that occur at approximately the same time in the life cycle, there is little research to support the idea that they are directly linked. None of the theories discussed earlier in this chapter can account for the age-related decline in spatial abilities while verbal skills remain high. Psychosocial and environmental explanations that are discussed in the next chapter account for this finding much better than any of the sex hormone theories.

CRITIQUE OF BIOLOGICAL HYPOTHESES

Biological and Environmental Interactions

Most of the biological theories discussed in this chapter have either failed to consider or have downplayed the fact that biology and the environment interact. For example, while it is possible that males are better at spatial skills because their cerebral organization is more lateralized than that of females, it might also be possible that because males excel at spatial skills or perform them more frequently, their hemispheres develop a more lateralized organization. Similarly, it is likely that young girls receive more verbal stimulation and are encouraged to read and speak correctly. Their early reliance on verbal skills could cause verbal skills to be developed at the expense of other types of abilities such as spatial skills. While the possibility that life experiences influence biological processes such as brain lateralization must be considered, it is also clear that biology influences the types of experiences to which people are exposed. For example, if boys are better than girls at spatial tasks for biological reasons, parents could differentially encourage this ability by buying them spatial toys (e.g., puzzles, erector sets) which in turn provides tham with more experience with spatial manipulations than their sisters would receive. Numerous other examples are possible.

As an example of the difficulty in disentangling biological from environmental influences, consider the following problem that has come to be known as the "twentieth century conundrum." Over the last two generations, girls have begun menstruating at an earlier age than their mothers who in turn experienced earlier menarche than their mothers (Frisch, 1983). While no one is really sure why this has been happening, it is probably related to improved nutrition, sanitation, and change in work environments. According to Waber (1977), early menarche implies early physical maturation, which is related to bilateral cerebral organization. Taken to its logical conclusion, we would have to conclude that the improved living conditions of the twentieth century have been detrimental to women's spatial ability! This is an unsatisfactory conclusion because it implies that conditions that are good for women's physical development are bad for their intellectual development. In addition, early menarche among twentieth century girls would also predict that the current generation of young women are less good at spatial skills than their mothers, who in turn are less good at spatial skills than their mothers. There is not only no evidence to support this possibility, all of the evidence suggests the reverse, that is, today's young women are better at spatial tasks than previous generations of women. Women have been entering traditional academic fields that require these skills at increasing rates over the last 20 years. Almost all engineering and architecture schools report that the proportions of women have increased substantially since the Women's Movement began in the 60s. Biological explanations cannot account for this phenomenon.

On the other hand, psychosocial variables cannot account for all of the data presented in this chapter. The strongest case for the importance of biological variables comes from the sex by handedness interactions described earlier in this chapter (Harshman, Hampson, & Berenbaum, 1983). In a large-scale study with three separate samples, cognitive abilities for women and men differed as a function of whether they were right or left handed. These results are interpretable only if handedness is accepted as an index of hemisphere organization. There is no plausible reason to believe that sex roles or any other psychosocial variable differ for right and left handed individuals of either sex. It is more plausible to interpret these results as, at least, partly due to sex differences in cerebral lateralization. A strong theory of brain organization that can relate lateralization differences to sex and cognitive abilities is still needed.

The Notion of Optimal Cerebral Organization, Optimal Hormone Balance, and Optimal Genetic Configuration

All of the biological theories began with the notion that there is a single optimal organization of hemisphere specialization, or an optimal hormone balance, or even an optimal genetic pattern that is associated with cognitive excellence. None of these theories consider the multidimensional nature of verbal and spatial tasks. Why should a single biological configuration be ideal for spatial visualization and spatial orientation tasks or for spelling, verbal reasoning, and language comprehension? It may even be that an optimal organization for males is not optimal for females. Perhaps bilateral organization is best when the hormones concentrations are female and lateralized cerebral organization is best when the hormone concentrations are male. The finding that males tend to be more lateralized and better at spatial tasks does not mean that they are better at spatial tasks *because* they are more lateralized. They could be better at spatial tasks for environmental reasons and more lateralized for biological reasons. It does not necessarily follow that lateralization is the optimal brain organization for spatial ability because it is found more frequently in the sex that tends to have better spatial ability. More studies are needed that examine the extent of lateralization with performance on spatial and verbal ability tests.

Much of the research on identifying the "best" brain, or hormone, or genetic pattern has been conducted with people with abnormalities in these biological systems. For example, the hypothesis that a minimal level of androgens must be present at puberty in order for spatial ability to develop was supported solely on research with males with abnormally low levels of these hormones (Hier & Crowley, 1982). How can we justify extrapolating these results to normal males and especially to normal females? In short, the notion that there exists a single best biology for the development of cognitive abilities needs to be questioned.

Intervening Variables

It is also possible that biology affects the development of cognitive skills in indirect ways that are generally not considered by proponents of the biological theories. Evidence was provided earlier in this chapter for the position that aggressive behavior is, at least in part, under hormonal control. Research with lower animals has clearly shown a link between prenatal hormones and later aggressive behavior and energy levels. While the research reviewed with humans is less clear, there is still good reason to believe that prenatal and possibly postnatal hormones play a role in human aggression and activity levels. Suppose that males tend to be more active because of higher levels of prenatal hormones. Individuals who are more active would be expected to develop better spatial skills because they move around the environment more often, roam farther at an earlier age, and interact with more objects. Thus, there could be biological reasons for sex differences in cognitive abilities, but they could be different ones from those being investigated.

A second intervening variable that could mediate between biology and environment is body type. Consider the notion that early maturing adolescents have poorer spatial skills than late maturing adolescents (Waber, 1977). As Waber pointed out, early maturing adolescents may not only have different patterns of cerebral lateralization, they also have different social environments. Shapely seventh grade girls and tall muscular seventh grade boys are responded to differently than their less developed peers. This could cause them to consider their math and science classes less seriously and create or increase differences in these areas that correlate with maturation rate. Support for these hypotheses is examined in the following chapter.

Body type is also a likely intervening variable for individuals with genetic or hormonal abnormalities. Much of the research in this area has used Turner's women to support or refute biological arguments. As stated earlier, these women have unfeminine body types (small breasts, thick necks). Their body type could cause them, consciously or unconsciously, to exaggerate feminine traits including eschewing stereotypically masculine cognitive skills. Hier and Crowley's (1982) research on minimal androgen levels utilized males with underdeveloped testes. While the finding that they are poorer on "masculine" tasks goes against the idea that they attempted to compensate for their feminine body type, it does seem likely that they sought certain experiences that would help them adjust to their body type. It is difficult to know how these special experiences affected their cognitive growth.

Differences and Deficiencies

Many people are concerned that if we concede that there are sex differences in the "underlying hardware" of human thought, then those who are anxious to keep women out of nontraditional occupations will use this finding to justify discrimination. Weisstein (1982) offered a stern caveat when she said, "Biology has always been used as a curse against women" (p. 41). It is important to keep in mind that sex differences are not synonymous with sexism. The empirical research that has been reviewed in this chapter is not antifemale. It is neither misogynist nor antifeminist to report that, on the average, males have superior spatial ability and math ability and females have superior verbal ability and that some of these differences could be biologically based.

It is also important to keep in mind that while the major focus of this book and research in this area is on sex differences, similarities are more often the rule. In McGlone's (1980) review of the cerebral asymmetry literature, she concluded, "Thus, one must not overlook perhaps the most basic conclusion, which is that basic patterns of male and female brain asymmetry seem to be more similar than they are different" (p. 226). Perhaps the most striking finding from all of the neuropsychological research is the overwhelming number of similarities between the sexes.

We know that there are sex differences in cognitive abilities, sex hormone concentrations, and probably patterns of cerebral organization. There are also undisputable sex differences in the reproductive organs and genitals. No one would argue that either sex has the better reproductive organs or genitals. They are clearly different, but neither sex would be considered deficient in these biological organs. However, when cognitive differences are considered there is sometimes an implicit notion of superiority. Is it better to be high in verbal skills or spatial skills? This is a moot question. The answer depends on the type of task that needs to be performed, the quantification of how much better, and individual predilection. To argue that female hormones are better than male hormones or that male brains are better than female brains is as silly as arguing which sex has the better genitals. It seems almost embarrassing and obvious to state that neither sex has the better biology for intellectual ability and that differences should not be confused with deficits.

Readers have probably noticed that a majority of the biological hypotheses have been concerned with sex differences in spatial ability. Only a few have addressed the differences in verbal ability, a fact that some reviewers have seen as basically sexist (Sherman, 1979). The greater concern with spatial ability is probably due to two factors. First, sex differences are greatest for spatial tasks, and second, they appear more often in the biological investigations. (Males with low levels of androgens at puberty showed low levels of spatial ability with no impairment of verbal ability, for example.) Future research needs to consider verbal ability sex differences if we are ever to untangle the web of relationships between biological systems and cognitive abilities.

Mathematical ability has also been underinvestigated in the biological literature. How do maturation rate and sex hormone levels relate to mathematical ability? Are the relationships similar to those found with spatial ability as would be predicted if spatial skill underlies success in mathematics? Or, is mathematics different? Does it require high verbal ability to decipher word problems and high spatial ability for analytic geometry and trigonometry? When it comes to biological explanations for cognitive processes, we still have more questions than answers. It remains the task of future scientists—both females and males—to ask questions and formulate answers about the mutual influences of biology and cognition.

CHAPTER SUMMARY

Three categories of biological influences on cognitive abilities were considered: (1) Genetic theories that posit an X-linked recessive gene for good spatial ability have been disproved. (2) Theories about sex-related brain differences are probably correct in asserting that there is sexual dimorphism in hemispheric specialization. In general, male brains may be more strongly lateralized or specialized for certain cognitive functions than female brains. These differences seem to be related to sex differences in physical maturation rate, but more research is needed relating degree of lateralization to cognitive abilities before the relationship among sex, brain organization, and cognitive abilities is understood. (3) Concentrations of sex hormones at puberty have also been implicated as affecting the development of cognitive abilities. The process by which they exert their influence is not known. They could direct brain organization or influence neural processes in some other way. Theories that posit either a minimal quantity of androgens or some optimal estrogen–androgen balance is needed for the development of spatial ability have received some support. Hypotheses concerned with age at puberty or other puberty/hormonal events cannot explain the cognitive sex differences that appear in early childhood; however it is possible that the earlier maturation rates of girls throughout childhood can explain some of the cognitive sex differences that are found among older children.

Our current knowledge of biological–cognitive influences remains sketchy and largely incomplete. Even those theories which have received empirical support remain open to criticism on methodological and logical grounds. Readers and researchers are urged to avoid interpreting sex differences as a cognitive deficiency for either sex.

5

Psychosocial Hypotheses

CONTENTS

The Importance of Psychosocial Variables
  Implications of Psychosocial Explanations
  Nonconscious Ideology
Sex Roles and Sex Role Stereotypes
  The Difference Between Sex Roles and Sex Role Stereotypes
  Sex Role Identification as a Mediator in Intellectual Development
  Theoretical Models
Sex-Linked Socialization Practices
  Childhood Experiences
  Adolescence
  Adulthood and Old Age
Ability Differences
  Spatial Ability
  Mathematical Ability
  Verbal Abilities
Extrapolating From Empirical Trends
Chapter Summary

THE IMPORTANCE OF PSYCHOSOCIAL VARIABLES

If you have been reading the chapters in order and just finished the preceding chapter that examined biological hypotheses as possible explanations of the sex differences in cognitive abilities, you probably spent much of the time considering alternative hypotheses. Whenever I teach this material to college classes, I always find that there are students who simply cannot wait to point out the ways in which differing life experiences for males and females could be used to explain the data. Hypotheses that favor the nurture side of the nature-nurture controversy are considered in this chapter. These two approaches are synthesized and conclusions about the relative merits of each are presented in the concluding chapter.

There is little doubt that environmental and social factors impact on the cognitive development of every member in our society. The crucial question for the purpose of understanding cognitive sex differences is, "How do socialization practices and other life experiences that differ for males and females influence the ability to perform intellectual tasks?" Of course, this question is based on the assumption that life experiences differ in systematic ways depending on biological sex. I have found that some people are willing to accept this assumption at face value, taking it as a statement of the obvious, and eager to consider the ramifications of these differences. Others, however, believe that sex differentiated socialization practices are a "thing of the past." These people believe the magazine and billboard ads that proclaim, "You've come a long way baby!" The underlying message is that contemporary women do the same sorts of things that men do, and sex-related differences in life experiences are either inconsequential or nonexistent. It is ironic to note the subtle influence of language as typified in this slogan that supposedly announces sexual equality. If women had, in fact, "come a long way," then they would not be referred to as infants or children, just as black men are no longer called "boy." (These ads, which you probably recognize, are designed to sell cigarettes. The incidence of lung cancer among women is now almost as high as that of men. The ad is correct with respect to lung cancer. Women have come a long way, but in this case, in the wrong direction.)

If anyone doubts that women and men still tend to perform different tasks in contemporary American society, a casual visit to a PTA meeting, or the restaurant in a large department store midweek, or a trade union hall, or a corporate engineering department will attest to the fact that while changes in the societal roles of women and men are occurring, there are still considerable differences in men's and women's experiences. High school cheer leaders are still virtually all female while shop classes remain virtually all male. Few girls play in the now "coed" little league games, and few boys elect to take home economics classes. Despite all of the efforts of those associated with the "women's movement," de facto sex-related life differences are alive and well.

Implications of Psychosocial Explanations

If we can use psychological and social explanations to understand cognitive sex differences, then the possibility of reducing or eliminating these differences is quite real. On the other hand, if we find that we are unable to explain these differences with psychosocial explanations, then there is little hope of being able to alter them by changing learning environments, attitudes, or educational and employment opportunities. Thus, the primary importance of psychosocial hypotheses is not in their heuristic value or for the development of some abstract theoretical model, but in the promise they hold for changing the status quo. Of course, if you are a champion of the status quo, then they are equally important, but for you they would represent a threat. In either case, the implications are clear. Psychosocial hypotheses devised to explain the origin of cognitive sex differences have important ramifications for the ways we want society to change or remain the same as we approach the twenty-first century.

Nonconscious Ideology

Perhaps one of the reasons for the tendency to underestimate sex differentiated experiences, messages, and expectations is that these differences are so prevalent and so ingrained in American life that we are often blind to them. In fact, for most of us, it is hard to imagine a society in which they didn't exist. Bem and Bem (1976) have used the term ''nonconscious ideology'' to describe this situation. We are simply unaware of the pervasiveness of sex differentiated practices. They have said that we are all like fish who are unaware that the water is wet. The clothes we wear, the way we furnish our rooms, the toys we were given as children, the hobbies we pursue, the salaries we receive at our jobs, the magazines we read, the household chores we perform, the language we use, and countless other examples all show differences between the sexes.

Consider, for example, the simple matter of the grammatically correct use of the pronoun ''he'' to mean he or she (or she or he). Somewhere in junior or senior high school, we were all taught that the grammatically correct singular pronoun when sex is unknown is ''he.'' Thus, it is correct to say, ''Everyone should do *his* homework.'' There have been many objections to the use of ''he'' to mean ''he or she.'' The use of ''he'' to refer to either sex has become known as the ''generic he'' to signify that its use is much like the use of generic labels for supermarket canned goods. One argument against changing from the generic he to either ''s/he'' or novel terms (e.g., te or E) is that the issue is trivial and of no real significance. Detractors have humorously labeled this debate as a case of ''pronoun envy,'' a take off on Freud's theory of penis envy as a major determinant of sex differences. Recent research has shown, however, that the issue is far from trivial. MacKay (1983) has studied the use of the generic ''he'' to determine its psychological significance. He has estimated that the generic ''he'' is used over 1,000,000 times throughout an individual's lifetime. In addition, he found that people tend to think of a male whenever the pronoun ''he'' is used. It is clearly not a sex neutral or generic term from a psychological perspective.

Do phrases like, ''No woman is an island'' or ''Now is the time for all good women to come to the aid of their party'' seem strange to you? One study on the use of the generic he found that high school women were less likely to respond to a job advertisement that used the pronoun ''he'' in its description than they were to respond to a similar ad that used the pronoun ''she'' (Bem & Bem, 1973). I remember once reading about the hardships encountered by early American pioneers and their wives. The nonconscious implication is that the women were not pioneers in the same sense that the men were.

There are countless other examples of the way American society has nonconsciously adopted sex differentiated practices. We expect to see little girls in the advertisements for Barbie dolls and little boys depicted on boxes that contain train sets and, therefore, never stop to consider the powerful messages they convey about sex appropriate interests and behavior. I remember receiving a

DENNIS THE MENACE

"When a lady never marries, she's an Old Maid."   "Then when a man never marries, is he an old butler?"

Reproduced by permission of Hank Ketcham and by News America Syndicate.

prize for serving as president of my high school's honor society. I was delighted with the bracelet I was given. I knew that all of the previous honor society presidents were male, and all of them had received a six-volume set of books by Winston Churchill. Yet, it had never occurred to me that the choice of this particular gift was an excellent example of sex differences in socialization practices. It wasn't until many years later that I was struck with the irony of the gift. Like most other people, I was simply unaware of the numerous subtle and not so subtle practices in our sex differentiated society.

SEX ROLES AND SEX ROLE STEREOTYPES

A stereotype is "a relatively rigid and oversimplified conception of a group of people in which all individuals in the group are labeled with the so-called group characteristics" (Wrightsman, 1977, p.672). As a society, we have stereotypes about racial groups (e.g., "Blacks are musical."), nations (e.g., "The Scots are thrifty."), sports groups (e.g., "Football players are dumb."), about people who wear eyeglasses, New Yorkers, redheads, obese people, cellists, Republicans, etc. Any of these stereotypes can influence interactions, feelings, and expectations. Sex role stereotypes are those stereotypes that relate to differences between the sexes. For the purposes of this discussion, the term "sex role stereotypes" will be used to encompass widely held assumptions about what females and males *are like,* as well as what they *ought to be like.* Readers should be aware that sometimes authors make a distinction between these two components of the term sex role stereotypes. Two questions concerning sex role stereotypes that have been raised are: Is there any evidence that they exist, and if so, can these stereotypes be used to understand sex differences in cognitive ability?

What are the stereotypes about women and men that exist in America today? This question has been researched extensively by psychologists, sociologists, and others over the last two decades. In the numerous studies that have been conducted (Bem, 1981; Broverman et al., 1972; Spence, Helmreich, & Stapp, 1974), two distinct clusters of traits have emerged. In general, (1) male stereotypic traits suggest competence and task orientation, a cluster of traits sometimes known as "instrumental," while (2) female stereotypic traits suggest warmth and expressiveness.

More recent studies of sex role stereotypes have gone beyond the notion that certain traits or characteristics are associated exclusively with being male or female. Deaux (1984), for example, examined the relative frequency with which traits are associated with either sex. As shown in Table 5.1, some characteristics are believed to be found more often in one sex or the other. Consider, for example, the role of "financial provider." According to Deaux's results, we expect about 83% of all males to be financial providers, while we expect only about 47% of females to assume this role. These data indicate that sex role stereotypes are alive and well in contemporary American society; however,

TABLE 5.1
Stereotypes of Males and Females
Probability Judgments

Characteristic	Judgment[a]	
	Men	Women
Trait		
Independent	.78	.58
Competitive	.82	.64
Warm	.66	.77
Emotional	.56	.84
Role behaviors		
Financial provider	.83	.47
Takes initiative with opposite sex	.82	.54
Takes care of children	.50	.85
Cooks meals	.42	.83
Physical characteristics		
Muscular	.64	.36
Deep voice	.73	.30
Graceful	.45	.68
Small-boned	.39	.62

[a]Probability that the average person of either sex would possess a characteristic. Copyright (1985) by The American Psychological Association. Reprinted by permission of the author.

instead of being attributed in an all-or-none fashion, most people acknowledge that there may be overlap between the sexes with regard to these characteristics.

The Difference Between Sex Roles and Sex Role Stereotypes

In a strict definitional sense, the term "sex role stereotype" refers both to those beliefs about what males and females are like and to those beliefs about what they ought to be like, while the term "sex roles" reflects actual differences between the sexes. Lueptow (1984) has operationalized the term "sex roles" as "any statistical difference between the sexes" (p. x). While this may be a starting point for a definition, Lueptow's reliance on statistical differences would include sex differences in height, for example, as a sex role. A more useful definition would emphasize the fact that sex roles are a societal construction based on sex differences in psychosocial variables such as traits and dispositions. As an example of the difference between these two terms consider beliefs about sex differences in sociability. A commonly held sex role stereotype is that females are more "social" than males; however, Maccoby and Jacklin's review of the literature (1974) has shown that this is not true—that there is no statistically significant difference in sociability between the sexes. This is an example in which the sex role stereotype does not agree with the finding that no sex differences exist in this area.

Recently, the term "sex roles" has come under attack (Lopata & Thorne, 1978). Those opposed to the term have argued that since we don't use terms like "race roles" or "class roles," why should researchers be so concerned with reifying (making a theoretical concept real or concrete by giving it a label) the concept of sex roles? It has also been argued that other roles in life, like that of student, or factory worker, or young adult, undergo changes as our life situations change, whereas, sex roles don't change because they are tied to biological sex. Numerous other academic arguments have been offered to suggest that the term "sex roles" is misleading and that sex roles are qualitatively different from other sorts of roles. Despite all of the rhetoric generated by this term, it is likely to remain in the psychological and sociological literature. One of the leading journals in the area of six differences is entitled "Sex Roles" and the term seems to have an intuitive meaning for people outside of academia. I believe that it is a useful term, even if it is used somewhat differently by different authors.

It is a widely held belief that sex role stereotypes, those beliefs about behaviors and dispositions that characterize males and females in our society, exert strong influences on male and female behavior. These stereotypes seem to be narrower or to allow fewer options for males, leaving boys and men fewer choices and dispositional alternatives. Generally, it is far more deviant for a male to engage in traditionally female activities (e.g., homemaker, nurse, or secretary) than it is for females to enter the traditional man's world (medicine, physics, trucking, plumbing). While young girls learn that they will be prized for their beauty, young men learn that they will be valued for their money and prestige. Accordingly, it should not be surprising to find that men outnumber women in the "hard" sciences that are both high paying and prestigious. Mathematics, for example, is a strongly masculine typed academic subject. One possible explanation for the disparity in sex ratios among mathematically gifted youth is the unwillingness of girls to be identified with mathematics and/or their unwillingness to devote their time to the rigorous demands of mathematics— time that could be spent on "appropriate" female activities like curling their hair and painting their nails. Sherman (1983) summarized the effect of traditional sex role stereotypes on female intellectual development when she said: "Data indicate that intellectual excellence is still enmeshed in a pattern of sex-role expectations contrary to the feminine sex-role" (p. 342).

The impact of sex role stereotypes comes from pervasive life long influences to conform to a pattern of behavior that is prescribed by sex. Sex differences in cognitive abilities mirror sex stereotypes about abilities, making it very difficult to determine the extent to which abilities differences and stereotype differences influence each other. The sex role literature is extensive. It contains numerous confirmations of the hypothesis that these stereotypes exert powerful influences on the way we think and behave.

Consider, for example, a recent study that investigated the way sex role stereotypes influence memory (Halpern, 1985). High school students were asked to read a fairly bland story about 2 days in the life of a protagonist. For half the high school students, the main character was named Linda: for the other half, the main character was named David. It was hypothesized that errors in memory for stated events and inferences about the main character's goals and motives would be biased toward conformity with sex role stereotypes. In general, the results confirmed the hypothesis that sex role stereotypes influenced the way the students remembered information that was presented in the story. When these results were described to the students who participated in this study, they were surprised. Most of the students were unaware of the extent to which they maintained sex role stereotypes and of the possiblity that these stereotypes were influencing how they think and remember. (For a more detailed discussion of the effect of stereotypes on memory and thought processes, see Halpern, 1984a).

Sex Role Identification as a Mediator in Intellectual Development

> *Many women in our present culture value mathematical ignorance as if it were a social grace.*
>
> —Osen (quoted in Burton, 1978, p.35)

Although there are numerous conceptions of the way sex role stereotypes operate to influence behavior, a modal or typical model assumes that individuals identify with and conform to a particular sex role stereotype. Consider, for example, the fact that mathematical ability is often perceived to be part of the male sex role stereotype. As boys learn their sex roles, they identify with the notion that they should excel at mathematics. Girls, on the other hand, learn that mathematical ability is unfeminine, and thus, avoid advanced mathematics courses.

Masculine and feminine stereotypes used to be viewed as separate and orthogonal or independent concepts. During the early 1970s, however, several psychologists (Bem, 1974; Constantinople, 1973; Spence, Helmreich, & Stapp, 1974) developed a multidimensional conception of the traits that constitute sex role stereotypes and the term "androgynous" became a buzz word in the literature. Individuals of either sex who reported both typical female and male traits were labeled androgynous. Some researchers also adopted the term "undifferentiated" to refer to individuals who reported very few feminine or masculine traits. Unlike their androgynous peers who exhibited both masculine and feminine traits, undifferentiated individuals seemed to exhibit very few of the traits associated with either sex role.

This type of research introduced a third construct into the literature—self-concept. For the purposes of this book, *sex role stereotype* refers to generalized beliefs about what women and men are like and what they ought to be like, *sex roles* refer to actual statistical differences between the sexes in psychosocial variables, and *self-concept* refers to individuals' beliefs about themselves. Thus, it is possible for someone to believe that men are and should be more aggressive than women, a sex role stereotype; since empirical evidence suggests that differences actually exist with respect to aggression, this same belief is a sex role difference; yet, any given woman may believe that she is more aggressive than most men, or any given man may believe that he is less aggressive than most women, reflecting their self-concept. Thus, while most of us maintain sex role stereotypes, we may or may not believe that we conform to them.

A plethora of research followed from the classification of self-reports of sex typed behaviors and dispositions into masculine, feminine, androgynous, and undifferentiated typological categories. It seems that these categories have been related to almost every conceivable variable. Very often the assumption underlying the research was that "androgyny is good." Androgyny has been examined as a mediating variable that affects success, career choice, psychosomatic problems, locus of control, self-esteem, and sexual behavior (Cook, 1985).

Given the immense popularity of sex role stereotypes and self-concept, it should not be surprising that they were also investigated as mediators of intellectual development. Using this framework, Mills (1981) tested the hypothesis that mathematics and verbal skill achievement would be related to sex role identification, or the extent to which someone identifies with the female or male sex role stereotype. She found a positive relationship between mathematical achievement and masculine traits for girls and between verbal skills achievement and feminine traits for boys. Based on this study, she concluded that cross-sexed characteristics seemed associated with success in traditionally masculine (i.e., mathematics) and traditionally feminine (i.e., verbal) content areas. Other studies, however, have shown that the actual relationship between achievement and personality characteristics is quite complex. The extent to which an individual perceives a cognitive ability as sex typed may also be predictive of performance in that area (Nash, 1979). It seems likely that a web of other contributing variables will have to be unraveled before any conclusive statements about the relationship between sex role identification and academic area of achievement can be made.

Theoretical Models

How are appropriate sex role behaviors acquired? Several theories have been proposed to answer this question. Four major theories designed to explain the acquisition of appropriate sex role behaviors—Freudian Theory, Learning Theory, Social Modeling, and Cognitive Theories—are briefly described. Each theory begins with a different notion about the nature of the forces that cause humans to conform to sex role stereotypes.

Freudian Theory

Sigmund Freud, the famous psychologist, proposed an influential theory around the turn of the century that encompassed developmental psychology, psychopathology, and personality. The foundation of Freudian theory was built upon the biological differences between the sexes, thereby representing a strong form of the belief that "biology is destiny." According to Freud, children come to identify with their same-sex parent, and through identification they imitate their appropriate sex role behaviors of their mothers or fathers. He maintained that all children at approximately 4- to 5-years-of-age enter a developmental period known as the "phallic state" so named because of their preoccupation with their genitals. (Freud used the term "phallic stage" to refer to the development of both girls and boys even though the term "phallic" is derived from a Greek word meaning "penis.") Children in the phallic stage go through a fairly involved sequence of parental alliances and jealousies that follows different paths depending on whether the child is a girl or a boy. It is during this developmental period that children resolve their early feelings of love and hate for their parents and ultimately identify with the same-sex parent.

Let's consider first how this process proceeds for boys because it is somewhat less complicated than the process Freud attributed to girls. The impetus to identify with their same sex parents for boys is the Oedipus complex, named for a 5th century B.C. play by Sophocles called *Oedipus Rex*. In this play, Oedipus unknowingly commits the unspeakable tragedy of killing his father and later marrying his mother and having children with her. Freud believed that this represented a universal theme of all boys' sexually longing for their mother. During the phallic stage, the young boy's newly discovered erotic feelings are vaguely directed toward his mother (or mother substitute), because she has been the source of pleasure in the past. At the same time, he also begins to feel jealous of his father, a "rival" for his mother's love. This is also the time in his development when he learns that girls do not have a penis, leading him to conclude that it must have been cut off for some terrible reason. He then reasons that the same thing could happen to him because of his sexual desire for his mother and his jealousy of his father. All boys at this age must resolve the problem of "castration anxiety" (an unconscious fear of being castrated). Boys resolve this dilemma the only way possible; they repress their erotic feelings for the mother and identify with the father.

How do girls come to identify with their mothers according to Freudian theory? There is a roughly analogous version of the Oedipus complex known as the Electra complex. Electra was the heroine in a Greek tragedy who convinced her brother to kill their mother, also a supposedly universal theme. During the preschool years, girls discover that they do not have a penis and immediately develop "penis envy," an intense desire to have male genitals. For reasons never clearly explained, the girl concludes that she must have once had a penis and was castrated. She holds the mother responsible for this sad state of affairs when she realizes that the mother also lacks the prized organ. Girls then turn to their fathers, and, like their brothers, have to resolve feelings of hatred and jealousy. Because of fear of reprisal from jealous mothers, girls shift their identification back to their mothers and imitate female sex role behaviors.

Thus, for Freud, the key to sex role identification is the presence or absence of a penis during critical years of child development (approximately 4- to 6-years-old) and the appropriate resolution of the Oedipus or Electra complex. Freudian theory is actually much more complex than this, but these are the basic assumptions underlying sex role identification. There are numerous problems with this aspect of Freudian theory. Most notably, research has shown that a large proportion of children in this age range don't have a conscious understanding about the anatomical differences between women and men (Katcher, 1955). Freudian theory has also been criticized for its antifemale (penis-centered) orientation, especially for its assumption that children of both sexes immediately perceive the superiority of male genitals over female genitals. In addition, it implies that children who are raised in homes without a same-sexed parent will fail to develop sex role appropriate behaviors. Research with children in single parent families has shown this prediction to be false (Lynn, 1974).

Learning Theory

In some sense, all of the theories being described here can be described as "learning theories" because they are all concerned with understanding the way sex role stereotypes are learned. Learning Theory, however, has a very specific meaning in psychology. It refers to the theory that most learning is contingent upon the rewards and punishments that follow behavior. Although terms like "reward" and "punishment" have an intuitive meaning, they have a precise meaning in the jargon of Learning Theory. A reward is anything that will increase the probability of a particular behavior, and a punishment is anything that will decrease the probability of a particular behavior. Learning theorists explain the acquisition of sex roles by positing that children are rewarded when they evince appropriate sex role behaviors and attitudes and punished for behaviors and attitudes that do not conform to the sex appropriate roles. We're all familiar with sex role statements like, "Boy don't cry" or "lady-like behavior." It's easy to imagine how rewards and punishments could function to reinforce sex role appropriate behavior.

Rewards and punishments can assume many different forms. A smile, pat on the back, an award, or some candy could all functionally serve to increase desired behavior. Similarly, a frown, scolding, physical punishment, or public humiliation could all serve to discourage or decrease the likelihood of some behavior. As children grow, they receive numerous rewards and punishments from parents and other socializing agents who want to influence their behaviors. Children and adults also receive rewards and punishments for certain intellectual activities. Mathematics, for example, is a highly sex typed academic subject (Sherman, 1983). One way that children come to learn this is through differential rewards and punishments. Numerous studies have shown that boys are more likely than girls to receive encouragement to work through difficult mathematics problems, and girls receive less praise than boys for correct answers in mathematics (Stage & Karplus, 1981). It is also likely that a sex differentiated pattern of rewards and punishments could be used to explain sex differences in verbal and spatial ability with girls encouraged to read more often than boys and boys encouraged to engage in spatial activities (blocks, erector sets, etc.) more often than girls. Thus, according to Learning Theory, through sex differentiated rewards and punishments children learn that mathematical and spatial activities are more appropriate for boys and that reading and other verbal activities are more appropriate for girls.

Social Modeling

Several prominent theorists have proposed that sex typed behaviors are learned in several ways (Bandura & Walters, 1963; Mischel, 1966). They believe that while direct rewards and punishments can produce sex role learning, imitation learning or modeling may be the more important mechanism for producing sex role appropriate behaviors. Because of the importance they attach to imitation or modeling in social situations, this theory is sometimes called Social Learning or Social Modeling. In addition to receiving rewards and punishments for behaviors that are either consistent or inconsistent with sex roles, children are also told in numerous ways that they are either a girl or a boy. Children then begin to notice similarities among other girls and among other boys. A list of possible examples would be quite long: Girls may wear bows and barrettes in their hair, but boys may not. Girls may wear almost any color clothing, while boys may not wear pink clothes. Very few boys will own doll carriages, a common girl's toy. Combat dolls like G.I. Joe are appropriate for boys, but not for girls. There are also obvious differences among adult models. Women may wear high-heeled shoes, make-up, nail polish, and dresses, while any man who wears these items is considered deviant.

According to Social Modeling Theory, children learn about sex role behaviors by observing between sex differences. They then imitate the behaviors and attitudes of same sex models. Social modeling theory differs from learning theory in that it does not assume that rewards and punishments must be received in order to shape behavior. Sex role learning can occur from observing others and imitating them. Appropriate imitation is likely to be rewarded, as in the case of a young girl who dresses up in her mother's shoes and old dresses. Inappropriate imitation is likely to be punished, as in the case of a young boy who dresses up in his mother's shoes and old dresses. Thus, through a combination of observational learning, modeling, and rewards and punishments, boys and girls learn society's sex roles.

Social Modeling is not restricted to the acquisition of sex roles in childhood. As adults, we also observe how each sex should act, imitate appropriate models, and receive rewards and punishments for these actions. Social influences to conform to behaviors deemed appropriate by society are extremely strong, even for adults. Few women feel comfortable as the only female in an all male mathematics course, and few men are comfortable in an all female nursing class. In this theoretical framework, it would be extremely important for women and men considering careers in these traditionally "sex-inappropriate" fields to have female mathematicians to serve as models for women and male nurses to serve as models for men.

Cognitive Theories

Cognitive Theories are a general class of theories that are based on the primary importance of children's and adults' knowledge of sex differentiated behaviors. Kohlberg (1966) has proposed a cognitive development theory to explain the acquisition of sex typed behavior by children. A more recent cognitive theory that explains sex role maintenance among adults is Gender Schema Theory, which was proposed by S. Bem (1981). Because each theory is designed for a different purpose, they are considered separately.

Cognitive Development Theory.   Kohlberg's Cognitive Development Theory begins with the notion that children's conceptions about the nature of the world change as they go through various developmental stages. Just as children's understanding of number concepts changes at different ages, so does their understanding of sex roles and sex appropriate behaviors. Around 3-years-of-age, children begin to label themselves as either a girl or a boy and somewhere during the next 2 years they learn to label other people's sex. During this developmental period, they also develop "gender constancy," which is the idea that gender or sex is an immutable part of one's identity. Once the child has developed a notion of his or her own sex, the child models the behaviors of same sex models.

In distinguishing the basic differences between Social Modeling or Social Learning Theory and Cognitive Development Theory, Kohlberg (1966) has said: "The social-learning syllogism is: 'I want rewards, I am rewarded for doing boy things, therefore I want to be a boy.' In contrast, a cognitive theory assumes this sequence: ' I am a boy, therefore I want to do boy things, therefore the opportunity to do boy things (and to gain approval for doing them) is rewarding" (p. 89). The basic difference between these two theories is that Social Modeling assumes that children conform to sex role stereotypes because they imitate sex role consistent behaviors which are reinforced; whereas Cognitive Development Theory assumes that children first develop an awareness of sex categories, then they form a sexual identity as part of their self-concept (I am a girl or I am a boy). After a sexual identity is formed, they perform sex role consistent behaviors which get rewarded.

Gender Schema Theory.   S. Bem (1981) proposed that our knowledge about sex differences form a "schema" or an organizing framework in which we process, interpret, and organize information. The term "schema" comes from cognitive psychology, the branch of psychology concerned with how we think and remember. The notion of a schema is very close to what we mean when we talk about stereotypes. It refers to the way we store information in memory and utilize that information. Hyde (1985) describes it this way: "A schema is a general knowledge framework that a person has about a particular topic. A schema organizes and guides perception" (p. 76).

When we interact with people, we use our schemas first to understand and then to remember what transpired. For example, Koblinsky, Cruse, and Sugawara (1978) showed that 10-year-old children remembered the masculine behaviors of boy characters and feminine behaviors of girl characters better than sex reversed behaviors. A similar effect was found by Liben and Signorella (1980) using a picture recognition task with first and second grade children.

The organization and structuring of information is a normal cognitive process with important consequences for how we think and remember (Halpern, 1985; Martin & Halverson, 1981). The propensity to interpret and remember information that is consistent with our schemas serves to perpetuate these schemas. Thus, once these cognitive categories are established, they will resist change because information that is inconsistent will tend to be either forgotten or changed. Thus our stereotypes or gender schemas will bias the way we interpret behavior.

Theory Comparisons

Each of the theories devised to explain the acquisition and maintenance of sex role stereotypes assumes a different perspective on the issue. Freudian Theory views the adoption of sex typed behaviors by young children as a necessary consequence of biological differences. Girls and boys will identify with the same-sex parent because of the need to resolve the Oedipus and Electra complexes. Learning Theory and Social Modeling Theory view sex differentiated rewards and punishments and modeling as primarily responsible for the adoption of sex role stereotypes by children. By contrast, cognitive theories posit that the way we develop and store information about sex role appropriate and inappropriate behaviors guides the way we interpret and remember information. It is difficult to determine which theory is *best* because there are areas of overlap among them. Nor do they necessarily represent mutually exclusive categories. It is likely that rewards and punishments, imitation of same sex models, and gender schemas all operate in the establishment and maintenance of sex role stereotypes.

TABLE 5.2
A Brief Summarization of Four Theories of Sex-Typed Behavior

Freudian Theory

> Development of penis envy in girls ➞ eventual identification with the mother ➞ conformity to female behavior
> Development of castration anxiety in boys➞ identification with the father ➞ conformity to male behavior

Learning Theory

> Girls and boys receive rewards for sex appropriate behavior and punishments for sex inappropriate behavior ➞ exhibit sex appropriate behavior

Social Modeling

> Boys and girls observe male and female behavior ➞ imitation of same sex models ➞ receive rewards for sex appropriate behavior and punishment for sex inappropriate behavior ➞ exhibit sex appropriate behavior

Cognitive Theories

> Cognitive Development
>
> > Girls and boys develop a sexual identity ➞ imitation of same sex models ➞ receive rewards for sex appropriate behavior and punishment for sex inappropriate behavior ➞ exhibit sex appropriate behavior

> Gender Schema Theory
>
> > Boys and girls development cognitive categories for sex differentiated behaviors and dispositions ➞ interpret and remember information according to these categories ➞ exhibit behavior consistent with cognitive categories

As you might probably guess, Freudian Theory has been most heavily criticized because of its "penis-centered" orientation. An alternative explanation is that the male role is preferred not because males have a penis, but because males have power and greater freedom in our society.

A brief summary of the salient points in the four theories of sex role stereotypes is presented in Table 5.2.

SEX-LINKED SOCIALIZATION PRACTICES

A common theme among the theories of sex role acquisition is that girls and boys receive rewards and punishments for sex role appropriate and inappropriate behaviors. Let's take a closer look at the nature of these rewards and punishments and other ways that sex role expectancies are communicated and learned. It is clear that the socialization practices we receive vary with age; therefore, a developmental perspective is assumed in examining this issue. For the purposes of this topic, the life span is broken up into three broad stages—childhood, adolescence, and adulthood and old age. The most salient aspects of sex role socialization practices in each of these broad stages are considered.

Childhood Experiences

Childhood is the time in life when socializing forces exert their greatest impact. Although almost any person or institution with which children come into contact can be considered socializing agents, we'll briefly examine three major forces in a child's life—parents, television and other media, and teachers and schools.

Without a doubt, parents play a major role in shaping their children's lives. As the primary socializing agents of the young, especially the very young, there are countless ways that parents could inculcate sex-typed behavior. Numerous studies have shown that parents respond differently to boy and girl babies, probably from birth (Rubin, Provenzano, & Luria, 1974). Stewart (1976), for example, found that within the first 6 weeks of life, male infants are handled more than female infants, and female infants receive more vocalizations. It is very possible that these early differences in home experiences provide the basis for later cognitive differences.

Block (1973, 1978) has found considerable differences in parenting practices as a function of child's sex. She has found that, in general, the parents of boys are more concerned with task oriented achievement for their child than the parents of girls. She also found that boys' parents reported that they were more concerned with punishment, negative sanctions, and sex typing than the parents of girls. What is the result of sex differentiated child rearing? Children as young

as 2-years-old express sex stereotypic ideas and make sex appropriate dispositional attributes (Kuhn, Nash, & Brucken, 1978). By age three, children can
ascribe sex appropriate attributes to other children and adults (Gettys & Cann,
1981; Haugh, Hoffman, & Cowan, 1980). It seems that by the time children are
able to express themselves verbally, they are able to report an awareness of sex
role stereotypes.

One major way in which parents influence the social and cognitive growth of
their children is in the toys they select for them. Etaugh (1983) noted big
differences in the kinds of toys purchased for girls and boys. Between the ages of
one to six, girls receive significantly more dolls and doll houses and boys receive
more building toys. For older children, parents provide more science related
activities for their sons than for their daughters, including microscopes, puzzles,
and chemistry sets. Of particular interest in understanding sex related mathematics differences, Graham & Birns (1979) reported that girls are less likely than
boys to have mathematical toys and games and individual instruction in mathematics.

Television and Other Media

Many people are amazed to learn that by age four, most children have spent
between 2,000 and 3,000 hours watching television (Stewart, 1976). What are
they learning about males and females during all of these hours? With only a few
exceptions (e.g., Sesame Street), media depictions of females and males parallel
commonly held sex role stereotypes (Deaux, 1985). Overwhelmingly, men and
boys are shown as active, hard working, goal-oriented individuals, while women
and girls are depicted as housewives and future housewives. In an analysis of 300
television commercials, Hoyenga and Hoyenga (1979) reported that over 90% of
the following activities or occupations were portrayed by females: baby and
infant care, inmate in nursing home, house cleaning, washing clothes and dishes,
shopping, cooking and serving food. Compare these with the following activities
and occupations which were portrayed by males over 90% of the time: farmer,
engaging in sports, driving a vehicle, office worker (not secretary), soldier, and
service station worker. Social Modeling theory would predict that children are
learning about sex roles by observing the activities and occupations of the female
and male characters they are viewing on television.

The prediction that children will be more likely to imitate same sex models
than other sex models has been difficult to demonstrate in the laboratory, possibly because of some of the constraints imposed by the nature of laboratory
investigations. A typical laboratory study of this phenomenon might consist of
exposing children to male and female models who engage in different sorts of
activities. The researchers then observe the girls and boys to see if they are more
likely to exhibit the activities of the same sex model than they are to exhibit the
activities of the other sex model. It is likely, however, that observational learning

followed by imitation of a same sex model occurs more frequently in real life where the child may have frequent contact with a model and a wider range of opportunities to demonstrate imitation.

Perry and Bussey (1979) have provided evidence in support of Social Modeling theory. They hypothesized that children learn sex-typed behavior by observing differences in the *frequencies* of sex-typed activities by female and male models. In a test of their hypothesis, they provided children with several male and female models. They found that children were more likely to imitate behaviors of same sex models than they were to imitate behaviors of other sex models. Perry and Bussey concluded that, "children are most likely to imitate persons whom they perceive to be good examples of their [own] sex role" (p. 1708). If, as Perry and Bussey suggest, repeated observations of the frequency of sex-typed behavior is the mechanism by which social modeling operates, then television should provide an optimal situation for such learning. Given the immense number of hours children and adults spend watching television, it is clear that television is a major socializing agent in modern American society. The sex stereotyped characterizations it depicts serve to reinforce sex role stereotypes.

Teachers and Schools

It would be preposterously naive to suggest that a B.A. degree can be made as attractive to girls as a marriage license.
—Grayson Kirk (former president of Columbia University)

Schools are the only institution in our society charged with the exclusive responsibility of educating our children. It is there that the intellectual abilities of all girls and boys should be nurtured so that every individual can develop to his or her full potential. Sadker and Sadker (1985) set out to find if there is any evidence that cognitive abilities are being differentially developed for girls and boys in our schools. In a 3-year-study of 100 fourth, sixth, and eighth grade classes in the District of Columbia, they found ample evidence of sex biases. At all grade levels in all subjects, boys dominated classroom discussions. Teachers paid more attention to the boys and praised them more often. "While girls sat patiently with their hands raised, boys literally grab teacher attention. They are eight times more likely than girls to call out answers" (p. 56). They reported that boys also received more dynamic and informative feedback to their classroom comments than the girls did. Sex differentiated treatment in the classroom could be directly responsible for or contributing to sex differences in mathematics and science achievement. If girls are taught that they will receive fewer rewards for scholastic success than boys will, learning theory suggests that they will seek success in other areas in which rewards are more probable. All of the teachers

Sadker observed reported that they treated boys and girls equally, yet observations conducted in their classrooms showed that their beliefs about their actions were untrue.

It seems that all of the major socializing agents of childhood act in ways that encourage sex differentiated cognitive development. It also seems that few of us are aware of the multitudinous pressures to conform to traditional sex roles and of the diverse ways these pressures are communicated to children.

Adolescence

Adolescence covers that time in the life span when boys and girls begin to develop secondary sex characteristics and ends when physical maturity is achieved. Considering the variety of individual differences in the timing of these developmental milestones, it can be roughly operationalized as beginning as early as age ten and extending to as late as age 18, recognizing, of course, that a few individuals begin puberty before age ten and a few continue physical maturity after age 18. Adolescence has already been identified in earlier chapters as a critical period in the development of cognitive sex differences. While sex differences in verbal, mathematical, and spatial ability are found only on selected ability tests (e.g., mental rotation, Water Level, and some tests of language proficiency) during childhood, differences clearly emerge during adolescence. Several biological hypotheses have been proposed that link the biological events of puberty to the emergence of cognitive sex differences during this time of life. However, along with the tremendous biological changes that occur during these years, there are also numerous and powerful psychosocial changes that occur during the preteen and teen years. Researchers who favor the nurture side of the nature/nurture controversy believe that the etiology of the cognitive sex differences is firmly rooted in the psychosocial forces that dominate the adolescent years.

Body Type and Developing Sexuality

Although biological definitions of puberty usually cite the development of adult patterns of body hair (the word puberty is derived from a Latin word meaning fine downy hair), psychosocial definitions of adolescence are more likely to stress romantic interest and concern with one's changing body. There are profound psychological consequences of the biology of adolescence.

The biological events that symbolize the ability to reproduce—menarche for girls and ejaculation for boys—have intense psychosocial significance. For each sex, these biological events signify that for the first time, the individual, along with a partner, can create life. Friendships with members of the other sex and preadolescent romances assume a new potential meaning when young adults develop sexually.

The biological changes associated with physical maturation have tremendous psychosocial significance. There is ample evidence to believe that girls and boys who attain puberty at an early age and develop adult-like body types before most of their peers are treated differently from their later maturing friends. As described in the preceding chapter, a major biological theory to explain cognitive sex differences is that early maturers don't develop spatial skills as well or as fully as later maturing adolescents, possibly because of the effect of sex hormones on brain organization. It is also possible however, that early maturers differ from late maturers for psychosocial reasons. Early maturing boys are more muscular and taller than later maturing ones; therefore, they experience greater peer group prestige (Hamburg & Lunde, 1966). There are numerous secondary gains from their physical stature. Their height gives them a competitive edge in sports such as basketball, volleyball, long jump, and soccer. The early growth of body hair allows them to cultivate a moustache while still in junior high school, and their developing biceps are likely to receive positive comments.

Puberty rate differences are even more pronounced for girls who soon learn that their "hour-glass" figures and growing breasts make them desirable dates and mates. They undoubtedly receive more attention from males, especially older males, than their less shapely girlfriends. It would seem that early maturers would be less concerned with academic pursuits than late maturers who still rely on good grades in school and teachers' praise as a major source of reward. Mazur and Robertson (1972) revealed the feelings of an anonymous girl who had experienced early puberty: "Sure, after I bloomed I always dressed so people could see how big my breasts were. After all, a pair of 48's can make a girl feel like a real person. Everybody pays attention" (p. 115).

It seems that early and later maturers have different social environments and receive different rewards. A psychosocial explanation of the sex related cognitive differences that emerge during puberty would suggest that it is these different life experiences that result from the hormonal events that trigger maturation and not hormonal events per se that underlie cognitive differences.

In one of the few examinations of commonly held stereotypes about early and late maturing girls and boys, Faust (1983) asked college students to describe individuals in these four categories. Early maturing girls were described as "attracted to the opposite sex, egocentric, absolutely boy crazy, and theatrical." By comparison, late maturing girls were described as "afraid of the opposite sex, unassuming, friends of both boys and girls, and exhibiting normal behavior." Early maturing boys were described as "liking football, sexy and outgoing, macho, slow learner, and a typical jock." Late maturing boys were described as "would rather read, fast learner, unmacho, and popular only with own friends." It seems that many people would agree with the research showing that early maturers have poorer intellectual skills and are more concerned with sex than later maturers.

Gender Intensification Hypothesis

The term "gender" is often used to refer to the psychological aspects associated with biological sex (Deaux, 1985). The term usually encompasses what I have been calling "sex role stereotypes." Adolescence has been identified as the time when boys and girls, but especially girls, respond to environmental pressures to conform to appropriate sex role behavior (Hill & Lynch, 1983). The psychological aspects of being female or male are intensified, hence the term "gender intensification." Adherence to traditional sex role stereotypes seem particularly important when boys and girls begin to interact in ways that are more characteristic of young women and men. Adolescence is a transitional period in life during which children undergo a metamorphosis from which they emerge as adults. Peer interactions are especially important and there are strict sanctions against sex role inappropriate behavior. The need to conform and be "just like everyone else" is high. Strict conformance to sex role stereotypes would require boys and girls to also conform to sex-typed cognitive activities which would translate into avoiding mathematics and science coursework for girls and avoiding poetry and literature for boys. Although the preteen and teen uniform changes with each generation—bobby socks and poodle skirts, denim jeans, and currently, brightly colored clothing—the unspoken code to conform exerts strong influences.

Several researchers have examined the relationship between conformity to traditional sex roles and intellectual development. Nash (1975) measured spatial visualization ability, sex role concepts, and sex role preferences among 11- and 14-year-old girls and boys. In accord with the usual research findings, she found that sex differences in spatial visualization ability did not emerge until age 14. However, the most interesting part of this study was the relationship between sex role preferences and spatial visualization ability. For males, viewing oneself as masculine was related to better spatial performance. For females, a preference for the male sex role was positively related to spatial performance. Thus, for both sexes, good spatial ability was associated with either an identification with or a preference for the male sex role. Good spatial ability is usually considered to be a masculine trait, and it was those girls and boys who positively viewed masculine traits that scored well on Nash's test of spatial ability. Nash also found that more girls than boys would prefer to be a member of the other sex and were more likely to feel that it is better to be the other sex.

One puzzling and distressing finding in the literature on adolescence is "adolescent intellectual decline." Campbell (1976) discussed replicated findings that a substantial proportion of adolescent girls show decrements in their IQ scores, while adolescent boys show a reverse trend toward increasing IQ scores. Although the magnitude of the actual losses and gains tends to be small, the sex differentiated pattern is consistently found. In Campbell's study of high school seniors, males gained an average of 1.62 IQ points and females lost an average of 1.33 IQ points relative to their scores in seventh grade. She hypothesized that girls who declined in IQ would conform to feminine sex role stereotypes more than the girls whose IQ's didn't decline because the feminine sex role stereotype is incompatible with academic or intellectual achievement. Her hypothesis was confirmed. Campbell concluded: ''[T]he girl decliners tended to express responses that were more typically stereotypic than did the total sample of girls'' (p. 634). The sex role message for adolescent girls is clear: It isn't feminine to be smart.

These results are most relevant to our interpretation of the report from Johns Hopkins University on the Study of Mathematically Precocious Youth (Benbow & Stanley, 1980, 1981, 1983). As reported in Chapter 3, a national search for mathematically precocious youth identified more males than females, with large sex ratios among the most highly gifted group. If adolescent girls learn that it is unfeminine to succeed at mathematics, then it is likely that a large proportion of mathematically gifted girls either declined to participate in the search or never pursued advanced mathematics courses. Tomizuka and Tobias (1981) note that such statistics are unfair because it may be difficult to identify the most gifted girls in such a talent search because of the social ostracism they would surely face for such inappropriate behavior during a time in life when sex role adherence is of particular importance.

Video Games, Sports, and Other Adolescent Activities

American female and male adolescents have always engaged in sex differentiated activities. Even recent attempts at legislation to end sex segregation in groups such as Boy and Girls Scouts and their adolescent counterparts, Explorer and Junior Scouts, and little league and Babe Ruth league have, for the most part, failed. Either the courts have ruled that sex segregation is legal, as in the case of scouting,or the lifting of sex restrictions has not in fact changed much, as in the case of adolescent baseball leagues which typically enroll few girls. Even in instances in which there is no formal sex segregation, boys and girls often self-segregate. One modern day example of this is billiards and video games which tend to attract a much higher percentage of boys than girls. Both billiards and video games seem to require spatial skill. It seems likely that repeated practice at these activities would lead to improvement in some spatial skills. Greenfield and Lauber (1985) believe that the visual analysis involved in these leisure time spatial activities transfers to academic disciplines such as the sciences which require spatial ability.

Adolescent boys also engage in more organized sports than adolescent girls. Football, a virtually exclusively male sport, requires considerable spatial analysis, especially if it includes carefully planned ''plays'' for passing. It is interesting to note that while the relationship between participation in sports and the development of spatial skills seems logical, it has never been tested empirically. There are some spatial activities that girls are more likely to engage in than boys. Embroidery, especially embroidery without a preprinted pattern would seem to be an excellent spatial skill, as would sewing without a pattern. However, these are activities that probably attract few girls, especially in relation to the number of boys who participate in traditionally male activities that contain spatial components. Reading is a somewhat sex-typed female activity. We really don't know what the majority of girls are doing while adolescent boys are engaged in sports. It seems likely that adolescent girls probably do read more than adolescent boys and probably watch more television, but these are untested "hunches."

Typically, girls are required to perform more housework chores. It is difficult to imagine how these chores could improve intellectual growth. For example, the type of mathematics used in recipes is arithmetic conversions, and isn't likely to require any mathematical skills beyond addition, subtraction, and fractions. In general, typical adolescent activities seem to favor the development of cognitive skills for males over females.

Adulthood and Old Age

The bulk of our lives is spent as adults and later as older adults. There are numerous psychosocial factors that maintain the sex role stereotypic behaviors we learned in our youth. Below is a brief survey of some of the factors which have implications for cognitive functioning.

Sex Related Power Differential

It is possible that psychologists who study cognitive differences are missing the most salient aspect of sex differences in human interactions. Meeker and Weitzel-O'Neill (1977) believe that many sex differences are merely an artifact of power and status differences. Men behave as they do because they hold all of the real power in society, and women behave as they do because they are essentially powerless, or at least less powerful than men. Men gain power and prestige through the status of their occupation and the size of their paycheck (Gould, 1974). Occupations that are typically male are more highly prized by society than occupations that are typically female. Even when a traditionally female and a traditionally male job require the same level of background or training (e.g., secretary and groundskeeper), the male job will most often pay substantially more.

Most of society's powerful people are men. Virtually all government leaders, corporate officials, leading scientists, bankers, and stock brokers are men. Society's power differential continues in most households. Even if men are no longer the sole breadwinner, in a vast majority of American households, they earn more than their wives. In most marriages, the husband not only earns more money, but he is also better educated, taller, and heavier than the wife. Thus, the power differential extends beyond money and prestige of occupation, it also includes the physical power associated with larger stature.

The occupations that require spatial and mathematical abilities are the same ones that offer higher prestige, power, and higher salaries. Children learn that if they want to become physicians, pharmacists, engineers, computer analysts, accountants, scientists, or veterinarians, they will have to excel in mathematics and sciences. Since these are examples of the high paying prestigious occupations that are primarily filled by men, boys learn that success in the academic areas that are prerequisites for these occupations is necessary if they are to fulfill their adult sex role. Occupations that are traditionally female, such as teacher, secretary, and homemaker, do not require excellent mathematical or spatial skills. Good communication or verbal skills are needed in these occupations, which is exactly the academic arena in which most females excel.

It is difficult to determine cause and effect when sex differences in occupations are considered. Females could dominate selected fields that require verbal ability because they are inherently better in verbal ability, or they could be better than males in verbal ability because they are educated for careers in these areas. Similar problems arise when considering the relationship between male abilities and male occupational preferences. The only conclusion that can be reached is that many prestigious, high paying jobs require mathematical and spatial skills and that these jobs tend to be filled primarily by men. However, it is important to remember when considering the relationship among ability, occupation, and sex that more than ability is involved in determining who fills the high status occupations. Traditionally, other demographic indicators like race, socioeconomic status, religion, and country of origin, independent of ability, have determined who will succeed in high status positions. Despite the fact that females have superior performance on *tests* of verbal ability, this has not translated into occupational success in high verbal fields like academia, or journalism that are associated with high prestige and/or high salaries which demonstrates the importance of psychosocial variables in determining occupational success. Even high status positions that primarily require verbal ability such as lawyer and politician are overwhelmingly male. Furthermore, it is difficult to think of any important occupation that does not require verbal ability because the ability to communicate is essential in all endeavors.

Performance Evaluations

One possible explanation for cognitive sex differences is that they don't really exist. We are misled into believing that they exist because we live in a sex biased society which evaluates female and male products differently. There is some evidence that a performance or product is evaluated differently depending on whether the evaluator believes that it was created by a man or a woman (Goldberg, 1968; Pheterson, Kiesler, & Goldberg, 1971).

Although it is likely that our stereotypes lead us to evaluate fine art or literature or architecture in different ways if we believe that they were created by a woman or a man because standards are more subjective in these areas, it is more difficult to apply this concept to standardized tests of mathematics and spatial ability. Some have argued that if a test reveals consistent sex differences, then the test should be declared invalid, and a new test should be found. This line of reasoning begins with the assumption that sex differences cannot truly exist; therefore, the fault must lie in the test. While it is always possible than any between-sex differences were due to some bias in the test itself (e.g., test uses examples that are unfamiliar to one sex), the standardized tests of spatial, mathematical, and verbal ability that have been used in a majority of the studies reviewed in this book are unlikely to contain many of these biases. Thus, while sex differentiated performance evaluations can account for some of the sex differences in success rates in certain occupations, it cannot account for the sex differences found with many standardized ability tests.

Achievement Motivation

Another possible explanation for the cognitive sex differences that are typically found is that they don't represent ability differences. Instead, it is possible that they are indicators of motivational differences. It is possible, for example, that women and men are equally able to learn higher level mathematical concepts, but for some reason, men are more motivated to put in the hard work needed to learn the concepts and/or more motivated to demonstrate their knowledge. Horner (1969) examined the possibility of sex differences in academic motivation. She asked college students to complete the following story which concerned a protagonist named either Anne or John: "At the end of first-term finals, Anne [John] finds herself [himself] at the top of her [his] medical school class." She found that college students wrote about many more negative consequences of academic success for the female protagonist than for the male protagonist. Examples of some of the negative consequences that followed Anne's success were: "Everyone hates and envies Anne" and "Anne feels unhappy and unfeminine." It seems that the female protagonist had become unsexed by success. These results led Horner to hypothesize that, in addition to the usual motivational tendencies that are found in both men and women, women possess a fear of success or a motive to avoid success because success often has negative consequences for women.

Although Horner's research on fear of success captured media headlines, it has not held up in replications. Like most psychological constructs, success motivation is more complex than a simple approach-avoid continuum. It seems that we also need to be concerned with "success at what?" Later research showed that there was little negative imagery when Anne was successful in traditional female occupations like nursing. In addition, males have also been found to be concerned with negative consequences of success. More recent research suggests that if fear of success is a valid motivational tendency, then it exists about equally in men and women. It seems that while many women may want to become more than just a "sex object," many men want to become more than just a "success object." Thus, the well publicized fear of success motivation cannot be used to understand cognitive sex differences. (See Spence & Helmreich, 1983 and Fogel & Paludi, 1984, for recent reviews of the literature.)

More recent examinations of achievement motivation have considered the multidimensional nature of this construct. Spence and Helmreich (1978, 1983) examined sex differences in achievement concerns in the areas of work (the desire to work hard and do a good job), mastery (the preference for challenging tasks and high performance standards), and competition (the enjoyment of interpersonal competition and the desire to do better than others). They found that, in general, women are more concerned with work achievement, and men are more concerned with achievement in competitive and mastery situations. Similar sex differences in competition are sometimes found with children (Halpern & Kagan, 1984). If males are more aggressive, more competitive, and more concerned with mastery throughout the life span, they might be expected to excel in the more competitive aspects of school and work. It is possible that a "competitive edge" or motivational achievement factor is underlying some of the cognitive sex differences. Since achievement is a major component of the male sex role stereotype, it should not be surprising to find that males are more achievement oriented, at least in competitive and mastery situations.

Family Life

> As much as women want to be good scientists or engineers, they
> want first and foremost to be womanly companions of men and to
> be mothers
> —Bruno Bettleheim

The overwhelming majority of adults marry and/or become parents. It is also true that despite recent social changes, women and men perform different roles and functions in most American homes. Although a majority of mothers now work outside of the home, most of these mothers still retain primary responsibility for childcare and housework (Allgeier, 1983). The result is severe strain and fatigue for women who want to maintain serious, demanding professional careers and a balanced family life. Recently, the Public Broadcasting Service aired a series exploring the lives of creative people. The diverse list of creative women they included all had one thing in common—none had children. This was, of course, not true for the creative men, most of whom had children. While many people regard children as an important asset in their lives and would gladly trade other forms of success for parenthood, one conclusion is that children require mothers to prioritize their time and effort in ways that are not required of many fathers. It does seem that traditional family life mitigates against academic and other professional success for women, although the number of women who have successfully combined motherhood, marriage, and demanding occupations is growing.

Family life commitments can explain sex differences in demanding occupations that require years of preparation such as physicist, mathematician, and engineer. They can also explain the cognitive sex differences that arise during puberty if we assume that teens direct their energies and select their coursework to prepare for their anticipated adult life roles.

ABILITY DIFFERENCES

Thus far in this chapter, we have considered the way psychosocial pressures to conform to sex role stereotypic behavior could operate to create or exacerbate cognitive sex differences. An alternate approach to the question is to consider the way each of the abilities that has been identified as the locus of sex differences could be affected.

Spatial Ability

Spatial ability is probably the most difficult of the three sex-related cognitive ability differences to describe or understand. As defined earlier, it consists of at least two component abilities—spatial visualization and spatial orientation. It is often measured with tests that require the mental rotation of a three dimensional figure in space, or finding a smaller figure embedded with the borders of a larger figure, or by having subjects indicate the water level of a tipped glass, or by having subjects position a rod within a rectangular frame so that the rod is vertically aligned. As reviewed earlier, almost all of these measures show consistent and sometimes substantial sex differences, with males performing more accurately than females.

It is difficult to relate these sorts of abilities to our usual notion of sex role stereotypes. It does not seem obvious that either sex should have the advantage when it comes to knowing that the water level remains horizontal in a tipped glass or in aligning a rod to the vertical position. If these results are related to sex role stereotypes, then you would expect that those individuals who are the most feminine sex typed would have the poorest skills and those who are the most masculine sex typed would have the best skills. Hyde, Geiringer, and Yen (1975) examined this hypothesis and found no support for this hypothesized relationship.

Sex role stereotypes could influence the development of spatial skills by providing each sex with different amounts and types of spatial experiences. This possibility was considered earlier in this chapter when video games and billiards were discussed as common adolescent activities among boys. If different experiences are responsible for the sex differences, then it should be possible to improve spatial abilities by providing appropriate training. Several psychologists have examined this possibility.

Spatial Skills Training

In a direct test of the hypothesis that boys develop better spatial skills than girls because of their experiences with spatial activities, Sprafkin, Serbin, Denier, and Connor (1983) gave 3 1/2- to 4-year-old children special training with preschool toys that are typically preferred by boys—blocks, dominoes, tinker toys, paper cut in geometric shapes. They believed that these typical "boys' toys" were important in the development of spatial ability. They found that the children who received the special training with these toys scored higher on a test of visual spatial ability than a control group of children who did not receive the special training. It seems clear that spatial ability can be taught, and that it can be taught to preschool children by increasing their exposure to typical male-preferred toys.

Support for the notion that differential experience underlies the spatial ability sex difference was obtained when spatial training was provided for first grade children. As discussed in Chapter 3, the Embedded Figures Test is a spatial ability test that yields large sex differences. When Connor, Schackman, & Serbin (1978) tested first grade children on a special children's version of the Embedded Figures Test, they found the usual sex difference with the boys performing more accurately than the girls. They then provided both the girls and the boys with an "overlay training procedure" in which they used transparent overlays to highlight the way smaller figures were embedded within the boundaries of the larger figures. They found that after this training both girls and boys improved significantly. Most importantly, the sex differential disappeared after the training. They believe that the reason that the girls benefited more from the training than the boys is because the girls typically have less experience with spatial activities and therefore would improve more with specific instruction. These results provide a strong case for the importance of sex differentiated environmental factors in the development of spatial skills. They clearly demonstrate that spatial skills are trainable.

The finding that girls profit more spatial training than boys has been replicated with other age groups of children. Vandenberg (1975) found that sixth grade girls, but not sixth grade boys, showed gains on a mental rotation task after receiving spatial training on building models with blocks. These results have been extended to eighth graders who also showed a significant increase in spatial ability following a 3-week training period which consisted of object manipulation exercises such as folding paper into geometric shapes (Brinkmann, 1966). There were no significant sex differences on the Spatial Relations Test for the eighth graders who participated in this program.

All of these studies point to one conclusion: Spatial ability can be improved with appropriate training. The question of whether girls benefit more from spatial skills training because they have fewer spatial experiences than boys is somewhat less clear. In a specific test of this hypothesis, Smith, Frazier, Ward, and Webb (1983) followed the same procedures as reported in several studies that found that spatial skills instruction had a differential effect on males and females. They found that instruction did improve scores on tests of spatial ability; however, unlike the earlier studies, the girls did not improve more than the boys. To date, evidence in support of the claim that girls benefit more from spatial skill training than boys is mixed, and no conclusive statement about this hypothesis can be made.

Despite these strong positive results that implicate environmental factors in the development of spatial skills, there are still some nagging inconsistencies that remain unexplained. The principle that water remains horizontal when a glass is tipped seems particularly difficult for girls to comprehend, and the large sex differences found on the Water Level Test cannot be explained by psychosocial factors. Thomas, Jamison, and Hammel (1973) reported very little success in teaching this principle to girls. In addition, even the strong results supporting the trainability of spatial skills do not rule out the possibility of a genetic-environmental interaction. It still remains possible, although unproven, that boys learn spatial principles more easily or readily than girls. It also seems reasonable to conclude that we should be providing all children with those toys that are typically labeled "boys' toys." There is enough evidence to suggest that experience with these toys may be useful in the development of spatial skills. We may be short changing the intellectual development of girls by providing them with only traditional sex stereotyped toys.

Another important implication of this research is the finding that spatial skills are trainable. Very few schools incorporate spatial skill training into their curriculum. One way to be certain that all individuals develop their spatial ability to their fullest capacity is to provide routinely such training to all students from their preschool through their high school years. Empirical results have shown that both girls and boys would benefit from such instruction.

Mathematical Ability

Sex differences in mathematics achievement are well documented and have been described in the previous two chapters. As discussed in the previous chapter, one biological hypothesis that has been suggested to explain this difference posits sex differences in brain lateralization. There are, of course, numerous psychosocial explanations that have been devised to explain mathematical sex differences. This class of theories places the "blame" squarely on socialization practices and the adherence to sex role stereotypes in contemporary American society.

Study after study has documented sex differences in the extent to which children are encouraged to pursue careers in mathematics, in mathematics role models, and in subtle pressures to eschew serious academic pursuits. Female mathematicians report that they were discouraged by others in their efforts to become mathematicians far more often than their male counterparts (Luchins & Luchins, 1981). Professor Martha Smith, a mathematician, described the negative stereotypes associated with being a female mathematician this way: "Many people on hearing the words 'female mathematician' conjure up an image of a six-foot, gray-haired, tweed suited oxford clad woman. . . . This image, of course, doesn't attract the young woman who is continually being bombarded with messages, direct and indirect, to be beautiful, 'feminine' and catch a man" (quoted in Ernest, 1976, p. 14). Our stereotypes exert strong social pressures. Few women would choose to identify with this stereotype, even if they were mathematically talented. An artist's rendition of this stereotypic image of a female mathematician is depicted in Fig. 5.1.

FIG. 5.1. Artist's conception of the stereotypical "woman mathematician" as described by Professor Marha Smith: "Many people on hearing the words 'female mathematician' conjure up an image of a six-foot, gray-haired, tweed suited oxford clad woman . . . This image, of course, doesn't attract the young woman who is being continually bombarded with messages, direct and indirect, to be beautiful, 'feminine' and catch a man" (Ernest, 1976, p. 14).

Hilton and Berglund (1974) designed a Background and Experience Questionnaire to assess sex related environmental differences in mathematics and science. Science interests and experience are often included in these studies because of its close relationship with mathematics as well as the corresponding sex differential in science achievement. They gave their questionnaire to boys and girls in seventh, ninth, and eleventh grades. They found that boys read more science books, report greater interest in mathematics, consider mathematics more useful in earning a living, talk more about science, and have parents who favor their continuing their education beyond high school more than the girls. While all of these differences were negligible at seventh grade, they increased with age so that by eleventh grade when career decisions are being made, sex differences were sizable.

Mathematics skills are extremely important in many occupations. Mathematics has been described as a "critical filter" which keeps women out of engineering, computer science, business, and accounting fields because only those individuals with a solid background in mathematics are able to enter these fields (Sherman, 1982b). The single best predictor of scores on mathematics achievement tests is the number of mathematics courses an individual has taken (Jones, 1984). Females take fewer mathematics courses than males (Sherman, 1982a). High ability women drop out of mathematics and science courses at greater rates than men beginning when the courses first become optional in high school and continuing into graduate school. For those concerned about the low participation of females in mathematically related careers, the solution seems to be simple: Encourage more females to take more mathematics courses. One program designed to encourage women in mathematics focused on the development of self-confidence and the awareness of the importance of mathematics as a key to many career options for women (MacDonald, 1980). Also incorporated in this program were cooperative learning strategies and optional tutoring. Although this was a small-scale study, the women who participated obtained higher class scores, had fewer dropouts, reported better attitudes toward mathematics, and were more likely to continue their mathematics education than a control group of women who did not participate in the program.

Models of Mathematical Achievement

The psychosocial variables that mitigate against female success in mathematics are numerous and interacting. Several multifaceted models have been proposed to explain the relationships among variables. Sherman (1980), for example has identified confidence in learning mathematics, perceived usefulness of mathematics, and attitudes of one's mother, father, and teacher toward learning mathematics as important determinants of mathematics achievement. As expected, males score higher on all of these variables than females. It seems intuitively obvious that these are important variables in understanding success in

SALLY FORTH by Greg Howard and by permission of News America Syndicate.

mathematics. Few people would persist in higher mathematics coursework if they believed that they did not have the ability to learn the material, if they felt that it was of litle value, or if they were routinely discouraged by their parents and teachers.

Sherman (1967, 1980) also believes that spatial ability is a key factor in understanding sex differences in mathematical ability. She found that scores on the Spatial Relations Test, a test of spatial visualization ability, were more important in predicting girls' decisions to continue in high school mathematics courses than they were for boys. Sherman suggests that by including spatial visualization training in school, the sex differential in both spatial and mathematics ability would be reduced or eliminated. Other researchers have also found a relationship between spatial visualization ability and scores on mathematics tests (Elmore & Vasu, 1980).

Sex differences in mathematics is an area that is ripe for expectancy effects. In one survey of teachers, 63% reported that they believed that boys were better than girls in mathematical ability, with the rest reporting no sex difference (Ernest, 1976). Harris and Rosenthal (1985) recently reviewed 135 studies on expectancy effects. They found that: "Teachers who hold positive expectations for a given student will tend to display a warmer socioemotional climate, express a more positive use of feedback, provide more input in terms of the amount and difficulty of the material that is taught, and increase the amount of student output by providing more response opportunities and interacting more frequently with the student" (p. 377). Simply put, teachers behave differently when they expect students to succeed than when they don't.

While, in general, mothers help their children more with all homework (Ernest, 1976), fathers are seven times more likely to be consulted for help with mathematics homework than mothers are (Sherman, 1983). In a recent study of the factors that affect women's enrollment in nontraditional vocations, Houser and Garvey (1985) found that the amount of support, encouragement, and discouragement the women received from significant others in their lives was the most significant factor influencing these decisions. In general, females receive less support and encouragement and more discouragement to pursue mathematics coursework and related occupations than their male counterparts.

The most comprehensive theoretical model designed to explain sex differences in academic achievement was proposed by Eccles (Parsons) et al. (1983). In this model they delineate the relationships among several important determinants of academic choices in general and mathematics choices specifically. In their psychological model of mathematics attitudes and behaviors, they posit a theoretical network composed of the following variables which will be described in ways that link them to the preceding discussion in this chapter:

Attitudes and Expectations of Others.   This variable includes the way the attitudes of others undermine confidence and determine how useful an academic area is perceived. In Eccles (Parsons) et al.'s study, they found that parents' and teachers' beliefs influenced students' self-concepts of mathematical ability.

Students' Beliefs About Appropriate Role Characteristics.   As already discussed, there are strong negative sanctions against females who opt to pursue the study of a "masculine" academic field like mathematics. In addition, most mathematics role models are male. Support for this statement comes from the finding that fathers provide more help than mothers with mathematics homework, most teachers in advanced mathematics courses are men, and teacher expectations are sex differentiated.

Students' Interpretations of Past Events.   There are clear differences in the early mathematical experiences of boys and girls. Traditional "boy's toys" have already been discussed as useful in training spatial ability, which in turn has been identified as important in determining mathematical success.

Goals and Self-Schemata.   Boys' career and life goals are more likely to include occupations that require mathematics than girls' career and life goals.

Self-Concept of Math Ability.   By the junior high school years, boys believe that they have more mathematical ability than girls, and girls' self-ratings of mathematical ability declines earlier and more than boys' throughout adolescence (Fennema & Sherman, 1977).

Perception of Difficulty of Math.   The term "math anxiety" has been coined to describe the irrational and debilitating fear of mathematics, an affliction more likely to be experienced by females than males. One possible reason for the greater fear of mathematics among girls is that it is representative of a loss of feminine identity. In support of this conclusion, Eccles (Parsons) et al. found that males rated mathematics as easier and requiring less effort than females in their study.

All of these variables influence how much students' value mathematics as well as their intentions to pursue higher level mathematics courses.

As Eccles (Parsons) et al. described, there is a complex web of psychosocial causative factors which all work against female excellence in mathematics. Many researchers in this area have been highly critical of any claim that sex differences in mathematics can be traced to a biological etiology given the large number of psychosocial explanations that both logically and empirically have been used to explain the data (Fox, Tobin, & Brody, 1979; Sherman, 1979). The Eccles (Parsons) et al. (1983) model is shown in Fig. 5.2.

Verbal Abilities

In some ways, verbal abilities has become the step-child of the cognitive sex differences literature. It is the one cognitive sex difference in which females have the advantage, and it is the least studied and discussed of the three ability differences. Few would argue that verbal ability is less important than spatial or mathematical ability. In fact, it would seem that it is the most important of the abilities since virtually every human interaction relies on verbal or language skills. Of all the ability differences, it is also the earliest to emerge. As reviewed earlier in this chapter, sex differentiated socialization practices begin at or before birth, with girl infants receiving more adult vocalizations than boy infants. It is also possible that when girls find mathematics and science courses closed to them, they then satisfy achievement needs in their language courses.

In a recent review of the cognitive sex differences literature, Bradshaw and Nettleton (1983) concluded that verbal abilities are more subject to environmental influences than spatial abilities. They based this conclusion on a review of ability studies in which correlations between parents and children, among siblings, and between identical and fraternal twins suggest that cultural and educational variables have a greater impact on verbal skills than spatial ones. Although this is an interesting possibility, correlational data can only provide weak support for this hypothesis and do not rule out the possibility of a biological-environmental interaction.

Although females outscore males on most verbal ability tests such as the Scholastic Aptitude Test, this advantage has not translated into exceptional occupational success. There have been no national searches for Verbally Precocious Youth similar to the search for Mathematically Precocious Youth. One might expect that a higher proportion of girls would be identified than boys, but since this search has never taken place there is no data to back up this prediction. It is difficult to understand why sex differences in verbal ability have not been investigated to the same extent as the other cognitive sex differences.

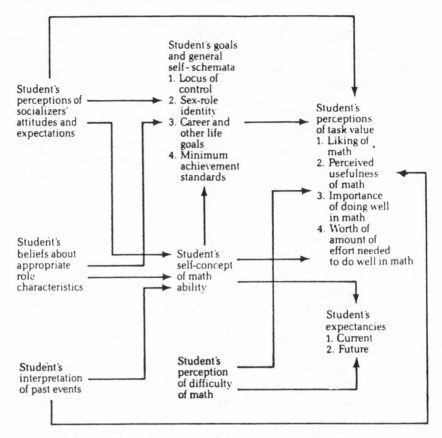

FIG. 5.2.   Model devised to explain how an interdependent network of values and expectations influence academic course selection in ways that discourage girls from pursuing mathematics courses in high school. From Expectations, values and academic behaviors. In J. T. Spence (Ed.), *Achievement and Achievement Motives* by Eccles (Parsons) et al., W. H. Freeman and Company, copyright 1983.

Bent Twig Hypothesis

One theory designed to explain female superiority in language areas was proposed by Sherman (1967). It has come to be known as the "Bent Twig Hypothesis" in reference to an old saying that goes something like this, "as the twig is bent, so the tree shall grow." Sherman begins with the assumption that girls talk at an earlier age than boys, although the evidence in support of this claim is somewhat mixed. Because of their early advantage with language, girls rely more on verbally and socially mediated approaches in their interactions with people and objects in their world. Boys, on the other hand, rely upon their better developed musculature to interact with people and objects, thus, they move about more, a fact that could contribute to the development of their spatial skills. Each sex develops somewhat fixed patterns or preferences for interacting, with the result that early developmental differences guide later actions.

It is interesting to note that the Bent Twig Hypothesis does not explain the initial sex difference with respect to verbal ability. It could be due to early differential reinforcement patterns for infant vocalizations or due to biologically based readiness to produce language or some interaction of these two possibilities.

If, as Sherman suggested, girls tend to rely upon verbal skills instead of utilizing spatial ones, then the finding that female's brains are less lateralized may, in fact, reflect strategy differences and not biolgical differences. In other words, the sex differences in lateralization that were discussed in the last chapter could be an artifact of verbal strategy preferences among females and not reflective of "hard wired" neurological differences. Suppose, for example, that females attempt to use verbal strategies or modes of information processing when faced with the Embedded Figures Test. A verbal strategy would be less efficient than a spatial approach to this problem. Females would then be expected to perform less well than males who are relying upon spatial modes of information processing when taking this test. If this hypothesis is true, then cognitive sex differences could be explained by the perseverative use of verbal strategies by females which leaves them at a disadvantage when performing spatial tasks.

EXTRAPOLATING FROM EMPIRICAL TRENDS

Perhaps one of the greatest sources of support for proponents of psychosocial explanations of cognitive sex differences can be captured in a quote from Bob Dylan: "The times, they are a-changin." Sex differences with respect to cognitive abilities have not remained static over the years that psychologists and other investigators have been studying them. As discussed earlier in this book (Chapter 2), the size of the sex differences is as important as the finding that there are sex differences. Rosenthal and Rubin (1982) have found that the effect size for studies of sex differences in cognitive abilities has been decreasing. As they aptly describe this state of affairs, ". . . in these studies, females appear to be gaining in cognitive skill relative to males rather faster than the gene can travel!" (p. 711). The only way that biological hypotheses can explain this finding would be to suppose that female and male biology has been rapidly changing over the last few decades, an assumption that flies in the face of everything that we know about biological and evolutionary trends.

Rosenthal and Rubin (1982) also note that one possible explanation for the decreasing effect size is that sampling differences have occurred over the years in which data on cognitive sex differences have been collected. Much of the research is conducted with college students. Colleges have been undergoing changes in their sexual composition with more young females pursuing college educations and more older women returning to college to complete a college career that was interrupted by marriage and family obligations. Thus, college women may be more representative of all adult women now than they were 20 years ago. Even with these differences in sampling, the fact remains that the most recent studies show substantial gains in cognitive performance by women relative to men, a finding which cannot be explained with biological explanations.

CHAPTER SUMMARY

Psychosocial explanations of cognitive sex differences are important because of their implications for change. If sex differences in cognitive abilities can be attributed to psychosocial variables, then these changes can be reduced or eliminated with appropriate societal changes. One of the difficulties in identifying the relevant psychosocial variables is the pervasiveness of sex role stereotypes in our society. The result has been a nonconscious ideology in which we are blind to many of the sex differentiated attributes and expectations that have become ingrained in contemporary society.

Children develop an awareness of and conformity to sex role stereotypes at a very young age. Freudian, Social Modeling, Learning, and Cognitive theories have been proposed to explain the acquisition and maintenance of sex stereotypic behavior patterns. Sex linked socialization practices which vary over the life span were examined in an attempt to understand the myriad of sex role stereotypic influences that are part of every male's and female's life.

The replicated finding that spatial ability can be trained lent strong support for psychosocial hypotheses that attempt to explain spatial ability sex differences by appealing to environmental variables. This position would be even stronger if there was clear cut evidence that females benefit more than males from such instruction; however, the data with respect to this second issue is mixed. A host of psychosocial variables has been used to explain sex differences in mathematics achievement. A complex interacting web of expectations, modeling influences, and perceived usefulness of mathematics provide a strong theoretical model for interpreting the usual sex differences results. Sex differences in verbal abilities have received the least experimental attention. The leading theoretical model in the area of verbal abilities builds on sex differentiated propensities to interact in either verbal or nonverbal ways.

The finding that effect sizes with respect to sex differences in cognitive abilities have been decreasing provides the strongest case for the importance of psychosocial variables. If the effect sizes continue to diminish in coming years, the question of cognitive sex differences will become an interesting part of historical thought.

6

Understanding Cognitive Sex Differences

CONTENTS

The Need for Cross-Cultural Research
  Myopia U.S.A.
  Outcomes of Cross-Cultural Research
The Winning Hypothesis Is . . .
  Data Psychosocial Hypotheses Cannot Explain
  Data Biological Hypotheses Cannot Explain
  A Continuum of Results
  Proportion of Explained Variance
  Multivariate Explanations
New Approaches to Old Problems
Into the Future
  Education for the Twenty-first Century
  Sex Differences, So What!

THE NEED FOR CROSS-CULTURAL RESEARCH

As presented in the preceding two chapters, biological and psychosocial hypotheses are two major categories of hypotheses designed to explain sex differences in cognitive abilities. Within any single society or culture these two types of variables are inextricably entwined because the psychosocial environment varies as a function of biological sex. In American society, for example, males receive more spatial toys as children and more rewards for engaging in spatial activities. They also have the male chromosome configuration, a preponderance of male hormones, and other biological indices that define them as male. Because biological sex and psychosocial environment are confounded, it is extremely difficult to ascertain the independent contribution of either of these variables. One possible way of doing this is to look to other cultures.

The underlying rationale of cross-cultural research in this area is that all females, everywhere in the world, share a similar biology, as do all males. Although there are obvious differences among people in their skin color, hair texture and curl, shape of eyes, etc., the biology of maleness and femaleness is the same everywhere. Except of medical anomalies, members of each sex have the same chromosome configuration for determing sex, internal reproductive organs, gonads (sex glands), genitals, and sex hormone balance. It also seems true that cognitive abilities are universal. In their seminal book on culture and thought, Cole and Scribner (1974) concluded; "we are unlikely to find cultural differences in basic component cognitive processes" (p. 193).

Societal and environmental milieu, however, differ from culture to culture. Consider, for example, the implications of cognitive sex difference research conducted in a society whose sex roles are very different from those of western cultures. Suppose that some hypothetical society existed in which sex role stereotypes were the reverse of those in America, such that girls were encouraged to succeed in the mathematics and science areas and boys were encouraged to be nurturant and to utilize their verbal skills. If we were to find the same cognitive sex differences that we typically find in American studies, then we would have strong support for the importance of sex-related biological variables in the determination of cognitive abilities. Conversely, if we were to find the reverse or a different pattern of cognitive sex differences, or no differences at all, then the psychosocial variables would have received a strong endorsement. Thus, one of the major advantages of cross-cultural research is that it allows the possibility of separating biological and psychosocial contributions to cognitive sex differences.

Myopia U.S.A.

Unfortunately, high quality cross-cultural research that employed comparable measures in a wide variety of cultures is rare. Fairweather (1976) used the term "myopia U.S.A." to describe the relative paucity of cross-cultural data designed to investigate the origins of cognitive sex differences. There are several reasons why researchers have been so nearsighted in their search for the answers to sex difference and other psychological questions. One of the primary reasons for the paucity of research is that cross-cultural data are difficult and expensive to collect. Unlike anthropologists who tend to examine other cross-cultural issues, few psychologists have the necessary connections in other countries to arrange for data collection. They also lack the necessary language skills to converse with subjects and foreign researchers. Subtle differences among languages and nuances that are lost in literal translations can render a research instrument that is valid in one culture invalid or even ludicrous when administered in another culture. There are also numerous controls that are necessary in cross-cultural research. For example, much of the early research designed to compare Mexican youth with American youth employed poor Mexicans and middle-class Americans as subjects. Not surprisingly, large cultural differences emerged; however, these so-called cultural differences were really created by differences in socioeconomic status.

Americans are not alone in their myopia. The majority of our knowledge about cognitive sex differences comes from research conducted with subjects in western industrialized nations by researchers living in those nations. Very little sex differences research is conducted in Third World countries. Sex differences research is simply not a priority in underdeveloped countries struggling to provide enough food for their citizens or in countries fighting for political survival.

There are also political ramifications to research of this sort. For example, the "emancipation of women" was one of the tenets of communism as defined by Marx and Engels. The Russian newspaper, *Pravda,* interpreted the failure of Americans to pass the Equal Rights Amendment as tantamount to endorsing sex discrimination. In fact, there are large numbers of women in the scientific community in the Soviet Union. Detractors are quick to point out, however, that the Soviet Union cannot claim to be a sex-egalitarian country because there are still very few women in positions of power in the government of the Soviet Union (Tavris & Offir, 1977). Whatever your political persuasion, the fact that the majority of engineers and scientists in the Soviet Union are women shows that if women are encouraged by society, they can demonstrate the ability to succeed in what has been construed by western society as "traditional men's fields."

Cross-cultural research is also complicated by the possibility that while biological indicators of sex are nonvariant, other concomitant variables could vary by sex between ethnic and racial groups. For example, it is likely that different ethnic groups mature at somewhat different rates. If maturation rate is an important determinant of cognitive sex differences, as some researchers believe, then between-group sex differences could be due to maturation rate differences and not sex per se. Unfortunately, the hypothetical example of a culture that differs from our own only in terms of its sex roles has never been found. It seems that cross-cultural research, like all of the other research that has been reviewed, cannot provide us with "the answer" about the etiology of cognitive sex differences, although it can provide support for or against any particular hypothesis.

Outcomes of Cross-Cultural Research

Williams and Best (1982) recently reported the results of an extensive cross-cultural project whose objective was "to identify the beliefs commonly held in many cultures about the psychological characteristics associated with men and women and to examine these sex-trait stereotypes for evidence of cross-national similarities and differences" (p. 13). They examined the sex role stereotypic beliefs of adults and children in thirty-nine different countries selected from six different areas of the world (Africa, Asia, Europe, North America, South America, and Oceania). They found a surprisingly high degree of similarity in sex role stereotypes. Williams and Best (1982) coined the term "pancultural generality" to describe the finding that instrumental or goal-oriented traits tend to be associated with being male, and expressive or interpersonal traits tend to be associated with being female.

Not only sex role stereotypes, but sex roles or actual statistical differences in traits or activities between the sexes tend to hold up across western industrialized societies, and it is from these societies that most of the available psychological data are collected. Men and women do play different roles in isolated cultures with little contact with modern industrialized society and have done so in other societies in the past (Leacock, 1980). Therefore, it is not true that women have always been "housebound" or the primary caretakers of the young and old, while the men always wandered from home. Unfortunately, we do not know much about sex differences in cognitive abilities in societies with social structures very different from our own.

Perhaps not surprisingly, when we look at other countries with sex roles similar to those in the United States, we find congruence between their patterns of sex differentiated cognitive abilities and the one discussed in this book. A London newspaper (*The Sunday Times,* September 9, 1984), for example, recently reported on the low level of participation by girls in science and technology courses. There are over four times as many boys as girls studying college preparatory physics in high school in England today. Research on schools in England has shown the same sex differentiated pattern of classroom interactions that was revealed by Sadker and Sadker (1985) in their research on American schools conducted in the Washington, D.C. area: Like their American counterparts, English boys are asked more questions by teachers; receive most of the teacher's attention; and "monopolise science laboratory equipment, consistently depriving girls of practical experience." It seems likely that classroom experiences reflect societal biases about what is appropriate girl and boy behavior. It should come as no surprise that the preponderance of males in math and science related courses and professions remains true for almost all industrialized societies except the Soviet Union. As stressed in several places throughout this book, sex differences in academic course selection and success in selected professions don't necessarily address the issue of ability since there are many factors that are unrelated to ability that could create this sex differential.

Studies that have addressed the abilities question also seem to suggest cross-cultural similarity. In Harris's (1978) review of the spatial ability literature, he concluded that the majority of cross-cultural studies report sex differences favoring males. In interpreting this sweeping statement it is important to realize that, cross-culturally, the average ratio of females to males enrolled in school also tends to favor males, with large disparities found in many countries (Dix, 1975, cited in Williams, 1977). Thus, what we may be interpreting as an ability difference may actually be due to unequal access to education. Even in countries with more equal participation between the sexes with respect to higher education, it is rare to find a study that does not report a male advantage on spatial ability tests. A Russian study (Kovac & Majerova, 1974), for example, reported that among children aged 9- to 15-years, males were superior to females on a standardized test of spatial memory, thus, even though Russian women are participating in science and mathematics professions at a higher rate, adolescent girls in Russia, like those in America, score lower than boys on spatial ability tests.

There are notable exceptions to Harris's conclusion that sex differences in spatial ability are universal. The most frequently cited exception is a study by

Berry (1966) that compared Canadian Eskimos from the Baffin Islands with the Temne tribe in Africa on a variety of spatial tests. Overall, the Eskimos outper-formed the Temne on every spatial test. Most interestingly from the perspective of the sex differences literature, there were no differences among the females and males in the Eskimo sample; whereas among the Temne, the males scored higher on the spatial ability tests than the females. One interpretation of these data is that for the Eskimos, the males and females tend to lead similar lives. For both sexes, traveling from home and hunting are important and frequent activities, and both of these activities should help to develop spatial skills. Among the Temne, traveling far from home is largely a male perrogative, and the sexes tend to be more segregated in their daily activities. While these results seem to favor environmental explanations of spatial ability sex differences, proponents of the biological position would be quick to point out that there may be genetic dif-ferences among isolated groups which have a restricted gene pool.

Another study that is of particular interest in resolving the nature/nurture controversy compared two different New Zealand ethnic groups, the Maori and Pakeha, on eight different cognitive tests (Brooks, 1976). Brooks found that male children in one ethnic group performed better on two different spatial tests; whereas, female children in the other ethnic group performed better on the same two spatial tests. Brooks concluded that different cultures through different pat-terns of socialization develop unique ability patterns for each sex. With respect to verbal abilities, the Pakeha seemed to have a clear-cut advantage. Brooks con-cluded from this finding that verbal ability is the most sensitive to cultural influences of the cognitive abilities. It is interesting to note that this is the same conclusion that was reported in previous chapters based on correlational research with twin and nontwin siblings.

Although cross-cultural studies are intriguing and interesting in their own right, they have not provided clear-cut support for either biological or psycho-social hypotheses. While Harris's general conclusion that spatial ability sex differences seem to hold up cross-culturally, this result is not particularly en-lightening as sex role stereotypes also seem to be largely the same across most of the societies studied. The studies that are exceptions to Harris's conclusion suggest the importance of environmental variables; however, unfortunately, there are several alternate explanations that could also be applied in interpreting these data. In summary, although cross-cultural investigations have the potential to differentiate between biological and psychosocial hypotheses, they are subject to an array of problems that don't permit a strong conclusion in either direction.

THE WINNING HYPOTHESIS IS . . .

Any reader who picked up this book in the hope of finding easy answers is probably frustrated by now. At one moment the data seem to favor one conclu-sion, yet upon further reflection or the accumulation of contradictory data, each theory seems inadequate, subject to alternative explanations, and sometimes wrong. This state of affairs is not unique to cognitive sex differences. It seems to be the norm in all areas of psychology and in the other sciences. In the search for understanding why the sexes differ in some abilities, we have amassed a considerable quantity of information and, we now understand much more about the nature of cognitive sex differences.

If you have been keeping score in the nature/nurture controversy, then you have already realized that the hypotheses in support of each of these two positions have "won some and lost some." Let's consider the nature of the wins and losses on the cognitive sex differences scoreboard.

Data Psychosocial Hypotheses Cannot Explain

The strongest data in support of biological or nature explanations is the finding that scores on tests of spatial ability and verbal ability depend on sex *and* whether an individual is right or left handed. Recall from Chapter 4, that at least among subjects with high reasoning ability, left handed males performed poorer on spatial ability tests than right handed males, but left handed males had the advantage over right handed males on verbal ability tests. The opposite pattern was found for females. Left handed females were better on the spatial ability tests than right handed females with an opposite pattern among females for the verbal ability tests. (See Chapter 4 for a more complete description of the sex by handedness interaction.) This is an important finding because there are no theories that suggest that sex role stereotypes or any other sex related environmental difference varies as a function of handedness. In other words, there is no reason to believe that right handed girls are socialized differently from left handed girls or that right handed boys are socialized differently from left handed boys. Handedness, used as an indicator of cerebral lateralization in these studies, strongly suggests that at least some of the sex differences in spatial and verbal abilities is due to sex differences in the way the brain is specialized to perform spatial and verbal tasks. There are really no other plausible hypotheses to explain these data. This conclusion is bolstered by studies cited in Chapter 4 that also found a link between a family history of left handedness (familial sinistrality) and sex differences in cognitive abilities.

The sex by handedness interactions make a more convincing case for the role of cerebral lateralization as a contributing factor in cognitive sex differences than the large body of data showing sex differences in lateralization. The finding that there are sex differences in lateralization and sex differences in cognitive abilities does not necessarily imply that laterality differences cause cognitive ability differences. It is possible for females, for example, to maintain a more bilateral representation of cognitive functions because of their biology and be better in verbal abilities and poorer in spatial and mathematical abilities because of their environment. However, when handedness is included as an index of laterality, the environmental explanation is no longer valid, and the causal links between sex differences in lateralization and sex differences in cognitive abilities become stronger. Of course I don't believe that we have the final word on this theory, nor has it emerged as the undisputed "winner" in the Best Hypothesis sweepstakes. Research in this area is proceeding at a rapid rate and today's favored theory can quickly become a theoretical dinosaur. It was only a few years ago that the now discredited theory of spatial ability as an X-linked genetic trait was enjoying similar success in its ability to explain sex differences in spatial ability.

The role of sex hormones in the development of cognitive abilities remains unclear. It is possible that they direct or are involved in sex differentiated brain lateralization patterns. It is also possible that, at least under extreme conditions for males, a minimal amount of androgens during puberty is needed for the development of spatial abilities (Hier & Crowley, 1982). The variety of research paradigms relating sex hormone type, quantity, and timing that were reviewed in the chapter on biological hypotheses all suggest that sex hormones are involved in the development of cognitive abilities. It remains the task of future researchers to determine the nature of the relationship.

A second type of data that seems relatively immune to psychosocial explanations concerns three spatial ability test results. Piaget's Water Level Test has been described in several places throughout this book. In this test subjects are required to draw in the water level in a picture of a tipped glass. The usual finding is that far fewer females draw a horizontal line to represent the water level than males. Females tend to draw their line parallel to the direction in which the glass is tipped. This is a robust result that has been replicated many times with samples ranging from elementary school-age children to college students. This task really requires two component skills: (1) Subjects must know that water will always remain horizontal even when its container is tipped; and (2) Subjects must be able to draw an approximately horizontal line. It is difficult to understand how either of these two skills could depend on sex related environmental differences. It does not seem likely that males have more or better experience with a tipped glass of water. In fact, one could argue that females, the primary cooks and dishwashers in many homes, might have more related experience with tipped glasses of water and other liquids than males. Nor does it seem likely that females are less able to express this knowledge with an approximately horizontal line. The ability to draw an approximately horizontal line is a "low level skill." Even if boys play with spatial toys like tinker toys and Lincoln logs more often than girls and are encouraged to pursue spatial professions like architecture and engineering, it does not seem intuitively obvious that these experiences are needed in order to be able to approximate a horizontal line. There is, of course, no simple or direct biological explanation for these results either. I do not believe that there is a genetic code for performance on the Water Level Test. Rather, it seems to be an example of a generalized sex differentiated spatial ability that emerges earlier in the life span (during the elementary school years) than some of the other spatial abilities tested.

Related to this problem is the finding that males score considerably higher on novel tests that require spatial visualization. The largest between-sex differences are found on tests that require subjects to mentally rotate a two-dimensional (i.e., drawn on paper) representation of a three-dimensional object in space. This is a novel task, and it is highly unlikely that anyone of either sex would have any direct experience with three dimensional mental rotations. Environmental hypotheses are somewhat more plausible in explaining this result than they are in explaining sex by handedness interactions or Piaget's Water Level Test because it is possible that males develop some generalized spatial skills through experience with spatial activities that are transferrable to novel spatial tasks. Even if this were true, the large size of the between sex difference on this task remains troublesome for those who prefer environmental hypotheses. While any sort of spatial experience could be helpful in preparing someone for any sort of spatial task, why are sex differences so much larger in this task than they are in other spatial tasks? There are still many unknowns in this area.

The third spatial ability test that is difficult to explain with environmental explanations is the Rod and Frame Test. As described earlier in this book, the Rod and Frame Test requires subjects to position a rod so that it is vertical within a tilted frame. The repeated finding that females perform this task less well than males is troublesome for the environmentalist position. Why should females be misled by a tilted frame more than males? Of course, it is possible that experimenters are unwittingly biasing the results so that they conform to their expectations, but given the fact that these results have been replicated many times by psychologists with strong feminist orientations, this explanation seems unlikely.

Moving along some hypothetical continuum in which experimental results are better explained by biological or psychosocial hypotheses, I would classify the finding that young girls tend to possess better verbal abilities as somewhat closer to the biological end than the psychosocial end of this continuum. In general, results that emerge very early in life are usually attributed to biological explanations since environmental intervention is minimal in very young infants. Unfortunately, the data in support of the finding that female infants are verbally precocious is somewhat weak, with differences clearly emerging in later childhood. Although the classification of these data is arguable, the early appearance of verbal superiority in young girl infants tips the balance for these results, albeit slightly, in favor of biological explanations.

Data Biological Hypotheses Cannot Explain

There have been drastic changes in the educational and professional aspirations of females and, to a lesser extent, males since the Women's Movement in the 1960s. Large numbers of women have begun entering medical school with the result that enrollments in medical schools are now approximately one-third female. Virtually every school of engineering and architecture, the two areas in which spatial ability is the *sine quo non* for success, has experienced dramatic increases in the number of female students enrolled and graduating. There is every indication that this figure has not begun to level off. The increasing number of women entering and succeeding in traditional *male* occupations demonstrates that they clearly have the ability to learn the required skills. Biological explanations simply cannot explain these data. Brains, hormones, genes, maturation rates, genitals, gonads, or any other between-sex biological differences have not changed over the last 2 decades. Female participation in the work force and professional aspirations have.

Psychosocial models designed to explain and predict academic course choices (e.g., Eccles (Parsons) et al., 1983) have been useful in identifying a web of psychosocial variables that influence decisions to pursue language, mathematics, and science courses. Because the number of courses taken in an academic area is the best single predictor of ability test scores in that area, models that explain why females and males tend to enroll in different academic courses are extremely important in understanding the origins of cognitive sex differences. Few would doubt that anyone's decision to enroll in an academic course is influenced by her or his belief that the course is important, parental beliefs and pressures, expectations of success, and the other psychosocial variables identified in these models.

The national search for mathematically precocious youth has shown that for most of the youngsters who participated, sex was not an important variable in predicting test scores. The average between-sex difference was small. When this difference is considered in light of the psychosocial variables that contribute to mathematics course selection and the male sex typing of mathematics, biological explanations seem less likely. The largest sex differences were among the most highly gifted group in which the number of males was substantially higher than the number of females. The extreme differences in sex ratios among the most gifted youth probably fit less well in the psychosocial camp than the results obtained with the rest of the sample. It is possible that mathematical geniuses, who obviously comprise a very small percentage of the general population, belong somewhat closer to the biological end of the continuum than the rest of us. This possibility, of course, is highly speculative. Additional research on this select group of individuals is needed before any firm conclusions about those who are outstandingly gifted in mathematical ability can be made.

The finding that the effect size for all cognitive sex differences is decreasing strongly tips our hypothetical scale in the direction of psychosocial explanations. In other words, the average between-sex difference has been decreasing over time (Rosenthal & Rubin, 1982). In agreement with this conclusion, results of the International Science Study showed that while American males in grades 5, 9, and 12, are more knowledgeable about scientific principles than females, this gap is smaller than it was in 1970 (Walton, 1985). If we were to extrapolate from this trend, the convergence of male and female scores on tests of cognitive abilities would make the reason for this book moot. Of course the finding that effect sizes have been decreasing does not necessarily imply that they will disappear.

The largest cognitive sex difference effect size is found with tests of spatial ability. The finding that sex differences among preschool and elementary school-age children can be reduced and eliminated with spatial training and experience with spatial activities weakens biologically based explanations (e.g., Connor, Schackman, & Serbin, 1978). It is clear that with appropriate training, girls can perform at least some spatial tasks as well as boys. We do not know if sex differences in spatial ability can be eliminated with early and repeated spatial training because the longitudinal experiment has not been conducted.

Psychosocial hypotheses are also needed to explain the fact that there are few women professionals in the prestigious occupations that require high level verbal abilities. A majority of lawyers, judges, journalists, authors, and poets are male. If women are, in fact, innately superior in verbal abilities, and even if they are superior in verbal abilities for environmental reasons, the only possible explanations for their traditionally low level of participation in these areas are psychosocial—societal expectations, sex role pressures, male preemption, and discrimination. This statistic is changing as an increasing number of women pursue higher education in these areas and as female achievement becomes recognized and rewarded.

A Continuum of Results

As described in the preceding two sections, each of the experimental results can be placed somewhere along a hypothetical continuum anchored at one end by biological explanations and anchored at the other end by psychosocial explanations. I have placed some of the cognitive sex differences results along this continuum, as shown in Fig. 6.1. The relative placement of each finding was determined by the extent to which it conforms to biological or psychosocial hypotheses. Two types of results have been placed midway to indicate that they do not seem to favor either of the end points. The general category of cross-cultural data has been placed midway along this continuum because of the consistency of sex role stereotypes across the industrialized societies in which virtually all of the data are collected, difficulties in interpreting cross-cultural research, the possibility of restricted gene pools in isolated cultures, and general paucity of good quality comparable data on the topic. The finding that cognitive sex differences emerge most clearly at puberty has also been placed midway of the continuum. Puberty is a time of great biological and psychosocial change. While the clear emergence of cognitive sex differences at puberty could be due to sex differences in maturation rate, it could also be due to the increased adherence to sex role stereotypes among budding adults.

Biological Hypotheses

Sex by Handedness Interactions - The finding that scores
on tests of spatial and verbal abilities depend on both
an individual's sex and preferred hand (Harshman, Hampson,
& Berenbaum, 1983).

Three Spatial Ability Tests

Piaget's Water Level Test - Males score consistently
higher than females on a test of the knowledge that
water level remains horizontal when a glass is tipped
(Harris, 1975).

Mental Rotation - Large effect sizes are reported on this
novel test of visual-spatial ability (Sanders, Soares, &
D'Aquila, 1982).

Rod and Frame Test - Females are less accurate than males
when positioning a rod within a tilted frame (Witkin et al.,
1962).

Precocious Female Verbal Ability- Female infants are more
advanced in their language skills than male infants
(McGuiness, 1976).

Sex Differences in Cerebral Lateralization - Females maintain
a less lateralized brain organization than males (Levy & Reid,
1978).

Androgen at Puberty - Males with extremely low levels of androgens at puberty have impaired spatial skills (Hier & Crowley, 1982).

Mathematically Gifted Youth - Large disparities are found in sex
ratios among extremely mathematically gifted youth (Benbow & Stanley,
1980, 1983).

Cross-Cultural Data - Paucity of quality data and the possibility
of alternate explanations place this midway on the continuum.

Events at Puberty - Cognitive sex differences emerge most clearly
at puberty; however, both biological and psychosocial explanations
are possible.

Spatial Skills Training - Scores on spatial ability tests can be
improved with training (Connor, Schackman, & Serbin, 1978).

Average Math Differences - Small effect sizes are found for the
overwhelming majority of males and females (Benbow & Stanley,
1980, 1983).

Decreasing Effect Sizes - The effect size for cognitive sex differences has been decreasing over the last 20 years (Rosenthal &
Rubin, 1982).

Academic Choices - The number of women entering the math and science
fields has been increasing dramatically over the last 20 years.

Sex Ratios in Prestigious Occupations That Require Verbal Ability -
Although females tend to excel in berbal abilities, prestigious
occupations that require these abilities are predominantly filled
by males.

Psychosocial Hypotheses

FIG. 6.1. Experimental results distributed along a hypothetical continuum anchored at one end by biological explanations and at the other end by psychosocial
explanations.

Proportion of Explained Variance

As shown in Fig. 6.1 neither biological nor psychosocial hypotheses have emerged as a clear winner in their ability to account for all of the cognitive sex differences. This is, of course, no surprise for anyone who has ever tried to unravel the multiple determinants of cognitive abilities. In a recent discussion about this topic with friends, they asked me to give them the "bottom line." They didn't expect me to conclude that cognitive sex differences were due to either biology or environment. Instead they wanted to know how much of the differences were attributable to each of these positions. Unfortunately, I had to disappoint them because simple numerical answers cannot capture the nature of the multiple variables involved and their complex interactions.

Although most of the research into the questions of sex differences in cognitive abilities can be interpreted within the framework of the nature/nurture controversy, it is, in fact, an unresolvable controversy. Any given individual is a complete biological organism living in an environmental context. Females and males differ from each other in their biology in a number of salient ways; they also differ in their psychosocial environments. Given that these two types of differences are fully confounded, it is impossible to decide which of these differences is more important. This controversy can only be resolved by some future society in which the psychosocial environment does not vary as a function of biological sex. It is clear from the current research that biology is not destiny. Even if biological differences underlie some portion of the cognitive differences, there is ample evidence to conclude that under environmental conditions that encourage the total intellectual development of males and females the size of the sex differential in cognitive abilities can be reduced, and possibly even eliminated.

Multivariate Explanations

The nature/nurture dichotomy has created a framework that has guided much of the research on cognitive sex differences. As noted in numerous places throughout this book, there are problems inherent in the nature of this dichotomy. A dichotomy requires an either/or answer, or, at best, a "more or less" type answer. Instead, the only answer we have been able to provide is "sometimes." That is, sometimes the data can be interpreted as requiring a primarily environmental answer; other times the data require a primarily biological answer. Simple answers have failed to capture the elusive nature of cognitive sex differences, which seem to depend on a multitude of variables such as experience, adherence to stereotypes, and biological differences within and between the sexes.

Ultimately, the answers we accept as explanations of cognitive sex differences will be much more complex than a single point along a biological-psychosocial continuum. Although laws of parsimony require researchers to accept the simplest explanation of a phenomenon, there is little likelihood that we will be able to explain sex differences in verbal, spatial, and quantitative abilities with a simple answer. Like most researchers, I find beauty and elegance in simple answers—a single explanation for all of the differences. However, I do not believe that cognitive abilities are simply determined, nor do I believe that a single answer like, "It's all in the hormones" or "It's all because of mothers' attitudes" will ever emerge as the origin of all sex differences in cognitive abilities.

Whenever psychologists are faced with knotty problems like this one, they weave a nomological net, which is an interrelated network of variables designed to explain a phenomenon. Theories that incorporate the independent and joint effects of biology and environment are needed if we want to capture the nature of cognitive sex differences. Research is needed in which such measures of handedness, laterality, age at puberty, endorsement of sex role stereotypes, parents' endorsement of sex role stereotypes, and academic background and attitudes are considered simultaneously and in selected interactions. I believe that multivariate approaches that examine the most likely biological and psychosocial variables within the same study will be more fruitful in untangling the web of possible variables that contribute to sex differences in cognitive abilities. This sort of design will allow direct comparisons of effect sizes for the variables investigated and their interactions. (Effect size data are important in understanding the magnitude of the underlying phenomena.)

One possible model of the joint influences of biological and psychosocial variables is presented in Fig. 6.2. As shown in this figure, biological determi-

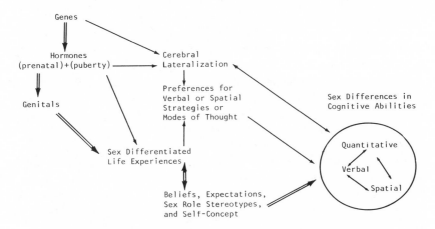

FIG. 6.2.   A model of the joint effects of biological and psychosocial variables on cognitive sex differences. The arrows linking these variables indicate the direction of an effect with double headed arrows representing the mutual effects of two variables on each other. Arrows drawn with single lines indicate weaker effects than arrows drawn with double lines.

nants of sex play a role in sex differentiation patterns of cerebral lateralization and in determining sex differentiated life experiences. Life experiences in turn affect self-concept including one's beliefs about her or his own abilities. The entire network of variables determine actual cognitive abilities. The arrows linking these variables indicate the direction of an effect with double headed arrows representing the mutual effects of two variables on each other. Arrows drawn with single lines represent weaker effects than arrow drawn with double lines.

NEW APPROACHES TO OLD PROBLEMS

Since the nature/nurture controversy has been found to be of limited usefulness, researchers need to construct new frameworks and new paradigms to answer old questions. For example, instead of arguing about the size of the sex difference in mathematical ability or whether it is better explained by biological or psychosocial explanations, researchers could be exploring the nature of the sex difference. Mayer (1985) reported that mathematical ability can be broken down into two component parts: (1) problem representation, which involves interpretation of the problem and some sort of mental representation of its salient features; and (2) problem solution, which involves manipulating the known information contained in the problem to derive the solution. These two parts of all mathematical problems can be investigated separately using methods currently available in cognitive psychology. Little is known about sex differences with respect to these component parts of mathematical ability. It would be useful to know if sex differences are found in one, both, or neither of these component parts.

Along similar lines, spatial ability and verbal ability can each be broken down into component parts. We know that all tests of spatial ability do not yield the same results. We should be analyzing the content of tests that consistently yield large sex differences and compare them to tests that usually yield small or no sex differences. By examining commonalities and differences among these tests, we could gain insight into exactly what it is that separates females from males on these tests. Verbal ability is also indexed in many ways, including word fluency, spelling, grammar, reading and oral comprehension. It would be useful to look at sex differences in each of these measures.

Another new or, at least underutilized, approach to the question of cognitive sex differences is to determine how sampling differences affect results. We know that sex differences in mathematical ability are large for adolescents who are extremely gifted in mathematics and small for the remaining majority of adolescents (Benbow & Stanley, 1983). We don't know if this finding is merely a statistical artifact of the way small mean differences affect differences in the tails of normally distributed distributions (as explained in Chapter 2) or whether mathematical geniuses are predominately male for an identifiable reason, either environmental, biological, or their interaction. For statistical reasons, we would expect similar differences among adolescents who are extremely gifted in verbal and spatial abilities with an overwhelming majority of the verbally gifted being female and a corresponding number of the "spatially gifted" being male. (The term "spatially gifted is never used, probably because it does not have an intuitive meaning, but it is a reasonable term in this context.) It would be interesting to see if these predictions are borne out.

A majority of the cognitive sex differences research has used students as subjects. Because only a small percentage of adults attend college, we may have been biasing our conclusions by extrapolating to all females and males from research conducted on a select group. Perhaps spatial skills are particularly high among males who attend college. It is possible that if we were to sample males in occupations that do not require a college degree, for example, salesmen, gas station attendents, laborers, gardeners, factory workers, we would not find them superior in spatial ability to a comparable group of females.

Sampling differences also need to be considered when discussing environmental variables. All Americans do not have similar environments. Research conducted with poor black, white, and Hispanic school children in large urban areas may not be applicable to wealthy children of any ethnicity in suburban areas or poor children in rural areas. Obviously, this caveat applies even more when researchers extrapolate their results as being applicable to all men and all women irrespective of their background or culture.

Another approach that is rarely used is to ask subjects directly about their mental processes. In one study where this technique was employed (Clarkson-Smith & Halpern, 1983), subjects who performed well on a mental rotation test reported that they used a mental rotation strategy while those subjects who performed poorly were unable to describe the strategy they used. As reported earlier (Chapter 3), we do not know why female performance is more variable in some visual spatial tasks and male performance is more variable in other sorts of visual spatial tasks. One way of investigating this question is to ask subjects what they are doing when they perform the task. It seems likely that we would find that subjects report strategy differences in how they approach these tasks.

It is also possible that we could learn a great deal by studying females with outstanding spatial and mathematical skills and males with outstanding verbal skills. Do they differ from other members of their sex in systematic ways? For example, do outstanding women mathematicians all come from families that rejected traditional sex role stereotypes or were they exposed to high levels of androgens when they were fetuses? Very little research has been conducted on subjects at the low end of the ability spectrum. What about males and females who are low in spatial ability or any other ability? Are they uniformly dull in all cognitive areas or does an uneven pattern of abilities help to suggest a cause for a specific deficit?

There is an endless list of research questions that can be generated. It remains the task of future research to find creative new ways of answering questions that may be as old as the human race.

INTO THE FUTURE

Unfortunately, there are no crystal balls to tell us about the changing nature of cognitive sex differences. No one believes that conclusions based on today's cognitive sex differences literature will remain unchanged even a few years from now. But where the changes will be and when they will occur is, of course, unknown. Predictions about future research results are always risky and sometimes humorous when viewed with the benefit of hindsight; yet, I believe that we will continue to find that the magnitude of all of the sex differences will diminish. Future technology may, however, create new sex differences. We know, for example, that many more males than females are pursuing careers in computer related fields (*Chronicle of Higher Education,* June 19, 1985). The nature of the skills required for success in computer-related occupations varies with different jobs. Some computer jobs, like documentation analyst or writer, require high verbal ability. Others, like programming in "low-level languages" require mathematical ability, and still others, like computer graphic designer, require spatial ability. It would seem that almost everyone could find a niche in a computer field. Yet, computer majors are predominantly male. If a major field of study becomes predominantly male or female, it seems likely that the skills stressed in that academic area will soon show sex differences.

Education for the Twenty-First Century

Today's young people are tomorrow's citizens, and our future is in their hands. How can we best prepare them for life in the twenty-first century and ensure that every individual develops her or his unique abilities to their fullest? Currently, we have reading and mathematics instruction in our schools with remedial programs for students with deficiencies in these areas. Given that we know that spatial skills are trainable, we should also be instituting spatial skills training for children from very young ages up through college. Remedial programs in spatial skills should also be offered for those with specific deficiencies in this area. We also need to try various ways of presenting material in all of the subject areas. Students should be taught how to solve problems using both verbal and spatial strategies, when appropriate. Spatial aspects of mathematics should be carefully diagrammed with special attention paid to converting word problems to other abstract representations and back again for all students—male and female.

We also need to provide role models of both sexes in all aspects of the curriculum and in occupations. We need male teachers in typing and home economics as much as we need female teachers in mathematics and science. Counselors and advisors need to assess carefully their own sex biases and stereotypes to be sure that they don't automatically steer students into sex stereotyped fields. Parents, the media, the corporate structure, and other aspects of society need to be educated, too. The collective mentality of our society needs to change so that Lincoln Logs, building blocks, erector sets, and models to be assembled—all toys that relate to the development of spatial abilities—are no longer labeled "Boy's Toys," while dolls, play kitchens, and pint-sized cleaning appliances are labeled "Girls' Toys." We cannot pretend that our children can choose for themselves when they have very little choice.

Sex Differences, So What!

What are the applied and practical implications of cognitive sex differences? Consider the following applied problem: It seems safe to assume that most Americans and American allies would agree that the U.S. Air Force should have highly qualified officers. In order to assure that this is so, prospective officers take a test (U.S. Air Force Officers Qualifying Test) that measures their verbal, quantitative, and spatial ability. In general, results obtained with this test agree with the sex differences literature in these areas, with females scoring higher on verbal ability and males scoring higher on quantitative and spatial ability. Since spatial ability seems particularly important for air force officers who often need to rely upon aerial landmarks and spatial coordinates, it is likely that many women are disqualified on the basis of this test.

In a recent examination of the question of whether females can, on the average, become as qualified for air force officer duties as men, McCloy and Koonce (1982) trained women and men on standard simulated flight maneuvers. They found that men were faster on learning the flight tasks than the women were. But, as they pointed out, is this the right question? The more important question concerns the level of ability after training. Were the women as good as men? The dependent measure in this study was number of trials to criterion. In other words, the women required more training trials than the men did to learn a particular task. Perhaps the most important point is that the women apparently were as good as the men when they completed the training. These results are in accord with the general finding that spatial skills are trainable.

We do not know why the women in this experiment required more trials to learn the same flight maneuvers as the men. It could be because of biological or psychosocial reasons, or both, or some other yet undiscovered difference between the sexes. While the etiology of cognitive sex differences is very important from a theoretical perspective, it is irrelevant in most applied settings. With appropriate training the sex differences can disappear. We also do not know if the women who received this training will be able to transfer their new spatial ability to other novel spatial tasks as quickly as the men can. In other words, if they are faced with a new and different spatial task, will they now perform it as quickly as their male counterparts? This remains as another important question for future research.

The example of the air force officers applies in other settings as well. Every teacher knows that some students will take longer to learn certain principles or concepts than others. If one student takes a half hour to complete a homework assignment and another student takes an hour, the difference is unimportant in most contexts. The important fact is that both students now know and understand something that they did not know before and, after training both are able to perform tasks that require the use of the newly acquired knowledge.

It is important to keep in mind a point that has been reiterated throughout this book. The experimental results that have been reviewed concern *average* differences obtained from groups of men and women, and no single individual is average. The data reviewed in this text are largely irrelevant when making decisions about individuals. They should never be used to justify or predict anyone's success or failure. There is considerable between-sex overlap with respect to these abilities, with large numbers of males demonstrating high verbal abilities and large numbers of females demonstrating high spatial and mathematical abilities.

The literature on sex differences has been proliferating in recent years because the questions are of profound human interest. The most important issue is not how men and women differ on the average. Keep in mind the words of Samuel Johnson, an eighteenth century British writer who was once asked who is smarter, men or women. He replied, "Which man—which woman?" The goal for future research and society is to find ways in which all people can develop their unique abilities and interests. We will need the best scientists, poets, and mathematicians, regardless of sex, if we are to survive as a society in the twenty-first century.

REFERENCES

Adair, J. G. (1973). *The human subject: The social psychology of the psychological experiment.* Boston: Little, Brown and Company.

Allgeier, E. R. (1983). Reproduction, roles and responsibilities. In E. R. Allgeier & N. B. McCormick (Eds.), *Changing boundaries: Gender roles and sexual behavior* (pp. 163–181). Palo Alto, CA: Mayfield Publishing Company.

Annett, M. (1980). Sex differences in laterality—meaningfulness versus reliability. *The Behavioral and Brain Sciences, 3* 227–263.

Backman, M. E. (1979). Patterns of mental abilities of adolescent males and females from different ethnic and socioeconomic backgrounds. In L. Willerman & R. G. Turner (Eds.), *Readings about individual and group differences* (pp. 261–265). San Francisco: W. H. Freeman.

Badger, M. E. (1981). Why aren't girls better at maths? A review of research. *Educational Research, 24,* 11–23.

Bandura, A., & Walters, R. H. (1963). *Social learning and personality development.* New York: Holt, Rinehart & Winston.

Baucom, D. H., & Welsh, G. S. (1978). In support of extreme groups design for studying masculinity–femininity and intelligence. *Intelligence, 2,* 6–10.

Becker, B. J., & Hedges, L. V. (1984). Meta-analysis of cognitive gender differences: A comment on an analysis by Rosenthal and Rubin. *Journal of Educational Psychology, 76,* 583–587.

Bem, S. L. (1974). The measurement of psychological androgyny. *Journal of Consulting and Clinical Psychology, 42,* 155–162.

Bem, S. L. (1981). Gender schema theory: A cognitive account of sex-typing. *Psychological Review, 88,* 354–364.

Bem, S. L., & Bem, D. J. (1973). Does sex-biased job advertising ''aid and abet'' sex discrimination? *Journal of Applied Social Psychology, 3,* 6–18.

Bem, S. L., & Bem, D. J. (1976). Training the woman to know her place: The power of a nonconscious ideology. In S. Cox (Ed.), *Female psychology: The emerging self* (pp. 180–190). Chicago: Science Research Associates.

Benbow, C. P., & Stanley, J. C. (1980). Sex differences in mathematical ability: Fact or artifact? *Science, 210,* 1262–1264.

Benbow, C. P., & Stanley, J. C. (1981). Mathematical ability: Is sex a factor? (Letters). *Science, 212*, 118–121.

Benbow, C. P., & Stanley, J. C. (1983). Sex differences in mathematical reasoning ability: More facts. *Science, 222*, 1029–1031.

Berenbaum, S. A., & Harshman, R. A. (1980). On testing group differences in cognition resulting from differences in lateral specialization: Reply to Fennell et al. *Brain and Language, 11*, 209–220.

Berry, J. W. (1966). Temne and Eskimo perceptual skills. *International Journal of Psychology, 1*, 207–229.

Bleier, R. (1984). *Science and gender: A critique of biology and its theories on women*. New York: Pergamon Press.

Block, J. H. (1973). Conceptions of sex roles: Some cross cultural and longitudinal perspectives. *American Psychologist, 28*, 512–526.

Block, J. H. (1976). Issues, problems, and pitfalls in assessing sex differences: A critical review of the Psychology of sex Differences. *Merrill Palmer Quarterly, 22*, 283–308.

Block, J. H. (1978). Another look at sex differentiation in the socialization behaviors of mothers and fathers. In J. A. Sherman & F. L. Denmark (Eds.), *The psychology of women: Future directions in research* (pp. 29–87). New York: Psychological Dimensions.

Bock, R. D., & Kolakowski, D. (1973). Further evidence of sex-linked major-gene influence on human spatial visualizing ability. *American Journal of Human Genetics, 25*, 1–14.

Boles, D. B. (1980). X-linkage of spatial ability: A critical review. *Child Development, 51*, 625–635.

Bouchard, T. J., Jr., & McGee, M. G. (1977). Sex differences in human spatial ability: Not an x-linked recessive gene effect. *Social Biology, 24*, 332–335.

Bradshaw, J. L., & Nettleton, N. C. (1983). *Human cerebral asymmetry*. Englewood Cliffs, NJ: Prentice-Hall.

Brinkmann, E. H. (1966). Programmed instruction as a technique for improving spatial visualization. *Journal of Applied Psychology, 50*, 179–184.

Brooks, I. R. (1976). Cognitive ability assessment with two New Zealand ethnic groups. *Journal of Cross-Cultural Psychology, 7*, 347–356.

Broverman, D. M., Klaiber, E. L., Kobayashi, Y., & Vogel, W. (1968). Roles of activation and inhibition in sex differences in cognitive abilities. *Psychological Review, 75*, 23–50.

Broverman, I. K., Vogel, S. R., Broverman, D. M., Clarkson, F. E., & Rosenkrantz, P. S. (1972). Sex-role stereotypes: A current appraisal. *Journal of Social Issues, 28*, 59–78.

Buffery, A. W. H., & Gray, J. A. (1972). Sex differences in the development of spatial and linguistic skills. In C. Ounsted & D. C. Taylor (Eds.), *Gender differences: Their ontogeny and significance* (pp. 123–157). Edinburgh: Churchill Livingstone.

Burnett, S. A., Lane, D. M., & Dratt, L. M. (1979). Spatial visualization and sex differences in quantitative ability. *Intelligence, 3*, 345–354.

Burnham, D. (1977). Biology and gender: False theories about women and blacks. *Freedomways, 17*, 8–13.

Burton, G. M. (1978). Why Susie can't—or doesn't want to—add. In J. E. Jacobs (Ed.), *Perspectives on women and mathematics* (pp. 35–57). Columbus, OH: Eric Clearinghouse for Science, Mathematics and Environmental Education.

Campbell, P. B. (1976). Adolescent intellectual decline. *Adolescence, 11*, 629–635.

Caplan, P. J., MacPherson, G. M., & Tobin, P. (1985). Do sex-related differences in spatial abilities exist? *American Psychologist, 40*, 786–799.

Carter, C. O. (1972). Sex-linkage and sex-limitation. In C. Ounsted & D. Taylor (Eds.), *Gender differences: Their ontogeny and significance* (pp. 1–12). Edinburgh: Churchill Livingstone.

Cattel, R. B. (1963). Theory of fluid and crystallized intelligence. *Journal of Educational Psychology, 54*, 1–22.

Christensen, L. B. (1985). *Experimental methodology (3rd Ed.)*, Boston: Allyn and Bacon, Inc.

Chronicle of Higher Education (June 19, 1985). Study funds 'gender gap' persists in high-tech jobs (p. 16).

Clarkson-Smith, L., & Halpern, D. F. (1983). Can age-related deficits in spatial memory be attenuated through the use of verbal coding? *Experimental Aging Research, 9*, 179–184.

Cohen, J. (1962). The statistical power of abnormal-social psychological research: A review. *Journal of Abnormal and Social Psychology, 65*, 145–153.

Cohen, J. (1965). Some statistical issues in psychological research. In B. B. Woleman (Ed.), *Handbook of clinical psychology* (pp. 95–121), New York: McGraw-Hill.

Cohen, J., & Cohen, P. (1983). *Applied multiple regression/correlation analysis for the behavioral sciences*. Hillsdale, NJ: Lawrence Erlbaum Associates.

Cole, M., & Scribner, S. (1974). *Culture and thought: A psychological introduction*. New York: Wiley.

Colley, A. (1984). Spatial location judgements by right and left-handers. *Cortex, 20*, 47–53.

Connor, J. M., Schackman, M., & Serbin, L. A. (1978). Sex-related differences in response to practice on a visual-spatial test and generalization to a related test. *Child Development, 49*, 24–29.

Constantinople, A. (1973). Masculinity-femininity: An exception to a famous dictum? *Psychological Bulletin, 80*, 389–407.

Cook, E. P. (1985). *Psychological androgyny*. New York: Pergamon Press.

Corballis, M. C., & Beale, I. L. (1983). *The ambivalent mind: The neuropsychology of left and right*. Chicago: Nelson-Hall.

Crosson, C. W. (1984). Age and field independence among women. *Experimental Aging Research, 10*, 165–170.

Dalton, K. (1976). Prenatal progesterone and educational attainments. *British Journal of Psychiatry, 129*, 438–442.

Day, J. (1977). Right-hemisphere language processing in normal right-handers. *Journal of Experimental Psychology: Human Perception and Performance, 3*, 518–528.

Deaux, K. (1984). From individual differences to social categories: Analysis of a decades research on gender. *American Psychologist, 39*, 105–116.

Deaux, K. (1985). Sex and gender. In M. R. Rosenzweig & L. W. Porter (Eds.), *Annual Reviews of Psychology, 36*, 49–81.

DeFries, J. C., Vandenberg, S. G., & McClearn, G. E. (1976). Genetics of specific cognitive abilities. *Annual Review of Genetics, 10*, 179–207.

de Groot, A. D. (1966). Perception and memory versus thought: Some old ideas and recent findings. In B. Kleinmuntz (Ed.), *Problem solving*. New York: Wiley.

Dimond, S. J., & Beaumont, J. G. (1974). Experimental studies of hemisphere function in the human brain. In S. J. Dimond & J. G. Beaumont (Eds.), *Hemisphere function in the human brain*. New York: Wiley.

Doering, C. H., Brodie, H. K. H., Fraemer, H., Becker, H., & Hamburg, O. (1974). Plasma testosterone levels and psychologic measures in men over a 2-month period. In R. C. Friedman & R. L. Vande Wiele (Eds.), *Sex differences in behavior: A conference*. New York: Wiley.

Eccles (Parsons), J. et al. (1983). Expectancies, values, and academic behaviors. In J. T. Spence (Ed.), *Achievement and achievement motives: Psychological and sociological approaches* (pp. 75–146). San Francisco: W. H. Freeman.

Ehrhardt, A. A., & Meyer-Bahlburg, H. F. L. (1979). Prenatal sex hormones and the developing brain: Effects on psychosexual differentiation and cognitive function. *Annual Review of Medicine, 30*, 417–430.

Elias, M. F., & Kinsbourne, M. (1974). Age and sex differences in the processing of verbal and nonverbal stimuli. *Journal of Gerontology, 29*, 162–171.

Eliot, J., & Fralley, J. S. (1976). Sex differences in spatial abilities. *Young Children, 31*, 487–497.

Elliot, R. (1961). Interrelationship among measures of field dependence, ability, and personality traits. *Journal of Abnormal and Social Psychology, 63,* 27–36.

Elmore, P. B., & Vasu, E. S. (1980). Relationship between selected variables and statistics achievement: Building a theoretical model. *Journal of Educational Psychology, 72,* 457–467.

Ernest, J. (1976). *Mathematics and sex.* Berkeley: University of California Press.

Etaugh, C. (1983). Introduction: The influences of environmental factors on sex differences in children's play. In M. B. Liss (Ed.), *Social and cognitive skills: Sex roles and children's play* (pp, 1–19). New York: Academic Press.

Evans, S. H., & Anastasio, E. J. (1968). Misuse of analysis of covariance when treatment effect and covariate are confounded. *Psychological Bulletin, 69,* 225–234.

Fairweather, H. (1976). Sex differences in cognition. *Cognition, 4,* 231–280.

Faust, M. S. (1977). Somatic development of adolescent girls. *Monographs of the Society for Research in Child Development, 42,* 1–90.

Faust, M. S. (1983). Alternative constructions of adolescent growth. In J. Brooks-Gunn & A. C. Petersen (Eds.), *Girls at puberty: Biological and psychosocial perspectives* (pp. 105–125). New York: Plenum Press.

Fennema, E., & Sherman, J. (1977). Sex-related differences in mathematics achievement, spatial visualization, and sociocultural factors. *Journal of Educational Research, 14,* 51–71.

Fennema, E., & Sherman, J. (1978). Sex-related differences in mathematics achievement and related factors: A further study. *Journal for Research in Mathematics Education, 9,* 189–203.

Fogel, R., & Paludi, M. A. (1984). Fear of success and failure or norms for achievement? *Sex Roles: A journal of Research, 10,* 431–434.

Fox, L. H., Tobin, D., & Brody, L. (1979). Sex role socialization and achievement in mathematics. In M. A. Wittig & A. C. Petersen (Eds.), *Sex-related differences in cognitive functioning* (pp. 303–332). New York: Academic Press.

Frisch, R. E. (1983). Fatness, puberty, and fertility: The effects of nutrition and physical training on menarche and ovulation. In J. Brooks-Gunn & A. C. Petersen (Eds.), *Girls at puberty: Biological and psycholosocial perspectives* (pp. 29–50). New York: Plenum Press.

Gelman, D., Carey, J., Gelman, E., Malamud, P., Foote, D., Lubenow, G. C., & Contreras, J. (1981, May 18). Just how the sexes differ. *Newsweek,* 77–83.

Geschwind, N. (1974). The anatomical basis of hemisphere differentiation. In S. J. Dimond & J. G. Beaumont (Eds.), *Hemisphere function in the human brain.* New York: Wiley.

Gersh, E. S., & Gersh, I. (1981). *Biology of women.* Baltimore, MD: University Park Press.

Gettys, L. D., & Cann, A. (1981). Children's perceptions of occupational sex stereotyping. *Sex Roles, 1,* 301–307.

Glass, G. V., McGaw, B., & Smith, M. L. (1981). *Meta-analysis in social research.* Beverly Hills, CA: Sage Publications.

Goldberg, P. (1968, April). Are some women prejudiced against women? *Transaction,* 28–30.

Golub, S. (1976). The effect of premenstrual anxiety and depression on cognitive function. *Journal of Personality and Social Psychology, 34,* 99–104.

Gottfried, A. W., & Bathurst, K. (1983). Hand preferences across time is related to intelligence in young girls, not boys. *Science, 221,* 1074–1076.

Gould, J. S. (1978). Women's brains. *Natural History, 87,* 44–50.

Gould, R. E. (1974). Measuring masculinity by the size of a paycheck. In J. H. Pleck & J. Sawyer (Eds.), *Men and masculinity* (pp. 96–100). Englewood Cliffs, NJ: Prentice-Hall.

Graham, M. F., & Birns, B. (1979). Where are the women geniuses? Up the down escalator. In C. B. Kopp & M. Kirkpatrick (Eds.), *Becoming female: Perspectives on development* (pp. 291–312). New York: Plenum Press.

Greenfield, P., & Lauber, B. (1985, March). *Cognitive effects of video games.* Paper presented at the Claremont Conference on Applied Cognitive Psychology. Claremont: CA.

Guilford, J. P. (1967). *The nature of human intelligence.* New York: McGraw-Hill.

Halpern, D. F. (1984a). *Thought and knowledge: An introduction to critical thinking*. Hillsdale, NJ: Lawrence Erlbaum Associates.

Halpern, D. F. (1984b). Age differences in response time to verbal and symbolic traffic signs. *Experimental Aging Research, 10,* 201–204.

Halpern, D. F. (1985). The influence of sex-role stereotypes on prose recall. *Sex Roles, 12,* 363–375.

Halpern, D. F. (in press). A different response to the question "Do sex differences in spatial abilities exist?" *American Psychologist.*

Halpern, D. F., & Kagan, S. (1984). Sex, age and cultural differences in individualism. *The Journal of Genetic Psychology, 145,* 23–35.

Hamburg, D. A., & Lunde, D. T. (1966). Sex hormones in the development of sex differences in human behavior. In E. E. Maccoby (Ed.), *The development of sex differences* (pp. 1–24), Stanford: Stanford University Press.

Hardyck, C., Petrinovich, L. F., & Goldman, R. D. (1976). Left-handedness and cognitive deficit. *Cortex, 12,* 266–279.

Harris, D. R., Bisbee, C. T., & Evans, S. H. (1971). Further comments-misuse of analysis of covariance. *Psychological Bulletin, 75,* 220–222.

Harris, L. J. (1975). Neurophysiological factors in the development of spatial skills. In J. Eliot & N. J. Salkind (Eds.), *Children's spatial development.* Springfield, IL: Charles C. Thomas.

Harris, L. J. (1978). Sex differences in spatial ability: Possible environmental, genetic, and neurological factors. In M. Kinsbourne (Ed.), *Asymmetrical functions of the brain* (pp. 405–522). Cambridge: Cambridge University Press.

Harris, M. J., & Rosenthal, R. (1985). Mediation of interpersonal expectancy effects: 31 meta-analyses. *Psychological Bulletin, 97,* 363–386.

Harshman, R. A., Hampson, E., Berenbaum, S. A. (1983). Individual differences in cognitive abilities and brain organization: Part I. Sex and handedness differences in ability. *Canadian Journal of Psychology, 37,* 144–192.

Haugh, S. S., Hoffman, C. D., & Cowan, G. (1980). The eye of the very young beholder: Sex typing of infants by younger children. *Child Development, 51,* 598–600.

Hays, W. L. (1963). *Statistics for psychologists.* New York: Holt, Rinehart & Winston.

Hays, W. L. (1981). *Statistics.* New York: Holt, Rinehart and Winston.

Hertzog, C., & Carter, L. (1982). Sex differences in the structure of intelligence: A confirmatory factor analysis. *Intelligence, 6,* 287–303.

Hier, D. B., & Crowley, W. F., Jr. (1982). Spatial ability in androgen-deficient men. *The New England Journal of Medicine, 306,* 1202–1205.

Hill, J. P., & Lynch, M. E. (1983). The intensification of gender-related role expectations during early adolescence. In J. Brooks-Gunn & A. C. Petersen (Eds.), *Girls at puberty: Biological and psychosocial perspectives* (pp. 201–228). New York: Plenum Press.

Hills, J. R. (1957). Factor analyzed abilities and success in college mathematics. *Educational Psychological Measurement, 17,* 615–622.

Hilton, T. L., & Berglund, G. W. (1974). Sex differences in mathematics achievement—A longitudinal study. *The Journal of Educational Research, 67,* 231–237.

Hines, M. (1982). Prenatal gonadal hormones and sex differences in human behavior. *Psychological Bulletin, 92,* 56–80.

Horner, M. S. (1969). Fail: Bright women. *Psychology Today, 3,* 36–38, 62.

Houser, B. B., & Garvey, C. (1985). Factors that affect nontraditional vocational enrollment among women. *Psychology of Women Quarterly, 9,* 105–117.

Hoyenga, K. B., & Hoyenga, K. T. (1979). *The question of sex differences: Psychological, cultural, and biological issues.* Boston: Little, Brown and Company.

Humphreys, L. G. (1978). Research on individual differences requires correlational analysis, not ANOVA. *Intelligence, 2,* 1–5.

Hunt, E. (1985). Verbal ability. In R. J. Sternberg (Ed.), *Human abilities: An information processing approach* (pp. 31–58). New York: W. H. Freeman.

Hyde, J. S. (1981). How large are cognitive gender differences? *American Psychologist, 36,* 892–901.

Hyde, J. S. (1985). *Half the human experience: The psychology of women* (3rd Ed.). Lexington, MA: D.C. Heath.

Hyde, J. S., Geiringer, E. R., & Yen, W. M. (1975). On the empirical relation between spatial ability and sex differences in other aspects of cognitive performance. *Multivariate Behavioral Research, 10,* 289–309.

Inglis, J., & Lawson, J. S. (1981). Sex differences in the effects of unilateral brain damage on intelligence. *Science, 212,* 693–695.

Janson-Smith, D. (1980). Sociobiology: So what? In the Brighton Women & Science Group. *Alice through the microscope* (pp. 62–86). London: Virago.

Johnson, C. D., & Gormly, J. (1972). Academic cheating: The contribution of sex, personality, and situational variables. *Developmental Psychology, 6,* 320–325.

Johnson, O., Harley, C. (1980). Handedness and sex differences in cognitive tests of brain laterality. *Cortex, 16,* 73–82.

Jones, L. V. (1984). White-black achievement differences: The narrowing gap. *American Psychologist, 39,* 1207–1213.

Kagan, J. (1982). The idea of spatial ability. *The New England Journal of Medicine, 306*(20), 1225–1227.

Kail, R., Carter, P., & Pellegrino, J. (1979). The locus of sex differences in spatial ability. *Perception & Psychophysics, 26,* 182–186.

Katcher, A. (1955). The discrimination of sex differences by young children. *Journal of Genetic Psychology, 87,* 131–143.

Keeton, W. T. (1967). *Biological science.* New York: W. W. Norton.

Kerlinger, F. N. (1979). *Behavioral research: A conceptual approach.* New York: Holt, Rinehart and Winston.

Kimura, D. (1969). Spatial localization in left and right visual fields. *Canadian Journal of Psychology, 23,* 445–458.

Kimura, D. (1983). Sex differences in cerebral organization for speech and praxic functions. *Canadian Journal of Psychology, 37,* 19–35.

Kimura, D. (1985). Male brain, female brain: the hidden difference. *Psychology Today, 19,* 50–52, 54, 55–58.

Kimura, D., & Durnford, M. (1974). Normal studies on the function of right hemisphere in vision. In S. J. Dimond & J. G. Beaumont (Eds.), *Hemisphere function in the human brain.* New York: Wiley.

Kitterle, F. L., Kaye, R. S. (1985). Hemispheric symmetry in contrast and oventation sensitivity. *Perception & Psychophysics, 37,* 391–396.

Koblinsky, S. G., Cruse, D. F., Sugawawa, A. I. (1978). Sex role stereotypes and children's memory for story content. *Child Development, 49,* 452–458.

Kogan, N. (1973). Creativity and cognitive style: A life-span perspective. In P. B. Baltes & K. W. Schale (Eds.), *Life-span developmental psychology: Personality and socialization.* New York: Academic Press.

Kohlberg, L. (1966). A cognitive-developmental analysis of children's sex-role concepts and attitudes. In E. E. Maccoby (Ed.), *The development of sex differences* (pp. 82–172). Stanford: Stanford University Press.

Kovac, D., & Majerova, M. (1974). Figure reproduction from the aspect of development and interfunctional relationships. *Studia Psychologica, 16,* 149–152.

Kuhn, D., Nash, S. C., & Brucken, L. (1978). Sex role concepts of two- and three-year olds. *Child Development, 49,* 445–451.

Lake, D. A., & Bryden, M. P. (1976). Handedness and sex differences in hemispheric asymmetry. *Brain and Language, 3,* 266–282.

Landauer, A. A. (1981). Sex differences in decision and movement time. *Perceptual & Motor Skills, 52,* 90.

Leacock, E. (1980). Social behavior, biology and the double standard. In G. W. Barlow & J. Silverberg (Eds.), *Sociobiology: Beyond nature/nurture* (pp. 465–488). Boulder, CO: Westview Press.

Leedy, P. D. (1981). *How to read research and understand it.* New York: Macmillan.

Lehrke, R. G. (1974). *X-linked mental retardation and verbal disability.* New York: Intercontinental Medical Book Corporation.

Levy, J. (1969). Possible basis for the evolution of lateral specialization of the human brain. *Nature, 224,* 614–615.

Levy, J. (1976). Cerebral lateralization and spatial ability. *Behavior Genetics, 6,* 171–188.

Levy, J., & Gur, R. C. (1980). Individual differences in psychoneurological organization. In J. Herron (Ed.), *Neuropsychology of left-handedness* (pp. 199–210). New York: Academic Press.

Levy, J., & Nagylaki, T. (1972). A model for the genetics of handedness. *Genetics, 72,* 117–128.

Levy, J., & Reid, M. (1978). Variations in cerebral organization as a function of handedness, handposture in writing, and sex. *Journal of Experimental Psychology: General, 107,* 119–144.

Levy-Agresti, J., & Sperry, R. W. (1968). Differential perceptual capacities in major and minor hemispheres. *Proceedings of the National Academy of Science U.S.A., 61,* 1151.

Liben, L. S., & Signorella, M. L. (1980). Gender-related schemata and constructive memory in children. *Child Development, 51,* 11–18.

Loehlin, J. C., Lindzey, G., & Spuhler, J. N. (1975). *Race differences in intelligence.* San Francisco: W. H. Freeman.

Loehlin, J. C., Sharan, S., & Jacoby, R. (1978). In pursuit of the ''spatial gene'': A family study. *Behavior Genetics, 8,* 27–41.

Lopata, H. Z., & Thorne, B. (1978). On the term ''sex roles.'' *Signs, 3,* 718–721.

Lott, B. (1985). The potential enrichment of social/personality psychology through feminist research and vice versa. *American Psychologist, 40,* 155–164.

Luchins, E. H. (1979). Women and mathematics: Fact and fiction. *American Mathematical Monthly, 88,* 413–419.

Luchins, E. H., & Luchins, A. S. (1981). (Letters) Mathematical ability: Is sex a factor? *Science, 212,* 116–118.

Lueptow, L. B. (1984). *Adolescent sex roles and social change.* New York: Columbia University Press.

Lynn, D. (1974). *The father: His role in child development.* Monterey, CA: Brooks/Cole.

Maccoby, E. E. (1966). Sex differences in intellectual functioning. In E. E. Maccoby (Ed.), *The development of sex differences* (pp. 25–55), Stanford: Stanford University Press.

Maccoby, E. E., & Jacklin, C. N. (1974). *The psychology of sex differences.* Stanford: Stanford University Press.

MacDonald, C. T. (1980). Facilitating women's achievement in mathematics. In L. H. Fox, L. Brody, & D. Tobin (Eds.), *Women and the mathematical mystique* (pp. 115–137). Baltimore, MD: The John Hopkins University Press.

MacKay, D. G. (1983). Prescriptive grammar and the pronoun problem. In B. Thorne, C. Kramarae, & N. Henley (Eds.), *Language, gender, and society* (pp. 38–53). Rowley, MA: Newbury House.

MacLusky, N. J., & Naftolin, F. (1981). Sexual differentiation of the central nervous system. *Science, 211,* 1294–1303.

Mandler, J. M., & Stein, N. L. (1977). The myth of perceptual defect: Sources and evidence. *Psychological Bulletin, 84,* 173–192.

Martin, C. L., & Halverson, C. F., Jr. (1981). A schematic processing model of sex typing and stereotyping in children. *Child Development, 52,* 1119–1134.

Mayer, R. (1985). Mathematical ability. In R. J. Sternberg (Ed.), *Human abilities: An information processing approach* (pp. 127–150). New York: W. H. Freeman.

Mazur, A., & Robertson, L. S. (1972). *Biology and social behavior.* New York: The Free Press.

McCloy, T. M., & Koonce, J. M. (1982). Sex as a moderator variable in the selection and training of persons for a skilled task. *Aviation, Space, and Environmental Medicine, 53,* 1170–1172.

McEwen, B. S. (1981). Neural gonadal steroid actions. *Science, 211,* 1303–1311.

McGee, M. G. (1979). Human spatial abilities: Psychometric studies and environmental, genetic, hormonal, and neurological influences. *Psychological Bulletin, 86,* 889–918.

McGlone, J. (1980). Sex differences in human brain asymmetry: A critical survey. *The Behavioral and Brain Sciences, 3,* 215–227.

McGuiness, D. (1976). Sex differences in the organization of perception and cognition. In B. Lloyd & J. Archer (Eds.), *Exploring sex differences* (pp. 123–156). New York: Academic Press.

McKeever, W. F., & Van Deventer, A. D. (1977). Visual and auditory language processing asymmetries: Influence of handedness, familial sinistrality, and sex. *Cortex, 13,* 225–241.

Meece, J. L., Eccles-Parsons, J., Kaczala, C. M., Goff, S. B., & Futterman, R. (1982). Sex differences in math achievement: Toward a model of academic choice. *Psychological Bulletin, 91,* 324–448.

Meeker, B. F., & Weitzel-O'Neill, P. A. (1977). Sex roles and interpersonal behavior in task-oriented groups. *American Sociological Review, 42,* 91–104.

Meyer-Bahlburg, H. F. L., & Ehrhardt, A. A. (1977). Effects of prenatal hormone treatment on mental abilities. In R. Gemme & C. C. Wheeler (Eds.), *Progress in sexology* (pp. 85–92), New York: Plenum.

Mills, C. J. (1981). Sex roles, personality, and intellectual abilities in adolescents. *Journal of Youth and Adolescence, 10,* 85–112.

Mischel, W. (1966). A social-learning view of sex differences in behavior. In E. E. Maccoby (Ed.), *The development of sex differences* (pp. 56–81). Stanford: Stanford University Press.

Money, J. (1975). Ablatio penis: Normal male infant sex-reassigned as a girl. *Archives of Sexual Behavior, 4,* 65–72.

Money, J., & Ehrhardt, A. A. (1972). *Man & woman, boy & girl.* Baltimore, MD: The Johns Hopkins University Press.

Moore, T. (1967). Language and intelligence: A longitudinal study of the first eight years. *Human Development, 10,* 88–106.

Nagae, S. (1985). Handedness and sex differences in selective interference of verbal and spatial information. *Journal of Experimental Psychology: Human Perception and Performance. 11,* 346–354.

Nash, S. C. (1975). The relationship among sex-role stereotyping, sex-role preference, and the sex difference in spatial visualization. *Sex Roles, 1,* 15–32.

Nash, S. C. (1979). Sex role as a mediator of intellectual functioning. In M. A. Wittig & A. C. Petersen (Eds.), *Sex-related differences in cognitive functioning: Developmental issues* (pp. 263–302). New York: Academic Press.

O'Kelly, C. G. (1980). *Women and men in society.* New York: Van Nostrand.

Orwin, R. G., & Cordray, D. S. (1985). Effects of deficient reporting on meta-analysis: A conceptual framework and reanalysis. *Psychological Bulletin, 97,* 134–147.

Perry, D. G., & Bussey, K. (1979). The social learning theory of sex differences: imitation is alive and well. *Journal of Personality and Social Psychology, 37,* 1699–1712.

Petersen, A. C. (1976). Physical androgyny and cognitive functioning in adolescence. *Developmental Psychology, 12,* 524–533.

Petersen, A. C., & Crockett, L. (1985, August). Factors influencing sex differences in spatial ability during adolescence. In S. L. Willis (Chair), Sex differences in spatial ability across the lifespan. *Symposium conducted at the Ninety-third Annual Convention of the American Psychological Association*, Los Angeles, CA.

Pheterson, G. I., Kiesler, S. B., & Goldberg, P. A. (1971). Evaluation of the performance of women as a function of their sex, achievement, and personal history. *Journal of Personality and Social Psychology, 19,* 114–118.

Piaget, J., & Inhelder, B. (1956). *The child's conception of space.* London: Routledge Kegan Paul.

Piazza, D. M. (1980). The influence of sex and handedness in the hemispheric specialization of verbal and nonverbal tasks. *Neuropsychologia, 18,* 163–176.

Plake, B. S., Loyd, B. H., & Hoover, H. D. (1981). Sex differences in mathematics components of the Iowa Test of Basic Skills. *Psychology of Women Quarterly, 5,* 780–784.

Plomin, R., & Foch, T. T. (1981). Sex differences and individual differences. *Child Development, 52,* 383–385.

Poole, C., & Stanley, G. (1972). A factorial and predictive study of spatial abilities. *Australian Journal of Psychology, 24,* 317–320.

Ray, W. J., Georgiou, S., & Ravizza, R. (1979). Spatial abilities, sex differences, and lateral eye movements. *Developmental Psychology, 15,* 455–457.

Ray, W. J., Newcombe, N., Semon, J., & Cole, P. M. (1981). Spatial abilities, sex differences and EEG functioning. *Neuropsychologia, 19,* 719–722.

Reinisch, J. (1981). Prenatal exposure to synthetic progestins increases potential for aggression in humans. *Science, 211,* 1171–1173.

Richardson, J. T. (1976). How to measure laterality. *Neuropsychologia, 14,* 135–136.

Rohrbaugh, J. B. (1979). *Women: Psychology's puzzle.* New York: Basic Books.

Rosenthal, R. (1966). *Experimenter effects in behavioral research.* New York: Appleton-Century-Crofts.

Rosenthal, R., & Rubin, D. B. (1982). Further meta-analytic procedures for assessing cognitive gender differences. *Journal of Educational Psychology, 74,* 708–712.

Rosenthal, R., & Rubin, D. B. (1985). Statistical analysis: Summarizing evidence versus establishing facts. *Psychological Bulletin, 97,* 527–529.

Rossi, J. S. (1983). Ratios exaggerate gender differences in mathematical ability. *American Psychologist, 38,* 348.

Rovet, J., & Netley, C. (1979). Phenotypic vs. genotypic sex and cognitive abilities. *Behavior Genetics, 9,* 317–321.

Rozeboom, W. W. (1960). The fallacy of the null-hypothesis significance test. *Psychological Bulletin, 57,* 416–428.

Rubin, J., Provenzano, F., & Luria, Z. (1974). The eye of the beholder: Parents' views on sex of newborns. *American Journal of Orthopsychiatry, 44,* 512–519.

Rudel, R. G., Denckla, M. B., & Spalten, E. (1973). The functional asymmetry of Braille letter learning in normal sighted children. *Neurology, 24,* 733–738.

Sadker, M., & Sadker, D. (1985). Sexism in the schoolroom of the 80's. *Psychology Today, 19,* 54–57.

Sanders, B., Soares, M. P., & D'Aquila, J. M. (1982). The Sex difference on one test of spatial visualization: A nontrivial difference. *Child Development, 53,* 1106–1110.

Sells, L. W. (1980). The mathematics filter and the education of women and minorities. In L. H. Fox, L. Brody, & D. Tobin (Eds.), *Women and the mathematical mystique* (pp. 66–75). Baltimore, MD: The Johns Hopkins University Press.

Seward, J. P., & Seward G. H. (1980). *Sex differences: Mental and tempermental, Lexington, MA: D. C. Heath.*

Shepard, R. N., & Metzler, J. (1971). *Mental rotation of three dimensional objects. Science, 171,* 701–703.

Sherman, J. A. (1967). Problems of sex differences in space perception and aspects of intellectual functioning. *Psychological Review, 74,* 290–299.

Sherman, J. A. (1977). Effects of biological factors on sex-related differences in mathematics achievement. In L. H. Fox, E. Fennema, & J. Sherman (Eds.), *Women and mathematics: Research perspectives for change* (pp. 137–206). Washington, D.C.: National Institute of Education.

Sherman, J. A. (1978). *Sex-related cognitive differences: An essay on theory and evidence.* Springfield, IL: Charles C. Thomas.

Sherman, J. A. (1979). Cognitive Performance as a function of sex and handedness: An evaluation of the Levy hypothesis. *Psychology of Women Quarterly, 3,* 378–390.

Sherman, J. A. (1980). Mathematics, spatial visualization, and related factors: Changes in girls and boys grades 8–11. *Journal of Educational Psychology, 72,* 476–482.

Sherman, J. A. (1982a). Continuing in mathematics: A longitudinal study of the attitudes of high school girls. *Psychology of Women Quarterly, 72,* 132–140.

Sherman, J. A. (1982b). Mathematics the critical filter: A look at some residues. *Psychology of Women Quarterly, 6,* 428–444.

Sherman, J. A. (1983). Girls talk about mathematics and their future: A partial replication. *Psychology of Women Quarterly, 7,* 338–342.

Shields, S. A. (1975). Functionalism, Darwinism, and the psychology of women. *American Psychologist, 30,* 739–754.

Shields, S. A. (1980). Nineteenth-century evolutionary theory and male scientific bias. In G. W. Barlow & J. Silverberg (Eds.), *Sociobiology: Beyond nature/nurture* (pp. 489–502). Boulder, CO: Westview Press.

Shuter-Dyson, R., & Gabriel, C. (1982). *The psychology of musical ability (2nd Ed.).* London: Methuen.

Singer, G., & Montgomery, R. B. (1969). Comment on "role of activation and inhibition in sex differences in cognitive abilities." *Psychological Review, 76,* 325–327.

Smith, W. S., Frazier, N. I., Ward, S., & Webb, F. (1983). Early adolescent girls' and boys' learning of a spatial visualization skill-replications. *Journal of Education, 67,* 239–243.

Spence, J. T., & Helmreich, R. (1978). *Masculinity and femininity: Their psychological dimensions, correlates, and antecedents.* Austin: University of Texas Press.

Spence, J. T., & Helmreich, R. L. (1983). Achievement-related motives and behaviors. In J. T. Spence (Ed.), *Achievement and achievement motives: Psychological and sociological approaches* (pp. 7–74). San Francisco: W. H. Freeman.

Spence, J. T., Helmreich, R. L., & Stapp, J. (1974). The personal attributes questionnaire: A measure of sex role stereotypes and masculinity-femininity. *JSAS Catalog of Selected Documents in Psychology, 4,* 43.

Sprafkin, C., Serbin, L. A., Denier, C., & Connor, J. M. (1983). Sex-differentiated play: Cognitive consequences and early interventions. In M. B. Liss (Ed.), *Social and cognitive skills* (pp. 167–192). New York: Academic Press.

Springer, S. P., & Deutsch, G. (1981). *Left brain, right brain.* New York: W. H. Freeman.

Stafford, R. E. (1961). Sex differences in spatial visualization as evidence of sex-linked inheritance. *Perceptual and Motor Skills, 13,* 428.

Stafford, R. E. (1963). An investigation of similarities in parent-child test scores for evidence of hereditary components. (RB-63-11). Princeton: Educational Testing Service.

Stafford, R. E. (1972). Hereditary and environmental components of quantitative reasoning. *Review of Educational Research, 42,* 183–201.

Stage, E. K., & Karplus, R. (1981). (Letters) Mathematical ability: Is sex a factor? *Science, 212,* 114.

Stanley, J. C., & Benbow, C. P. (1982). Huge sex ratios at upper end. *American Psychologist, 37,* 972.

Stewart, V. (1976). Social influences on sex differences in behavior. In M. S. Teitelbaum (Ed.), *Sex differences: Social and biological perspectives* (pp. 138–174). Garden City, NY: Anchor Books.

Stones, I., Beckmann, M., & Stephens, L. (1982). Sex-related differences in mathematical competencies of pre-calculus college students. *School Science and Mathematics, 82*, 295–299.

Tavris, C., & Offir, C. (1977). *The longest war: Sex differences in perspective.* New York: Harcourt Brace Jovanovich.

Teng, E. L. (1981). Dichotic ear difference is a poor index for the functional symmetry between the cerebral hemispheres. *Neuropsychologia, 19*, 235–240.

Thomas, H. (1983). Familial correlational analyses, sex differences, and the x-linked gene hypothesis. *Psychological Bulletin, 93*, 427–440.

Thomas, H., Jamison, W., & Hammel, D. D. (1973). Observation is insufficient for discovering that the surface of still water is invariantly horizontal. *Science, 181*, 173–174.

Thurstone, L. L., & Thurstone, T. G. (1941). *Factorial studies of intelligence.* Chicago: University of Chicago Press.

Tiger, L. (1970, October). Male dominance? Yes, Alas. A sexist ploy? No. *The New York Times Magazine* (pp. 35–37, 124–127, 132–138).

Tinkcom, M., Obrzut, J. E., & Poston, C. S. (1983). Spatial lateralization: The relationship among sex, handedness and familial sinistrality. *Neuropsycholia, 21*, 683–686.

Tomizuka, C., & Tobias, S. (1981). (Letters) Mathematical ability: Is sex a factor? *Science, 212*, 114.

Unger, R. K. (1979). *Female and male: Psychological perspectives.* New York: Harper & Row.

Vandenberg, S. G. (1968). Primary mental abilities or general intelligence? Evidence from twin studies. In J. M. Thoday & A. S. Parkes (Eds.), *Genetic and environmental influences on behavior* (pp. 146–160). New York: Plenum.

Vandenburg, S. G. (1969). A twin study of spatial ability. *Multivariate Behavioral Research, 4*, 273–294.

Waber, D. P. (1976). Sex differences in cognition: A function of maturation rate? *Science, 192*, 572–574.

Waber, D. P. (1977). Sex differences in mental abilities, hemispheric lateralization, and rate of physical growth at adolescence. *Developmental Psychology, 13*, 29–38.

Walton, S. (1985). Girls and science: The gap remains. *Psychology Today, 19*, 14.

Wechsler, D. (1955). *Manual for the Wechsler Adult Intelligence Scale.* New York: Psych Corp.

Weisstein, N. (1972). *Psychology constructs the female.* In V. Gornick & B. K. Moran (Eds.), *Women in sexist society* (pp. 207–224). New York: New American Library.

Weisstein, N. (1982, November). Tired of arguing about biological inferiority? *Ms.*, 41–46, 85.

Westkott, M. (1979). Feminist criticism of the social sciences. *Harvard Educational Review, 49*, 422–430.

Williams, J. E., & Best, D. L. (1982). *Measuring sex stereotypes. A thirty-nine nation study.* Beverly Hills, CA: Sage Publications.

Williams, J. H. (1977). *Psychology of women: Behavior in a biosocial context.* New York: W. W. Norton.

Williams, J. H. (1983). *Psychology of women: Behavior in a biosocial context* (2nd Ed.). New York: W. W. Norton.

Winograd, E., & Simon, E. V. (1980). Visual memory and imagery in the aged. In L. W. Poon, J. L. Fozard, L. S. Cermak, D. Arenberg, & L. W. Thompson (Eds.), *New directions in memory and aging: Proceedings of the George A. Talland Memorial Conference* (pp. 485–506). Hillsdale, NJ: Lawrence Erlbaum Associates.

Witelson, S. F. (1976). Sex and the single hemisphere: Specialization of the right hemisphere for spatial processing. *Science, 193*, 425–427.

Witkin, H. A. (1950). Individual differences in ease of perception of embedded figures. *Journal of Personality, 19*, 1–15.

Witkin, H. A., Dyk, R. B., Faterson, H. F., Goodenough, D. G., & Karp, S. A. (1962). *Psychological differentiation.* New York: Wiley.

Witkin, H. A., Lewis, H. B., Hertzman, M., Machover, K., Meissner, P. B., & Wapner, S. (1954). *Personality through perception.* New York: Harper & Row.

Wittig, M. A. (1985). Metatheoretical dilemmas in the psychology of gender. *American Psychologist, 40,* 800–811.

Wrightsman, L. S. (1977). *Social psychology, 2nd Ed..* Monterey, CA: Brooks/Cole.

Yeo, R. A., & Cohen, D. B. (1983). Familiar sinistrality and sex differences in cognitive abilities. *Cortex, 19,* 125–130.

Author Index

Number in *italics* indicate pages with complete bibliographic information.

A

Adair, J. G., 24, *163*
Allgeier, E. R., 131, *163*
Anastasio, E. J., 26, *166*
Annett, M. 91, *163*

B

Backman, M. E., 64, *163*
Badger, M. E., 57, *163*
Bandura, A., 117, *163*
Bathurst, K., 88, *166*
Baucom, D. H., 30, *163*
Beale, I. L., 48, *165*
Beaumont, J. G., 82, *165*
Becker, B. J., 26, *163*
Becker, H., 100, *165*
Beckmann, M., 58, *173*
Bem, D. J., 109, *163*
Bem, S. L., 109, 110, 114, 118, 119, *163*
Benbow, C. P., 58, 63, 127, 158, *163, 164, 172*
Berenbaum, S. A., 29, 86, 87, 103, *164, 167*
Berglund, G. W., 57, 136, *167*

Berry, J. W., 149, *164*
Best, D. L., 147, *173*
Birns, B., 122, *166*
Bisbee, C. T., 26, *167*
Bleier, R., 4, 98, *164*
Block, J. H., 35, 121, *164*
Bock, R. D., 71, *164*
Boles, D. B., 72, *164*
Bouchard, T. J., Jr., 49, 63, 72, *164*
Bradshaw, J. L., 139, *164*
Brinkman, E. H., 134, *164*
Brodie, H. K. H., 100, *165*
Brody, L., 139, *166*
Brooks, I. R., 149, *164*
Broverman, D. M., 10, 100, 111, *164*
Broverman, I. K., 10, 111, *164*
Brucken, L., 122, *168*
Bryden, M. P., 82, *169*
Burnett, S. A., 48, 50, 57, 59, 63, *164*
Burnham, D., 77, *164*
Burton, G. M., 113, *164*
Bussey, K., 123, *170*

C

Campbell, P. B., 126, *164*
Cann, A., 122, *166*
Caplan, P. J., 49, *164*
Carey, J., 61, 63, *166*

Carter, C. O., 70, *164*
Carter, L., 65, *167*
Carter, P., 50, *168*
Cattel, R. B., 5, 24, *164, 165*
Clarkson, F. E., 10, 111, *164*
Clarkson-Smith, L., 51, 101, 159, *165*
Cohen, D. B., 89, *174*
Cohen, J., 27, 60, 62, *165*
Cohen, P., 27, *165*
Cole, M., 146, *165*
Cole, P. M., 82, 84, *171*
Colley, A., 89, *165*
Connor, J. M., 133, 154, *165, 172*
Constantinople, A., 114, *165*
Contreras, J., 61, 63, *166*
Cook, E. P., 114, *165*
Corballis, M. C., 48, *165*
Cordray, D. S., 38, *170*
Cowan, G., 122, *167*
Crocket, L., 51, 62, 84, 97, *170, 171*
Crosson, C. W., 55, *165*
Crowley, W. F., Jr., 98, 104, 151, *167*
Cruse, D. F., 119, *168*

D

Dalton, K., 95, *165*
D'Aquila, J. M., 49, 62, *171*
Day, J., 82, *165*
Deaux, K., 11, 111, 122, 126, *165*
DeFries, J. C., 72, *165*
de Groot, A. D., 56, *165*
Denckla, M. B., 85, *171*
Denier, C., 133, *172*
Deutsch, G., 56, 78, 83, 90, *172*
Diamond, S. J., 82, *165*
Doering, C. H., 100, *165*
Dratt, L. M., 48, 50, 57, 59, 63, *164*
Durnford, M., 82, *168*
Dyk, R. B., 53, 54, *173*

E

Eccles (Parsons), J., 138, 139, 153, *165*
Ehrhardt, A. A., 75, 95, 96, *165, 170*
Elias, M. F., 51, *165*
Eliot, J., 69, *165*
Elliot, R., 54, *166*
Elmore, P. B., 137, *166*
Ernest, J., 10, 135, 137, 138, *166*
Etaugh, C., 122, *166*
Evans, S. H., 26, *166, 167*

F

Fairweather, H., 146, *166*
Faterson, H. F., 53, 54, *173*
Faust, M. S., 83, 125, *166*
Fennema, E., 18, 49, 59, 138, *166*
Fach, T. T., 61, *171*
Fogel, R., 131, *166*
Foote, D., 61, 63, *166*
Fox, L. H., 139, *166*
Fraemer, H., 100, *165*
Fralley, J. S., 69, *165*
Frazier, N. I., 134, *172*
Frisch, R. E., 102, *166*

G

Garvey, C., 138, *167*
Geiringer, E. R., 55, 59, 65, 132, *168*
Gelman, D., 61, 63, *166*
Gelman, E., 61, 63, *166*
Georgiou, S., 82, *171*
Gersh, E. S., 57, 75, *166*
Gersh, I., 57, 75, *166*
Geschwind, N., 78, 79, *166*
Gettys, L. D., 122, *166*
Glass, G. V., 36, *166*
Goldberg, P. A., 129, *166, 171*
Goldman, R. D., 87, *167*
Golub, S., 101, *166*
Goodenough, D. G., 53, 54, *173*
Gormly, J., 46, *168*
Gottfried, A. W., 88, *166*
Gould, J. S., 9, 77, *166*
Gould, R. E., 128, *166*
Graham, M. F., 122, *166*
Greenfield, P., 127, *166*
Guilford, J. P., 5, *166*

H

Halpern, D. F., 5, 11, 17, 51, 101, 113, 119,
    131, 159, *165, 167*
Halverson, C. F., Jr., 119, *170*
Hamburg, D. A., 125, *167*
Hamburg, O., 100, *165*
Hammel, D. D., 134, *173*
Hampson, E., 29, 87, 103, *167*
Hardyck, C., 87, *167*
Harley, C., 89, *168*
Harris, D. R., 26, *167*
Harris, L. J., 52, 63, 148, *167*

Harris, M. J., 136, *167*
Harshman, R. A., 29, 86, 87, 103, *164, 167*
Haugh, S. S., 122, *167*
Hays, W. L., 37, *167*
Hedges, L. V., 26, *163*
Helmreich, R. L., 111, 114, 131·, *172*
Hertzman, M., 55, *174*
Hertzog, C., 65, *167*
Hier, D. B., 98, 104, 151, *167*
Hill, J. P., 126, *167*
Hills, J. R., 59, *167*
Hilton, T. L., 57, 136, *167*
Hines, M., 95, 96, *167*
Hoffman, C. D., 121, *167*
Hoover, H. D., 57, *171*
Horner, M. S., 130, *167*
Houser, B. B., 138, *167*
Hoyenga, K. B., 122, *167*
Hoyenga, K. T., 122, *167*
Humphreys, L. G., 30, *167*
Hunt, E., 59, *168*
Hyde, J. S., 46, 55, 59, 61, 62, 63, 65, 91, 119, 132, *168*

I

Inglis, J., 83, *168*
Inhelder, B., 52, *171*

J

Jacklin, C. N., 28, 35, 46, 50, 51, 59, 61, 112, *169*
Jacoby, R., 72, *169*
Jamison, W., 134, *173*
Janson-Smith, D., 4, *168*
Johnson, C. D., 46, *168*
Johnson, O., 89, *168*
Jones, L. V., 57, 58, 136, *168*

K

Kagan, J., 49, *168*
Kagan, S., 131, *167*
Kail, R., 50, *168*
Karp, S. A., 53, 54, *173*
Karplus, R., 117, *172*
Katcher, A., 116, *168*
Kaye, R. S., 79, *168*
Keeton, W. T., 75, *168*
Kerlinger, F. N., 23, 65, *168*
Kiesler, S. B., 129, *171*

Kimura, D., 82, 83, 90, 93, *168*
Kinsbourne, M., 51, *165*
Kitterle, F. L., 79, *168*
Klaiber, E. L., 100, *164*
Kobayashi, Y., 100, *164*
Koblinsky, S. G., 119, *168*
Kogan, N., 53, *168*
Kohlberg, L., 118, 119, *168*
Kolakowski, D., 71, *164*
Koonce, J. M., 161, *170*
Kovac, D., 148, *168*
Kuhn, D., 121, *168*

L

Lake, D. A., 82, *169*
Landauer, A. A., 16, *169*
Lane, D. M., 48, 50, 57, 59, 63, *164*
Lauber, B., 127, *166*
Lawson, J. S., 83, *168*
Leacock, E., 148, *169*
Leedy, P. D., 24, *169*
Lehrke, R. G., 73, *169*
Levy, J., 77, 80, 81, 82, 84, 85, 87, 89, *169*
Levy-Agresti, J., 80, *169*
Lewis, H. B., 55, *174*
Liben, L. S., 119, *169*
Lindzey, G., 49, *169*
Lochlin, J. C., 49, 72, *169*
Lopata, H. Z., 112, *169*
Lott, B., 9, *169*
Loyd, B. H., 57, *171*
Lubenow, G. C., 61, 63, *666*
Luchins, A. S., 135, *169*
Luchins, E. H., 59, 135, *169*
Lueptow, L. B., 112, *169*
Lunde, D. T., 125, *167*
Luria, Z., 121, *171*
Lynch, M. E., 126, *167*
Lynn, D., 116, *169*

M

Maccoby, E. E., 28, 35, 46, 50, 51, 59, 61, 99, 112, *169*
MacDonald, C. T., 136, *169*
Machover, K., 55, *174*
MacKay, D. G., 13, 109, *169*
MacLusky, N. J., 93, *169*
MacPherson, G. M., 49, *164*
Majerova, M., 148, *168*
Malamud, P., 61, 63, *166*

Mandler, J. M., 49, *169*
Martin, C. L., 119, *170*
Mayer, R., 158, *170*
Mazur, A., 125, *170*
McClearn, G. E., 72, *165*
McCloy, T. M., 161, *170*
McEwen, B. S., 93, *170*
McGaw, B., 36, *166*
McGee, M. G., 49, 63, 72, 99, *164, 170*
McGlone, J., 83, 84, 90, 105, *170*
McGuiness, D., 47, 56, *170*
McKeever, W. F., 86, 89, *170*
Meece, J. L., 58, *170*
Meissner, P. B., 55, *174*
Metzler, J., 51, *171*
Meyer-Bahlburg, H. F. L., 95, 96, *165, 170*
Mills, C. J., 114, *170*
Mischel, W., 117, *170*
Money, J., 12, 75, *170*
Montgomery, R. B., 100, *172*
Moore, T., 47, *170*

N

Naftolin, F., 93, *169*
Nagae, S., 89, *170*
Nash, 115, 122, 126, *168, 170*
Netley, C., 74, *171*
Nettleton, N. C., 139, *164*
Newcombe, N., 82, 84, *171*

O

Obrzut, J. E., 89, *173*
Offir, C., 147, *173*
O'Kelly, C. G., 5, *170*
Orwin, R. G., 38, *170*

P

Paludi, M. A., 131, *166*
Pellegrino, J., 50, *168*
Perry, D. G., 123, *170*
Peterson, A. C., 51, 62, 84, 97, 98, *170, 171*
Petrinovich, L. F., 87, *167*
Pheterson, G. I., 129, *171*
Piaget, J., 52, *171*
Piazza, D. M., 89, *171*
Plake, B. S., 57, *171*
Plomin, R., 61, *171*
Poole, C., 48, *171*

Poston, C. S., 89, *173*
Provenzana, F., 121, *171*

R

Ravizza, R., 82, *171*
Ray, W. J., 82, 84, *171*
Reinisch, J., 94, *171*
Richardson, J. T., 86, *171*
Robertson, L. S., 125, *170*
Rohrbaugh, J. B., 73, *171*
Rosenkrantz, P. S., 10, 111, *164*
Rosenthal, R., 24, 41, 64, 137, 141, 142, 153, *167, 171*
Rossi, J. S., 58, *171*
Rovet, J., 74, *171*
Rozeboom, W. W., 24, *171*
Rubin, D. B., 24, 64, 141, 142, 153, *171*
Rubin, J., 121, *171*
Rudel, R. G., 85, *171*

S

Sadker, D., 10, 123, 148, *171*
Sadker, M., 10, 123, 148, *171*
Sanders, B., 49, 62, *171*
Schackman, M., 133, 154, *165*
Scribner, S., 146, *165*
Sells, L. W., 57, *171*
Semon, J., 82, 84, *171*
Serbin, L. A., 133, 154, *165, 172*
Seward, G. H., 83, *171*
Seward, J. P., 83, *171*
Sharan, S., 72, *169*
Shepard, R. N., 51, *171*
Sherman, J. A., 12, 13, 18, 49, 53, 55, 59, 74, 87, 105, 113, 136, 138, 139, 140, *171, 172*
Shields, S. A., 9, *172*
Shuter-Dyson, R., 56, *172*
Signorella, M. L., 119, *169*
Simon, E. V., 51, *173*
Singer, G., 100, *172*
Smith, M. L., 36, *166*
Smith, W. S., 134, *172*
Soarles, M. P., 49, 62, *171*
Spalten, E., 85, *171*
Spence, J. T., 111, 114, 131, *172*
Sperry, R. W., 80, *169*
Sprafkin, C., 133, *172*

Springer, S. P., 56, 78, 83, 90, *172*
Spuhler, J. N., 49, *169*
Stafford, R. E., 72, 74, *172*
Stage, E. K., 117, *172*
Stapp, J., 111, 114, *172*
Stanley, G., 48, *171*
Stanley, J. C., 58, 63, 127, 158, *163, 164, 172*
Stein, N. L., 49, *169*
Stephens, L., 58, *173*
Stewart, V., 121, 122, *172*
Stones, I., 58, *173*
Sugawawa, A. I., 119, *168*

T

Tavris, C., 147, *173*
Teng, E. L., 86, *173*
Thomas, H., 73, 134, *173*
Thorne, B., 112, *169*
Thurstone, L. L., 5, 22, *173*
Thurstone, T. G., 5, 22, *173*
Tiger, L., 101, *173*
Tinkcom, M., 89, *173*
Tobias, S., 127, *173*
Tobin, D., 139, *166*
Tobin, P., 49, *164*
Tomizoka, C., 127, *173*

U

Unger, R. K., 11, *173*

V

Vandenberg, S. G., 72, 73, *165, 173*
Van Deventer, A. D., 86, 89, *170*
Vasu, E. S., 137, *166*
Vogel, S. R., 10, 111, *164*
Vogel, W., 100, *164*

W

Waber, D. P., 82, 83, 97, 102, 104, *173*
Walters, R. H., 117, *163*
Walton, S., 153, *173*
Wapner, S., 55, *174*
Ward, S., 134, *172*
Webb, F., 134, *172*
Weisstein, N., 5, 105, *173*
Welsh, G. S., 30, *163*
Weitzel-O'Neill, P. A., 128, *170*
Westkott, M., 1, *173*
Williams, J. E., 147, *173*
Williams, J. H., 61, 148, *173*
Winograd, E., 51, *173*
Witelson, S. F., 48, 84, *173*
Witkin, H. A., 53, 54, 55, *173, 174*
Wittig, M. A., 8, *174*
Wrightsman, L. S., 110, *174*

X, Y, Z

Yen, W. M., 55, 59, 65, 132, *168*
Yeo, R. A., 89, *174*

Subject Index

A

Abilities
  use of term, 12–13
  see also Cognitive abilities; Mathematical
    abilities; Quantitative abilities; Spatial
    abilities; Verbal abilities
Ability tests, 5, 6
Academic choice
  cross-cultural research on, 148
  medical schools and, 152–153
  variables in, 138–139
Achievement
  sex differences in, 65, 66
  spatial ability and, 59
Achievement tests, 6
Adolescence
  body type and developing sexuality in, 124–
    125
  cognitive differences in, 100
  gender intensification hypothesis in, 125–
    127
  sex-differentiated activities in, 127–128
  socialization and, 124–128
  visual-spatial abilities and, 51
Adrenal glands, 95
Adulthood
  performance evaluations in, 129–130
  power differential in, 128–129
  sex hormones and, 101–102
  socialization and, 128–131

Age
  brain lateralization differences and, 83–84
  cross-cultural research and, 147
  psychosocial significance of body changes
    with, 124–125
  sample issues in research and, 28
  quantitative abilities and, 57
  verbal ability differences and, 47–48
  visual-spatial abilities and, 51
Aggressive behavior
  variables in development of, 104
  prenatal development and, 94–95
American College Tests (ACT), 48
Androgen, 91
  prenatal abnormalities and, 94–96
  Turner's syndrome and, 96–97
  variables in studies of, 104
  visual spatial ability and, 98, 104, 106
  see also Sex hormones
Androgyny, 114
Anecdotal evidence in research, 17
Animal studies
  generalizations from, 28
  prenatal sex hormones on, 92–94
Autosomes, 70

B

Barr bodies, 75
Billiards, 127

Binomial Effect Size Display (BESD), 64
Biological hypotheses, 67–106
    biological determination theory and, 68–69
    body type and, 104–105
    critique of, 102–106
    differences seen as deficiencies in, 105–106
    empirical trends and, 141–142
    environmental factors and, 102–103
    factors not explained by, 152–154
    genetic theories in, 69–75
    intervening variables and, 104–105
    model of joint influences of psychosocial
        variables and, 157–158
    sex hormones and, 91–102
    sex-related brain differences in, 75–91
    similarities between sexes and, 105
Blacks
    brain structure and intelligence and, 77
    see also Race
Body type, 104–105
Braille, 84–85
Brain
    cognitive abilities and, 85
    cortical hormone differences in, 75–76
    dominance of hemisphere in, 78
    handedness and cognitive similarities in,
        87–89
    hearing and, 78
    hemispheric specialization in, 77–79
    lateralization differences in, 81–86
    maturation rate and, 83–84
    prenatal development and, 96
    research needs in, 89–90
    sex-differentiated asymmetries in, 80–81
    sex-related differences in, 75–91
    size, weight, and complexity of, 77
    social values in research on, 9
    vision and, 78–79
    see also Lateralization in brain

C

Card rotation test, 62
Castration anxiety, 116
Causal link in research, 18–19
Censorship in science, 11
Central tendency measures, 33–34
Chess, 55–56
Child rearing
    sex differentiated, 121–122
    socialization and, 131
    sociobiology on, 4

Childhood
    sex differences in, 100
    sex hormones in, 97–100
    socialization and, 121–123
Chromosome patterns
    generalizations about, 27–28
    sex-linked versus sex-limited in, 69–70
Classroom behavior
    commonly held stereotypes and, 10
    cross-cultural research on, 148
    intelligence and, 46
    sex differentiation treatment in, 123
Cognitive abilities
    age and, 100
    biological explanations for, 10–11
    brain asymmetries and, 81
    effect size for, 64, 153–154
    genetic abnormalities in research on, 74–75
    handedness and, 81, 87–89
    hemispheric dominance and, 78
    hemispheric specialization and, 77–79
    margin of error in tests of, 6–7
    performance evaluations and, 129–130
    prenatal development and, 95–96
    sex differences in, 6
    sex hormones and, 151
    teachers and socialization and, 123
    tests on, 5–7
    as theoretical construct, 7
    theories on, 5
Cognitive development theory of sex roles,
        118–119, 120–121
Cognitive styles
    definition of, 53
    visual-spatial abilities and, 53–55
Cognitive psychology, 5
Cognitive sex differences
    empirical evidence for, 45–66
    nature/nurture controversy on, 2–4
    sociobiology and, 4–5
Cohort effect in studies, 40
College students in samples, 142, 159
Competition, 131
Computer-related fields, 160
Correlational data in research, 18–20
Cross-cultural research
    nature/nurture controversy and, 149
    need for, 145–149
    outcomes of, 147–149
    relative paucity of, 146–148
    underlying rationale for, 145–146
Cross-sectional studies, 40–41

D

d (measurement), 38
DES (hormone), 95
Developmental issues
 cross-sectional vs. longitudinal studies in, 40–41
 research on sex differences and, 39–41, 59
 sex hormones and, 91–102
 visual-spatial abilities and, 55, 59
Developmental psychology, 115
Differential Aptitude Tests, 63
Distribution of scores, 31–33
Dyslexia, 89

E

Education
 access to, 148
 future needs and, 160–161
 role models in, 160–161
 see also Teachers; Training
Effect size
 cognitive abilities and, 64, 153–154
 measurement and, 8, 35–38
 quantitative abilities and, 63–64
 sex differences evidence and, 60–61
 verbal abilities and, 61–62
 visual-spatial abilities and, 62–63, 154
Elderly, see Old age
Electra complex, 116
Embedded Figures Test
 cognitive styles and, 54, 55
 maturation rate and, 97
 sex differences in, 65, 66
 spatial skills training and, 133
 verbal skills and, 141
Environmental factors
 biological hypotheses and, 102–103
 cross-cultural research and, 146
 experiments and, 22
 importance of, 107–108
 sampling differences in, 159
 spatial skills and, 133
 verbal abilities and, 139
 see also Psychosocial hypotheses
Equal Rights Amendment, 2, 147
Eskimos, 149
Estrogen, 91, 101; see also Sex hormones
Ethnicity
 cognitive abilities and, 64
 cross-cultural research and, 147
 perceptual functioning and, 48–49
Evaluation of research, 42–43
Experiments
 hypothesis testing with, 23–25
 summarizing research with, 24–25
 true, 21–22

F

Factor analysis
 intelligence studies with, 5
 research use of, 22–23
 sex differences in, 64–66
Family life, and socialization, 131
Fathers, and mathematical achievement, 137
Fear of success, 130
Female sex roles, see Sex roles; Sex role stereotypes
Feminist scholarship
 goals of, 9
 methods used in, 10
 science and, 9–10
Fetal development, see Prenatal development
Field-articulation, 53
Field-dependence and independence, 53–55
Football, 127
Freudian theory on sex roles, 115–116, 120–121
Frontal lobes, 9

G

Games, 127
Gender, use of term, 11–12
Gender constancy, 119
Gender intensification hypothesis, 125–127
Gender schema theory of sex roles, 118, 119, 120–121
Gene-environment transaction, 69
Generalizations from samples, 27–28
Genetic theories, 68, 69–75
 abnormalities as basis for research in, 74–75, 104
 gene-environment transaction in, 69
 mathematical skills heritability in, 74
 optimal cerebral organization concept for, 103–104
 research strategies in, 69
 sex-linked versus sex-limited in, 69–70
 sociobiology and, 4–5

spatial skills heritability in, 70–73
verbal skills heritability in, 73
Genotype, 69

H

Handedness
biological and environmental interactions in,
103
cognitive abilities and, 81, 87–89
hemispheric specialization and, 77–78
psychosocial hypotheses and, 150
spatial skills and, 86
Hearing, and brain structure, 78
Hormones
brain lateralization and, 82
generalizations about, 27–28
see also Sex hormones
Housework chores, 127–128, 131
Hunter-gatherer societies, 5
Hypothalamus
menstruation and, 75
prenatal development and, 94
Hypotheses
continuum of results in, 154, 155
lack of clear conclusion in, 149–150
logic of testing, 23–25
null, 23–24
proportion of explained variance in, 156
summarizing research with, 24–25

I

Intelligence and intellectual development
adolescence and, 126
brain size, weight, and complexity and, 77
commonly held stereotypes on, 10
empirical evidence for, 45–47
gender intensification hypothesis in, 126
handedness and, 87
heritability of, 70
interest in, 5
job classification and, 45–46
multiple, 46
research on, 46–47
sample issues in research on, 27
school achievement and, 46
self-concept and, 114
sex role identification and, 113–115
use of term, 5
verbal and visual-spatial abilities and, 48

Intelligence tests
sex differences and, 45, 46
verbal abilities on, 47–48

J

Job classification
intelligence and, 45–46
performance evaluations of, 129–130
quantitative abilities and, 57–58
sex-related power differential in, 128–129
see also Occupational choice

L

Language
nonconscious ideology and, 109
terminology use in research and, 11–13
Language ability
bent twig hypothesis for, 140–141
brain lateralization differences and, 80–86
empirical evidence for, 47, 48
sex hormones and, 89
Lateralization in brain
biological and environmental interactions in,
102
Braille learning and, 84–85
cognitive abilities and, 85
electroencephalograms (EEC's) in, 84
empirical evidence for sex differences in,
81–86
hemispheric specialization and, 77–79
maturation rate and, 83–84
optimal cerebral organization concept for,
103–104
psychosocial hypotheses and, 150
sex-differentiated asymmetries and, 80–81
sex hormones and, 97
Learning ability, and lateralization in brain,
84–85
Learning theory
sex roles and, 116–117, 119, 120–121
teachers and socialization and, 123
Left-handedness, see Handedness
Longitudinal studies, 40–41

M

Male sex roles, see Sex roles; Sex role
stereotypes
MANOVA, 31

Maori, 149
Margin of error in tests, 6–7
Mathematical ability
  academic choices in, 138–139
  achievement models in, 136–139
  achievement motivation and, 130
  achievement tests in, 6
  adolescence and, 126–127
  anxiety in, 138
  biological hypotheses on, 106
  commonly held stereotypes on, 10
  component parts of, 158
  encouragement and, 134–135, 136, 138
  exceptional talent in, 58, 63, 153
  expectancy effects of teachers of, 136–138
  females in research on, 159
  future needs and training in, 160
  gender intensification hypothesis in, 125–126
  heritability of, 74
  issues in testing for, 8
  learning theory on, 117
  occupational choice and, 135
  performance evaluations of, 129–130
  predictive value of tests in, 7
  prenatal development and, 95–96
  sample issues in research on, 25
  self-concept of, 138–139
  sex-related power differential in, 128–129
  sex role identification and, 114
  socialization and, 122, 135
  spatial relations test and, 59
  training and, 136–137
  see also Quantitative abilities
Maturation rate, see Age
Measurement
  central tendency measures in, 33–34
  d (measurement) in, 38
  distribution of scores in, 31–33
  effect size in, 35–38
  interaction of variables in, 38–39
  issues in research on, 8, 29–39
  meta-analysis in, 35–38
  multivariate indicators in, 30–31
  ω^2 (omega squared) in, 36–38
  sex and, 29–30
  sex-role orientation and, 30
  situational variables in, 39
  statistical and practical significance in, 34–35
  variability of scores in, 31–34

Media, and socialization, 122–123
Medical schools, 152–153
Memory
  sex role stereotypes and, 113
  visual-spatial ability in chess and, 56
Menarche, 102–103
Menopause, 100
Menstruation
  brain structure and, 75–76
  sex hormones and, 101
Mental rotation task
  age and sex differences in, 100
  effect size for, 62, 63
  visual-spatial abilities and, 51, 152
Meta-analysis
  d (measurement) in, 38
  measurement and, 35–38
  ω^2 (omega squared) in, 37–38
Minorities, see Race
Mothers and mothering
  mathematical achievement and, 138
  sociobiology on, 4
Motivation, sex differences in, 65, 66
Multivariate indicators, 30–31, 156–158
Musical ability, 55, 56–57

N

Nature/nurture controversy
  cognitive sex differences and, 2–4
  cross-cultural research on, 149
  experiments and, 22
  research and, 2–4
  sociobiology and, 4–5
Null hypothesis, 23–24

O

Objectivity in science, 7–9
Observational techniques in research, 20–21
Occupational choice
  achievement motivation and, 130–131
  family life and, 131
  mathematical ability and, 135–136
  medical schools and, 152–153
  role models in, 160–161
  sex role stereotypes and, 112–113
  verbal ability and, 154
  see also Job classification
Oedipus complex, 115–116

Old age
   performance evaluations in, 129–130
   power differential in, 128–129
   sex hormones and, 101–102
   socialization and, 128–131
   ω^2 (omega squared), 36–38
Orientation factor in visual-spatial abilities, 49,
      59, 132

P

Pakeha ethnic group, 149
Parents
   mathematical achievement and, 138
   socialization and, 121–123
Parietal lobes, 9
Peer group effect in studies, 40
Penis envy, 116
Perception, racial differences in, 48–49
Performance
   sex-related evaluations of, 129–130
   use of term, 12–13
   visual-spatial abilities and, 50–51
Phallic state, 115–116
Phenotype, 69
Pituitary gland, 94
Prenatal development
   abnormalities in, 94–96
   aggressive behavior and, 94–95, 104
   animal studies on, 92–94
   cognitive abilities and, 95–96
   DES and, 95
   sex hormones and, 91–97
Problem representation, 158
Problem solution, 158
Progesterone, 91, 101; see also Sex
      hormones
Pronouns, use of, 13
Psychology
   interest in intelligence issues in, 5
   nature/nurture controversy and, 3
Psychosocial hypotheses, 107–143
   biological hypotheses and, 103
   extrapolating from empirical trends in, 141–
      142
   factors not explained by, 150–152
   implications of, 108
   importance of, 107–110
   intellectual development and, 113–115
   language use and, 109
   mathematical ability and, 134–139

model of joint influences of biological vari-
      ables and, 157–158
   nonconscious ideology and, 109–110
   sampling differences and, 142
   sex roles and sex role stereotypes in, 110–
      121
   socialization and, 121–131
   spatial ability and, 132–134
   verbal abilities and, 139–141
   see also Environmental factors
Puberty
   psychosocial significance of body changes
      in, 124–125
   sex hormones and, 97–100
Punishments, in learning theory, 117

Q

Quantitative abilities
   age and, 57
   components of, 58
   effect size for, 63–64
   empirical evidence for, 47, 57–59
   job classification and, 57–58
   sex differences in, 5
   test interpretation in, 58–59
   visual-spatial abilities related to, 59–60
   see also Mathematical ability

R

Race
   brain structure and intelligence and, 77
   perceptual functioning and, 48–49
   research and views on, 9
   stereotypes about, 110
Random assignment of subjects, 19, 21–22
Reasoning ability, and handedness, 87–88
Recessive genes
   abnormalities as basis for research in,
      74–75
   basic theory of, 70–71
   mathematical skills heritability in, 74
   predictions using, 71–72
   spatial skills heritability in, 70–73
   validity of, 73
Remedial programs, 160
Replication of research, 28–29
Reproductive behavior
   biological determination and, 68
   sociobiology on, 4

Research, 15–43
  anecdotal evidence in, 17
  censorship in, 11
  central tendency measures in, 33–34
  continuum of results in, 154, 155
  correlational approach to, 18–20
  cross-sectional vs. longitudinal studies in,
      40–41
  d (measurement) in, 38
  developmental issues and, 39–41
  distribution of scores in, 31–33
  effect size in, 35–38
  evaluating claims in, 42–43
  factor analytic approaches to, 22–23
  feminist scholarship methods and, 9–10
  generalizations in, 27–28
  hypothesis testing in, 23–25
  interaction of variables in, 38–39
  meta-analysis in, 35–38
  myth of objectivity in, 7–9
  measurement issues in, 29–39
  multivariate indicators in, 30–31
  nature/nurture controversy and, 3–4
  need for, 15–17
  new approaches to, 158–160
  ω^2 (omega squared) in, 36–38
  personal beliefs and values influencing, 8
  plausibility of theories in, 19–20
  replication of results in, 28–29
  sampling issues in, 25–29
  scientific method in, 16
  selective nature of reviews of, 13–14
  self-fulfilling prophecies and, 41–42
  situational variables in, 39
  social environment and, 8–9
  statistical and practical significance in, 34–
      35
  summarizing with hypotheses in, 24–25
  surveys used in, 17–18
  terminology used in, 11–13
  true experiments in, 21–22
  types of investigations in, 17–23
  understanding results of, 23–39
  variability of scores in, 31–34
Rewards
  learning theory and, 117
  teachers and, 123
Right-handedness, see Handedness
Rod and Frame Test
  cognitive styles and, 53–54, 55

  psychosocial hypotheses and, 152
  sex differences in, 65, 66

S

Samples
  age by sex interactions in, 28
  comparison between sexes in, 25–26
  empirical trends and, 142
  generalizations from, 27–28
  issues in research and, 8, 25–29
  replication of results in, 28–29
  representative population in, 25, 142, 159
  results affected by, 158–159
  size in, 8, 26–27
  statistical control in, 25–26
Scholastic Aptitude Test (SAT), 48, 57, 58,
      63, 138
School behavior, see Classroom behavior
Science
  censorship in, 11
  feminist scholarship methods and, 9–10
  myth of objectivity in, 7–9
  personal beliefs and values influencing, 8
  sex differences in, 135, 153
  social environment and, 8–9
Scientific method, 16
Secondary sex characteristics, 97, 99
Self-concept
  mathematical ability and, 138–139
  sex role stereotypes and, 114
Self-fulfilling prophecies in research, 41–42
Sex, use of term, 11–12
Sex chromosomes, 70–71
  abnormalities as basis for research in, 74–75
  brain structure and, 75
  mathematical skills heritability and, 74
  prenatal development and, 91–92
  spatial skills heritability and, 70–73
  verbal skills heritability and, 73
Sex differences
  biological explanations for, 10–11
  commonly held stereotypes in, 10
  current interest in, 1–2
  factor analysis of, 64–66
  nature/nurture controversy on, 2–4
  political and social ramifications of, 10–11
  political climate and view of, 2
  sexism different from, 105
  similarities between sexes and, 105
  sociobiology on, 4–5

use of term, 12
see also Cognitive sex differences
Sex hormones
  adulthood and, 100–101
  aggressive behavior and, 94–95
  animal studies on, 92–94
  biological hypotheses using, 68, 91–102
  childhood and puberty and, 97–100
  cognitive abilities and, 95–96, 151
  elderly and, 101–102
  methematical ability and, 95–96
  optimal cerebral organization concept for,
    103–104
  prenatal, 91–97
  psychosocial significance of body changes
    with, 124–125
  secondary sex characteristics and, 97, 99
  spatial ability and, 98–99
  Turner's syndrome and, 96–97
  visual ability and, 98
Sexism, 105
Sex-related differences
  use of term, 12
  see also Sex differences
Sex roles
  cognitive development theory on, 118–119
  comparison of theories on, 120–121
  Freudian theory on, 115–116
  gender schema theory on, 118, 119
  intellectual development and identification
    in, 46, 113–115
  learning theory on, 116–117
  mathematical ability and, 114
  psychosocial hypotheses with, 110–121
  sex role stereotypes different from, 112–113
  socialization practices linked with, 121–131
  social modeling and, 117–118
  sociobiology on, 4
  theoretical models of, 115–121
Sex role stereotypes
  androgyny in, 114
  cross-cultural research on, 147
  definition of, 110
  existence of, 111–112
  gender intensification hypothesis in, 125–
    127
  memory and, 113
  occupations and, 112–113
  psychosocial hypotheses with, 110–121
  ramifications of, 10
  self-concept and, 114

sex role different from, 112–113
use of term, 110–111, 112
Significance of test scores, 34–35
Situational variables, 39
Size of samples, 8, 26–27
Skills, use of term, 12–13
Socialization
  achievement motivation and, 130–131
  adolescence and, 124–128
  adulthood and old age and, 128–131
  body type and developing sexuality and,
    124–125
  family life and, 131–132
  gender intensification hypothesis in, 125–
    127
  importance of, 107–108
  mathematical ability and, 125–126, 134
  performance evaluations and, 129–130
  power differential and, 128–129
  psychosocial hypotheses with, 121–131
  sex-differentiated activities and, 127–128
  sex-differentiated child rearing and, 121–
    122
  Social Modeling theory and, 122–123
  sports and, 127
  teachers and schools and, 123
  television and other media and, 122–123
  toys and, 122
  verbal abilities and, 139
  video games and, 127
Social modeling theory
  sex roles and, 117–118, 119, 120–121
  socialization and, 122–123
Social values, and research, 8–9
Sociobiology, 4–5
Socioeconomic status (SES)
  cognitive abilities and, 64
  cross-cultural research and, 146
Soviet Union, 147, 148
Spatial abilities
  age and differences in, 51, 83–84, 100,
    101–102
  biological and environmental interactions in,
    102–103
  brain lateralization differences and, 80–86
  chess and use of, 55–56
  cognitive styles and, 53–55
  components of, 49, 158
  cross-cultural research on, 148–149
  developmental data and, 55
  effect size for, 62–63, 154

Spatial abilities (*cont.*)
  Embedded Figures Test and, 54, 55
  empirical evidence for, 47, 48–57
  factor analytic studies of, 48–49
  females in research on, 159
  field dependence and, 53–55
  future needs and training in, 160
  gender intensification hypothesis in, 126
  genetic abnormalities in research on, 74–75, 104
  handedness and, 87, 89
  heritability of, 70–73
  learning theory on, 117
  mathematical achievement and, 136
  mental rotation task and, 51
  multivariate indicators in testing for, 30–31
  musical ability and, 55, 56–57
  old age and, 101–102
  orientation factor in, 49, 59, 132
  performance predictions in, 50–51
  performance evaluations of, 129–130
  psychosocial hypotheses and, 150, 151–152
  quantitative abilities related to, 59–60
  racial or ethnic differences in, 48–49
  Rod and Frame Test and, 53–54, 55
  sex differences in, 5
  sex differentiated activities and, 127
  sex hormones and, 96–97, 98–99, 104, 106
  sex-related power differential in, 128–129
  sociobiology on, 5
  sports and, 127
  test score interpretation in, 55
  test score variability for, 49–50
  toys and, 132–133, 134, 151
  training for, 132–134
  verbal abilities distinct from, 48
  video games and, 127
  visualization factor in, 49, 59, 132, 136, 152
  water level task and, 51–52
Sports, 127
Statistical significance, 34–35
Statistics
  hypothesis testing with, 23
  sample control with, 25–26
Stereotypes, *see* Sex role stereotypes
Students
  commonly held stereotypes and, 10
  sample selections with, 142
  see also Classroom behavior

Stuttering, 48, 89
Subjects in research
  random assignment of, 19, 21–22
  true experiments and, 21–22
Success motivation, 130
Surveys, 17–18

T

Teachers
  commonly held stereotypes and, 10
  cross-cultural research on, 148
  mathematics ability and, 136–138
  socialization and, 123
Television, and socialization, 122–123
Temne tribe, 149
Testosterone, 91
  animal studies of prenatal, 92, 93–94
  spatial ability and, 98
  see also Sex hormones
Tests
  ability, 5, 6
  achievement, 6
  cognitive abilities on, 5–7
  cognitive styles and, 53–55
  distribution of scores in, 31–33
  hypothesis testing with, 23
  interpretation of, 7
  margin of error in, 6–7
  multivariate indicators in, 30–31
  predictive value of, 7
  sex differences and, 6
  variability of scores in, 31–34
  verbal abilities on, 47–48
  see also Measurement *and specific tests*
Third World countries, 146–147
Toys
  socialization and, 122, 161
  spatial skills training and, 132–133, 134, 151
Training
  ability level after, 161–162
  future needs and, 160–161
  mathematics, 135–136
  sex differences and, 161
  spatial skills, 132–134, 136
True experiments, 21–22
Turner's syndrome
  androgen insensitivity in, 96
  research using, 74, 104

Twin studies
  spatial skills heritability in, 70
  verbal skills heritability in, 73

U

Underdeveloped countries, 146–147

V

Values, and research, 8–9
Variability of test scores
  central tendency measures in, 33–34
  distribution in, 31–33
Variables
  interaction of, 38–39
  situational, 39
Variance, and ω^2 (omega squared), 36–38
Verbal abilities
  age and differences in, 47–48, 83–84
  bent twig hypothesis for, 140–141
  biological and environmental interactions in,
    102
  brain asymmetries and, 80, 81
  components of, 47, 158
  cross-cultural research on, 149
  differences seen as deficiencies in, 105–106
  effect size for, 61–62
  empirical evidence for, 47–48
  environmental factors and, 139
  genetic abnormalities in research on, 74–75
  handedness and, 87–89
  heritability of, 73
  learning theory on, 117
  males in research on, 159
  occupational choice and, 154
  psychosocial factors in, 139–141, 150
  sex differences in, 5
  sex hormones and, 96, 100
  sex-related power differential in, 129
  socialization and, 139
  visual-spatial abilities distinct from, 48
Video games, 127
Visual abilities
  age and, 51
  brain structure and, 78–79
  chess and use of, 55–56
  cognitive styles and, 53–55
  components of, 49
  developmental data and, 55

effect size for, 62–63
Embedded Figures Test and, 54, 55
empirical evidence for, 47, 48–57
factor analytic studies of, 48–49
field dependence and, 53–55
genetic abnormalities in research on, 74–75
mental rotation task and, 51
musical ability and, 55, 56–57
performance predictions in, 50–51
quantitative abilities related to, 59–60
racial or ethnic differences in, 48–49
Rod and Frame Test and, 53–54, 55
sex hormones and, 96–97, 98
test score interpretation in, 55
test score variability for, 49–50
verbal abilities distinct form, 48
water level task and, 51–52
Visualization factor in visual-spatial abilities,
  49, 59, 133, 136, 152
Visual memory, 56
Visual-spatial abilities, *see* Spatial abilities;
  Visual abilities

W

Water level task
  age and sex differences in, 100
  psychosocial hypotheses using, 151–152
  visual-spatial abilities and, 51–52, 134
Wechsler Adult Intelligence Scale
  (WAIS), 47–48
Wechsler Intelligence Scale for Children
  (WISC), 47
Women's Movement, 2, 103, 108
Work, *see* Job classification; Occupational
  choice

X

X chromosomes, 70–71
  brain structure and, 75
  mathematical skills heritability in, 74
  spatial skills heritability and, 70–71, 72
  verbal skills heritability in, 73

Y

Y chromosomes, 70–71
  brain structure and, 75
  spatial skills heritability and, 71